QUANTUM LEARNING
BEYOND DUALITY

Taruga

Thank ~

This book would

have been published

without your tremendous

help.

Love

Conrad

VIBS

Volume 113

Robert Ginsberg
Executive Editor

Associate Editors

QUANTUM LEARNING
BEYOND DUALITY

Conrad P. Pritscher

Amsterdam – New York, NY 2001

The paper on which this book is printed meets the requirements of "ISO 9706:1994, Information and documentation - Paper for documents - Requirements for permanence".

ISBN: 90-420-1387-7
©Editions Rodopi B.V., Amsterdam – New York, NY 2001
Printed in The Netherlands

CONTENTS

FOREWORD

David Geoffrey Smith

Conrad P. Pritscher and I first met in the early 1990s at one of the annual conferences of the *Journal of Curriculum Theorizing*. I had just given a presentation on the Buddhist understanding of *prajnaparamita* (the perfection of wisdom) in relation to teaching. Standing outside the main building afterwards, to breathe some fresh air, I was suddenly aware of a certain presence beside me. Turning to my right, my eyes set on a man who said that he too had been studying Buddhism. Minutes into our conversation, I knew instinctively that I had met a spiritual brother, and a true friend. After that, our acquaintance was very limited. But as in all true friendships, paucity of contact has had no bearing at all on the underlying experience of knowing deeply that since we had found each other in the great ocean of being, somehow our friendship is "for life," in all senses of those words.

When Pritscher invited me to write a brief guest foreword for this book, of course I was honored. Mysteriously, reading the manuscript has evoked again the same sensation—I am in the presence of someone, and it is a unique presence, with a voice that resonates with uncommon wisdom and grace. The book is the man. Together they call the reader to attention, to attend to life in a way now almost completely suffocated by the dominant order of things.

Like most North American academics today, I live a severely harried existence. Even though I practice meditation, and try to dwell as fully as possible in the present moment, still I am caught in a daily round that breathes the distinctive pathology of technical rational culture organized around capital modes of production. This is the pathology constructed from a temporal dualism that believes the full resolution of life is always in the future. No matter how hard one works, there is always more work to be done. No matter how fast one goes, one could always go faster. So in this spirit, I picked up the manuscript, determined to read it as quickly as possible. Get the job done, so you can get on with the next job. Imagine even thinking like that with respect to the work of a brother that you love. Yet I did.

True to form, the older brother taught me a lesson. This book simply cannot be read quickly. As most fundamentally a meditative text, it comes from a person who has resolved what the Chinese call the unity of the heart-mind. In Chinese, the word for mind implies the heart, and *vice versa*. So there is only one word, *h'sin*, meaning heart-mind. Issuing from such a place, a text must be what it is talking about, that is, there must be no disjuncture between what is being spoken about and the way of getting there. Actually, in this context, the way is the thing spoken about; therefore, the text itself must be the way, that is, reveal the way through its own manner, and not just point to it as a futurity. And the first requirement of a reader is to slow down, to read one's way into the still point around which the work revolves. There are no short-cuts. Skimming will not do. Indeed, something here is in the nature of a call to personal responsibility, to take responsibility for one's delusions, and to heal oneself of cultural diseases as an act of communal care. "When I heal myself, I heal the world," said eco-philosopher Wendell Berry. It is slow, difficult work, requiring close attention to the details of one's life.

Quantum learning: beyond duality? A foreword is not the place for summaries, but a few remarks may be in order, even if order isn't really the right word at all. More than anything, this book is a weird (OED, "uncanny") and wonderful event, a revealing of multiple visions and ethical concerns, all guided by a basic understanding that everything is always already everywhere present, for us, in spite of us, and that we find our original nature not in defining ourselves against this pre-given reality (a conceit we inherit from Aristotle's theory of substance), but quite precisely in it. The work required is not ego-logical, that is, the work of pure ego struggling to affirm itself against all odds, all Others. Under that condition, the skills to be honed are all largely expressive, and based on the will to power. Instead, the work is that of attunement, which privileges listening and paying attention; speaking when necessary, but honoring silence too. Really, what is called forth in Pritcher's book is nothing short of an understanding of human life that stands in almost complete alterity to what, in this crazy age, we euphemistically call "life." His hermeneutic, may be, in his language, the "chosen dualism" that people everywhere may increasingly be called upon to take up in confrontation with the dominant myths of contemporary order.

Paradoxically, I was reading this manuscript at the same time as another that I was asked to review, John McMurtry's *Unequal Freedoms: The Global Market as an Ethical System* (Toronto: Garamond Press, 1998). This is one of the most lucid and insightful deconstructions of the neo-liberal market theory currently underwriting the push for economic globalization. It is a very dark book, for it reveals the human and environmental costs of the totalistic formula of profit maximization that is making its way around the world. Reading Pritscher and McMurtry together reminded me forcefully of what the Pritscher vision is up against. Fortunately he is not alone. An emerging critical mass of concerned souls recognize the essential madness of our current economistic determinism, wherein The Economy is god, even though increasing numbers of people are suffering greatly under it.

A saying, I believe of Dogen, is, "The world cannot be made more beautiful." This is a statement about the way that everything that is required for us to live well is already present in the world, and that human difficulties are what we suffer because our delusions, and the enculturated constraints of perception and interpretation. Pritscher's book signals many ways through which we might better understand what Dogen was talking about, especially as it pertains to our present contexts in education as they stand in relation to the shifting sands of national and global identity.

The book resonates with deep pedagogical sensitivity, and profound moral concern for what both students and teachers suffer under conventional assumptions regarding epistemology, and even dualistic assumptions about the duality of the teacher-student relation. One last thing I remember about Conrad P. Pritscher personally: the wonderful twinkle in his eyes. I think you will find that in the book too. Happy reading!

International Forum on Education and Society
University of Alberta, Edmonton, Alberta, Canada

ACKNOWLEDGMENTS

Thanks to my family, colleagues, and Bowling Green State University for their cherished contributions. I thank my brother, Thomas Pritscher, for his insight, ideas and encouragement. I give my deep gratitude to Haju Sunim, P'arang Gerri Larkin, and Samu Sunim for telling me nothing, for teaching me no concepts whatsoever, and for helping me begin to realize that attainment, as Layman Hsiang said, gains nothing, and loss loses nothing. Thanks to Malcolm Campbell, David Doane, William Geismann, James Guinan, Todd May, David Geoffrey Smith, and Daniel Tutolo for their generous help and thoughtful contributions. Thanks to Sherry Haskins and Judy Maxey for their care and thoughtfulness in assembling this book. Thanks to Robert Ginsberg for his wisdom and openness to experience. Thanks to Tavia Rowan for her outstanding editorial skill. All mistakes are mine. Thanks to my wife, Kay, for her many thoughtful suggestions, loving kindness, and support.

Much of the material for this book comes from notes from conferences, books, journals, magazines, and private interviews. When the source of my writing is known that source is given. Unfortunately, some information and ideas were noted, but the exact source was not given. I apologize for any inconvenience this may cause readers.

While we are dualistic, clear distinctions are made between forewords and afterwords, between prologues and epilogues, between beginnings and endings. After reading this book, my hope is that you will still see distinctions when you choose to, but you will also be open to seeing a whole with interchangeable parts, where no difference may occur between forewords and afterwords.

Please do not mistake this for an enlightened teaching. With gratitude to everyone and everything, and may all beings be at ease.

INTRODUCTION

Plutarch said, "Music, to create harmony, must investigate discord." Is time nature's way for preventing everything from happening all at once? When everything happens at once, discord seems to arise. If this were a quantum introduction, I would say everything simultaneously. In order to communicate, I will make differences between this and that and attempt to show connections between learning in the previous millennium and possible aspects of quantum learning in a new millennium.

As quantum computers use the given of quantum physics that sub-atomic particles can be regarded as a wave and as particles, quantum learning could profitably use the idea that learners can be simultaneously nondual (whole) and dual (part). To help see this simultaneousness, I quote David Geoffrey Smith's superb work *Pedagon*,

> What is the silence that comes over an audience after fine poetry reading, a well played piece of music or a superb dramatization? If we describe the performance as 'brilliant,' we indicate our sense of something shining through the ordinary routine of things. But even more important is the effect of the performance on us—what it calls forth in our deep experience. The silence which reigns after the playing of the last note may be understood as a sign of our being 'taken up' by that which has just been given into a new way of self-understanding, and a new way of being together.[1]

A new way of being together about which Smith is writing is connected to recombining what has been separated. Quantum physics has reunited aspects of thought which had been separated by earlier thinking regarding the physical world. Learning activities in a Quantum Age could profit from recombining what has been made separate within and between individuals and groups.

What we do with, to, and for others and ourselves, in schools and society, "depends on who I think the Other is, and who I think I am in relation to them," to quote Smith again.[2] Our learning, if it is to be long-lasting and fruitful for ourselves and society, could profitably relate to recombining parts of ourselves that have been separated by earlier thought and a culture which cherished separations and distinctions. The intent of the earlier separating was to provide greater clarity in thought and expression. The greater clarity may have come at the expense of rigidifying thought and behavior which may close-off people from new experience.

As Carl Reiner has asked, why don't we sing only the last note when it is only after the last note that we applaud? The answer to why we applaud is obvious, but what contributes to the silence of the audience and what is the ground out of which the silence arises after a fine poetry reading, etc.?

This writing attempts to say more about some near-ineffable ponderings at the basis of our scientific endeavors. What I say is partly based on scientific findings and partly based on hypotheses on which scientific hypotheses themselves are grounded.

I ask you to look at quantum learning as that which unites parts into wholes and then wholes into larger wholes and then those larger wholes into very large wholes. As fractal geometry shows similarities between shore lines when viewed from 1,000th of a millimeter and 100,000 meters above, so does Quantum Learning show similarities between studying parts of atoms and studying groups of galaxies as far as we can see, and between inconsequential matters such as, "my shoes are brown," to matters of great consequence such as how we may better notice what is going on in and around us as it is going on.

This writing will reconsider clarity in thought and expression. If fuzziness, or murkiness, or a blurring of distinctions is considered, what might be said of that which hovers between the clearly defined concepts? What are the limits of conceptual thought? Do we need concepts to explore those limits? Nonduality exists beyond duality, but what are the dangers of conceptualizing nonduality?

Research shows that creative thinkers were unable to describe or explain how they solved the problems they creatively solved. They knew what they could not tell. Is there a difference between knowing "about" something and knowing directly? Did these creative thinkers "know directly?" This writing will pay attention to nonduality. In days gone by, nonduality was frequently referred to as some brand of Eastern thinking. This nondual "knowing" holds that what you know and want to communicate, must move "down" to the realm of concepts, and use a variety of agreed-upon common meanings, words, that contribute, at times, to the difficulty in making your meaning known.

We use pairs of opposites to describe and explain. The listener selectively perceives what is being said. Unquestionably, the intellect has a function, yet we may stimulate human growth by considering how we know in ways beyond using only the intellect. Recombining our thinking occurs when balancing thinking with feeling and open noticing. What kind of knowing can arise from the synergy of newer kinds of integrating/combining in a Quantum Age?

Reconsider the value of "not knowing." In a strictly conceptual sense, knowing is delusion. Nondually, not knowing conceptually is knowing. Are too many experts knowing more and more about less and less? At the outer limits of each of these experts' area of expertise may be a unified field/super symmetry of which each area of expertise partakes. Might that field go beyond string/unified field theory/supersymmetry of physics? This book takes a look at that possibility.

I will be looking at how "difference" is viewed as figure within a ground of "same." How can we "avoid reducing difference to the logic of the same," as Todd May asks? What "difference" would it make if we avoided that reducing? What if we did not avoid reducing? What difference does "making differences" make? What comes next?

I frequently want to know what will happen next. If my knowledge is extensive, I will have a greater chance of knowing what will happen next. My knowledge helps me predict. My ability to predict helps me control my environment and myself. We relegate present experience to an inconsequential place in our lives. Most of our schooling and our general experience is designed to help us to know, predict, and control. When we only know for predicting, and when we only predict to control, we avoid our present experience.

Avoiding present experience has become excessive to the point where knowing, predicting and controlling prevent us from exploring. As a result, my skill at exploring, and perhaps yours, is minimal. According to three Nobel Prize winners I interviewed, original research is a small portion of research. We excel at replicating experiments but original/breakthrough type findings are meager. Exploring is an activity for which one needs some knowledge, some ability to predict and some ability to control, but exploring goes on in the present. Replicating previous research is a step removed from exploring.

Exploring is an end in itself which contributes to our convenience, our being at ease, and our wisdom, whereas knowing, predicting, and controlling, by themselves, without exploring to help us notice what is happening as it is happening, contributes to our deluding ourselves. We delude ourselves when we are not open to explore. We will not know what is explorable until we explore.

For instance, if we wanted to explore how to explore where would we begin? We begin now even though our beginning is a decision to delay further effort now. My knowing, predicting, and controlling frequently prevent me from being in the present. When I am thinking of "next" I am not here. I am not here now because my knowing, predicting, and controlling have their purpose in what is next. What will happen next is not now.

What is the point of all this "next" talk? This may be difficult to believe because it sounds odd even to me. The point is what will happen next is a fantasy called, "the future." As we know, tomorrow never comes. Tomorrow is not now. It is then. All of my ideas about "next" are to argue against our excessive need to know in advance what will happen before it happens. My statements are designed to allow us to pay more attention to the present by helping us notice how much we avoid the present by frequently dealing with what is going to happen next.

Many think stretching our imaginations is good. Our closed, narrow schooling has led us to occasionally know what is going to happen next and to hold out the hope that we can better know what is going to happen next. This closed conceptioning controls by making the world static and unreal. Albert Einstein said about the laws of mathematics that, insofar as they are uncertain, they relate to reality, but insofar as those laws are certain, they do not relate to reality. Dealing with what is next is unreal unless we are aware of what we are doing as we are doing it.

Stretching the imagination can only happen in the present or it happens not at all. We learn to stretch our imaginations by stretching our imaginations. For schools to help us stretch our imaginations, they would need to permit much more stretching than is now the case. Schools would need to cherish imagination stretching until the stretching approached the borders of excess. Our schools and society have been over the border of "non-exploring" for quite some time. Evidence for non-exploring in schools continues.

Sometimes when we stretch our imaginations, we stretch too far. When imaginations are stretched too far, they are unpredictable. Unpredictability does not fit with our training to know so that we can predict, control, and avoid uncertainty. Most of us have been taught to avoid uncertainty at almost all costs. One of my goals is to provide evidence that the cost of avoiding uncertainty has been excessively high.

When we stretch our imaginations, we do not know the product of the stretching before the stretch. That is to say, we do not know what is going to happen next. So knowing what is going to happen next may prevent us from being aware of our present experience. This prevents the stretching from occurring. Our concern with what is going to happen next keeps us in the dark about our avoiding our present experience. Excessive concern with "next" focuses on knowing in order to predict and control what will happen next, which continues the avoidance.

When I am so focused on what will happen next, I keep my present awareness closed to what is happening in and around me. When I do not know what is happening in and around me, I cannot choose to have it happen or have something else happen. In a sense, I lose control over my present experience when I am not aware of what is happening in the present. So the paradox to this knowing, predicting, and controlling is that we are less aware of what is happening as it is happening, and as a result, we have less control. That is what is hard to believe.

This lowered awareness of present experience generates a need for more control. The cycle continues, but it can be broken. When knowing, predicting, and controlling have their purpose in the activity of exploring, then the present moment is opened to be viewed; and it is viewed in a way that is "more" than conceptual. Exploring can only be done in the present and this exploring of our present experience increases the chances for all beings to be at ease, and for everyone to better know what they want and how to get it. What is beyond duality is nonduality. Within nonduality, exploring and being at ease are identical, but we must expend great effort in order to arrive at an effortless state.

I will later talk about infinitesimals, a notion used in calculus of variables so small that they are immeasurable or incalculable, and how they might help us be aware of our present experience. This writing is partly about how the cycle of avoiding present awareness in schools and society can be broken. Some of us do not want the cycle to be broken because is it is more convenient, temporarily, to deal with past and future and avoid the uncertainties of the present. Avoiding uncertainty has been a hidden agenda of schools and society. This avoidance has been so hidden we do not notice it.

Paul B. Baltes and Ursula M. Staudinger state, "Wisdom may be beyond what psychological methods and concepts can achieve," yet the general practice of wisdom is that in which knowledge, prediction, control, and exploring find their meaning and purpose.[3] In Chapter Fourteen, I mention Hermann Hesse who said, "The wisdom which a wise man tries to communicate always sounds foolish.... Knowledge can be communicated but not wisdom."[4]

The notion of wisdom has not frequently been used in scientific writings. Only recently has it begun to emerge on a more than occasional scale. Baltes and Staudinger report that G. Stanley Hall, the first president of the American Psychological Association, wrote about wisdom, but he wrote about it anonymously in a 1921 issue of the *Atlantic Monthly*.

The Baltes and Staudinger article is evidence that views of reality are changing in scientific circles beyond physics, chemistry, and biology. They state,

The primary focus of this article is on the presentation of wisdom research conducted under the heading of the Berlin wisdom paradigm. Informed by our cultural-historical analysis, wisdom in this paradigm is defined as an expert knowledge system concerning the fundamental pragmatics of life. These include knowledge and judgment about the meaning and conduct of life and the orchestration of human development toward excellence while attending conjointly to personal and collective well-being.[5]

One of the criteria that the authors of this article use in measuring wisdom, a wise person, is "recognition and management of uncertainty."[6] Uncertainty has been long accepted by physicists. Chapter Fifteen below looks at the possible positive effects of a society and its schools that may yet move to the point of accepting the reality of uncertainty as something to be cherished rather than avoided.

Other criteria used by Baltes and Staudinger for the determination of wisdom through their analysis of their data are: "rich factual and procedural knowledge, lifespan contextualism, and relativism of values in life priorities."[7] The last two and the one earlier mentioned, recognition and management of uncertainty, are what the authors hold as metacriteria essential to wisdom. Their research helps unveil a possible noosphere of which Pierre Teilhard de Chardin wrote about more than fifty years ago.[8] Teilhard de Chardin's metaphor, "omega point," may be an aspect of nonduality toward which learning in a Quantum Age is moving.

Baltes and Staudinger quote the Roman emperor, Marcus Aurelius: "It is better to limp slowly along the right path than to walk stridently in the wrong direction."[9] Some of the ideas on the following pages suggest that intelligence/wisdom be integrated into a unit which allows us to see powerful means moving in the direction of ends which help all sentient beings become wise, compassionate, and at ease. The book also suggests the possibility of an interchangeability of these means and ends.

New and unusual discoveries in physics and astronomy show how we may recombine parts to better order our experience. We can recombine more of our experience by looking at the murkiness of nonduality and present experience. Quantum physics has recombined what was separated by earlier thinking about physical events. Quantum learning attempts to provide conditions whereby we may recombine various other processes and events which are abstracted from what we can directly sense. "Beyond duality" approaches a singularity called nonduality of which nothing may be directly said. As a whole is more than the sum of its parts, near-nonduality attempts to recombine large wholes into very large wholes. The arrangement of the parts of the whole is itself an element in the whole which cannot be seen unless the whole is experienced as a whole: something toward which words can only point.

Pointing is partially done by reconsidering clarity in thought and expression. We may use the discontinuity of murkiness in order to provide a greater clarity of continuity as disorder may be used to increase order. Ideas of quantum physicists, astronomers and others are given to show that the universe, as J. D. Bernal, a British scientist suggested, is not only weirder than we imagine: the universe, part of which is quantum learning, is weirder than we *can* imagine.

Part One

SIMILARITIES BETWEEN
QUANTIFYING QUALITY
AND QUALIFYING QUANTITY

One

RECOMBINING SEPARATIONS

Quantum computers today are similar to a newly-formed fetus in a mature adult, digital world. Quantum computers can now do work less than a calculator. Scientists are now evolving a conscious machine using genetic algorithms, neural nets and "machine evolution." Gary Taubes thinks evolution should be a good way of creating chips that are very adaptable, and can run anywhere in a wide variety of conditions, in systems that happen to be rapidly changing.[1] Researchers are attempting to find solutions to problems that humans have trouble designing into a system, computer chips that evolve themselves. Taubes refers to the evolving of complex chips as weird, and he thinks those chips are something like our brains.

Genetic algorithms and evolutionary computation are now doing jobs in distilleries that are done in one-seventh of the time taken by five expert workers. Machine evolution of efficient systems now does in hours what biological evolution did in eons.

One computer expert asks who needs the kind of equipment we now have for computers when we can connect to the Internet through a tiny telephone implanted in our heads?

John Yaukey says quantum mechanics is the only science that addresses the question, "what existed before the big bang?"[2] Nothing existed before the big bang. "Nothing" refers to what is called the "quantum vacuum" in quantum mechanics. Particles arise and vanish like bubbles on boiling water in the quantum vacuum. The bubbles are so ephemeral as to be essentially nothing, which is possibility without actuality.

These ephemeral particles are similar to infinitesimals about which I will later write. Yaukey says that some experts believe the quantum vacuum is what ignited the big bang. Cosmologist Andreas Abecht, from the University of California, Davis, says, "In this vacuum, there is actually a lot going on.... It's a very interesting place where it is never impossible for a universe to start."[3]

A recent article about computers and the future includes interviews with a number of computer experts, but quantum computers were not mentioned. Perhaps those experts thought a larger quantum computer cannot be developed because of the use of small particles, lasers, and crystals. A small quantum computer exists today, and its developers project startling results. Quantum computing uses a different computational paradigm. It uses magnetic resonance imaging rather than the "chips" of a digital computer.

In order to see those projected results, a hypothetical problem that is given to illustrate the power of a future quantum computer is to find a missing item in a three thousand-room hotel. A digital computer would need to look in each room separately for the missing item. A quantum computer looks in all rooms simultaneously. Some knowledgeable person compared a quantum computer to a digital computer as a hydrogen bomb is to a firecracker. An unnamed expert estimated that a quantum computer would solve a problem a billion times faster than a digital computer. DNA computers may be able to apply their logic to everything from code-breaking to finding the most efficient way to visit multiple destinations, even though they are now slow and clumsy. One gram of DNA could hold as much data as a trillion CDs.

The *Encyclopedia of Philosophy*, under philosophical implications of quantum mechanics says, "But the initial skepticism natural in professional philosophers should not obscure the big departure from philosophical tradition that is built into the very heart of quantum mechanics."[4] In the same article regarding uncertainty relations the encyclopedia says,

> Concepts which the nineteenth century had sundered, as a matter of scientific logic, to be recombined in our time. It has been the triumph of quantum mechanics to achieve a largely satisfactory recombination. The recognition on the nature of this triumph, however, leads directly to a qualitative appreciation of the uncertainty relations.

I use the term "quantum" as a gross quantity or bulk, that into which uncombined parts could now profitably be recombined into a whole that is more than the sum of its parts. The whole is more than the parts because the arrangement of the parts, which cannot be seen outside the whole, is itself an element of the whole.

I refer to one more sense of "quantum," namely, that quantum effects are simultaneous. Everything is happening all at once and this is it. "When you talk about how atoms bind together, you are talking about quantum mechanics," says Nobel Prize-winning Cornell University chemist, Roald Hoffmann.[5] "It is this theoretical framework of how atoms connect," he says. Connection, simultaneity, and some necessary uncertainty are central to quantum physics and quantum learning.

John G. Cramer's ideas about quantum nonlocality will help demonstrate some translogical elements of quantum functioning and quantum learning.[6] Nonlocality has often been demonstrated in laboratory experiments. Cramer uses the word "mysterious" in referring to the ability of nature to enforce correlations when separated, but what Cramer called "entangled parts" of a quantum system move faster-than-light to ensure that the separated but entangled parts are made to match. Nonlocality, according to Cramer, means that correlations in quantum systems are not possible through simple memory yet are being enforced faster-than-light across space and time.

Cramer speaks about Albert Einstein's dislike of quantum mechanics as developed by Paul Dirac, Werner Heisenberg, and others. Quantum mechanics did not properly fit with Einstein's understanding of the universe. One of Einstein's objections to quantum mechanics Einstein called "spookiness at a distance." Cramer says that Einstein's "spookiness" is now referred to as nonlocality. Cramer calls this nature's mysterious ability. If we allow mystery in quantum physics, we may find using mystery in quantum learning when the learning combines previously separated but entangled parts.

Although Einstein spoke of "spookiness" of what is now a fact of quantum systems, according to Judith Orloff, author of *Second Sight*, Einstein believed the distinction between past, present, and future is only a persistent illusion. She believes modern physics is confirming that our common view of reality is limited. I mention Einstein and Orloff to help pave the way for noticing quantum learning. We frequently see what we believe, but we rarely see what we do not believe.

Some writers hold that Rupert Sheldrake's theory of morphic resonance and morphic fields relates to nonlocality as Cramer is using the term. According to conventional ways of thinking, some of quantum mechanics, and what I say about quantum learning and nonduality, seem weird.

The vast separation of scientific concepts, differences which the scientific community has made over the past centuries, could now be recombined into a whole to which the nondual/holistic paradigm refers. The whole includes not only digital functioning, but also analog functioning, and the simultaneous aspects of quantum functioning. This whole is more than the string/unified field theory of which physicists are trying to more fully develop to unify all physical forces. As John Yaukey implies, scientists had to learn to surf the weirdness rather than fight it. Yaukey is referring to quantum mechanics. If we surf enough, may we find a singularity/nonduality?

Although change continues to occur, technology is accelerating change to the point where rapidity of change is now frequently considered. Norbert Wiener, the initiator of cybernetics, talked about our not being able to build a machine that we theoretically could not criticize, but because we are so slow relative to machines, criticism of machines may come long after it is relevant.

I am not referring to a possible machine takeover, although Wiener is. I am talking about a person/machine joint venture in which many of us, during the next fifty years, will think that machines are conscious. Machine consciousness will be a part of this larger whole to which I am referring.

Looking at present differences between current digital computers and projected quantum computers, digital computers use, at any given instant, zeroes or ones for a "yes" or a "no," open or closed circuits. Quantum computers use zeroes and ones simultaneously. In a digital computer, an electronic signal in a wire represents a one, whereas the absence of electronic signal represents a zero. Digital computers use differences, and quantum computers use samenesses and differences, until an integration is called for.

Erwin Schrödinger devised equations in the 1920s that define particles as waves, a cornerstone of quantum theory. One effect of the use of quantum physics in computers is that subatomic particles can be waves and also particles until the computer system designer arranges for them to be either waves or particles, which can then be integrated into a single reality. This is a factor in how a quantum computer can simultaneously "look" into three thousand rooms.

Change is occurring very rapidly, and wisdom moves us to develop ourselves so that we can more conveniently adapt to rapid change. Nowhere in American society is the need to adapt to change greater than in our nation's schools and universities. I am offering a paradigm different from a static, Newtonian paradigm to facilitate the acceptance of change. This paradigm is as different from the present-day dualistic paradigm as quantum theory is different from classical, "uncombined," Newtonian science. This different paradigm may help us adapt to change more conveniently.

Patterns emerge from individual threads as Todd May reminds us. May reminds us that, "a problem here, an inconsistency there, a perspective on a particular issue to be worked out" is what most thinkers use thought for.[7] May says, "this is the stuff of the daily life of most philosophers… What that pattern is might be reinterpreted by later generations…. A pattern that might not have been noticed beforehand, might now make sense."[8] May alludes to the idea that frequently a pattern is rarely noticed until attention is given to it, often by wide variety of thinkers.

This book does not deal with a clearly defined problem here, or a definite inconsistency there, or an agreed upon perspective of a particular issue that a number of scholars agree needs to be worked out. This writing explores recombining now more of what had been separated then. We want to be clear and explicit in thought and expression, yet when everything is happening simultaneously, difficulties arise. We can become more open, however, by paying attention to murkiness/uncertainty and by focused noticing of what is going on around us as it is going on. I am dealing with an uncommon notion that thoughtfulness/mindfulness can be enhanced by reducing the quantity and broadness of conceptioning. Conceptioning more frequently deals with past and future than with a person's present experience.

The pattern that has emerged from poststructuralist and postmodern thinkers, mainly French, concerns difference and its valorization. May says, "It has become clear that the articulation of an adequate concept of difference, as well as a proper sense of how to valorize it, is the overriding problem that occupies recent French thought."[9] The problem, according to May, is "How to avoid reducing difference to the logic of the same."[10]

While words relate to experience, and words can be used in an infinite variety of ways, one way of using words, from a nondual perspective, is that the word "same" could be viewed differently when it is used in the sense of "the logic of the same." To use logic implies that subjects and objects exist, and that the object be other than the subject; otherwise, a statement is tautological. Saying red is red is not frequently illuminating or informative.

"Difference," from a dualistic perspective, cannot be reduced to "same." Nonduality is not a framework, or a paradigm, but I will express nonduality as a framework for my purposes here. Paradoxically, "difference" is none other than "same" from a nondual framework. When May alludes to "avoiding reducing difference to the logic of the same," he is moving toward more balance between two poles. I contend that this movement could profitably continue toward the nondual pole partly because of the many years of excessive attention given to the dualistic pole.

The problem of how to avoid reducing difference to the logic of the same is contrived, as are other problems from a nondual view. For example, a person has a problem because he has no shoes. When he meets a person who has no feet, his problem temporarily vanishes. The problem emerges again when the person with no feet is forgotten. Another illustrative story is a person is walking out of a grocery store carrying several bags of food. The person bumps into someone and falls down with all the food lying all over the ground. Just as the grocery carrier is about to finish saying, "Hey! Are you bli...," she notices that the person she bumped into is blind. Perspective immediately changes. The nondual paradigm will more easily have the effect of helping one remember the person with no feet or that a person bumped may be blind.

But the problem has more to do with the noticing than with memory. Nonduality includes no difference between having or not having feet. We can notice few large wholes more easily than we can notice billions of details simultaneously. The paradox we run into is that only details exist, but these details have been recombined in quantum mechanics, and we now profitably see that we have made differences, separations, what my brother Tom describes as "tears in the fabric of our being," only since we have been deluded. In this quantum world, each part is the whole. The whole is in the part.

We cannot verify this general recombining within our traditional view of science. We need to consider that we can know more than we can tell, and have intuitive understanding which often is at the foundation of what is later verified. We often fail to notice the present details; instead, we deal with concepts/abstractions from present reality. These abstractions relate to the past and future and prevent us from seeing large, presently-operating wholes.

At any time when using a nondual paradigm, one can choose to use a dualistic paradigm. The dualistic paradigm is the paradigm in which we are so immersed that we rarely notice the possibility of nonduality. Nondualists hold that a dualistic paradigm is a subset of nonduality. Your understanding is enhanced when you hold that you can be nondual and dual simultaneously, as in quantum theory particles can be waves and particles simultaneously.

From a nondual framework, all problems are not only temporary. Problems are also contrived in the sense that a problem is only a problem when a person perceives one. The problem is not thoughtfulness/mindfulness. The problem is the aspect of what is sometimes considered to be thought-fulness/mindfulness, conceived as conceptioning, which creates the differences and the problems. Without differences, problems would not exist. Nonduality holds that neither differences nor problems exist. There is no "there" different from here. Only enlightenment and illusion exist, and they are not two and not one, and "it" cannot be said. If "it" can be said, "it" is not "it." But please do not give up yet. You will see that "it" does make some sense when seen in a larger quantum context.

Regarding inconsistencies, when things are consistently inconsistent, while looking nondually, we may say that they are quantumly consistent which is similar to total consistency. With respect to a particular issue that needs to be worked out, near-nondualists consider inconsistency to be simply another way of stating that a problem needs to be solved, but again, the problem is a problem only when a person conceives a problem.

While I do not consider nonduality to be equal to the logic of the same, I have been writing from a perspective that tends to be nondual. May is writing from a less nondual perspective. Is one perspective correct and the other wrong? The answer is probably "yes" from a dualistic perspective. From a nondual perspective, the dualistic perspective is embodied by the nondual. We can use a dualistic perspective when a dualistic perspective helps us avoid delusion. Viewed nondually, various conceptions are delusions since conception implies "this" is separate from "that."

Most Westerners are born in a dualistic milieu. Some Westerners, through focused attention, have moved beyond a dualistic framework to a more open, nondual way of being. Those who have made such a movement hold that they did not move at all but rather, through opening their minds, they see they are always nondual. Only through making differences, total separations that they did not see, were they deluded.

This nondual non-point-of-view emphasizes action rather than theory, and emphasizes what may be called direct or intuitive vision rather than interpretation. All theories, therefore, are interferences to this intuitive, direct seeing.

Although the origins of talk about nonduality arose in India, nondual ways of being moved to most of Asia. Since nondual thinking has increased in the West during the last fifty years, I will not refer to nondual thinking as Eastern thinking. To view the differences between dualistic and nondual ways of being, I refer to the article by Kaiping Peng and Richard E. Nisbett, "Culture Dialectics, and Reasoning About Contradiction," to review some interesting ideas about dualistic thinking and nondual ways of being.[11] The authors, when referring to what is near-nondualism, use the language, "principles of Eastern naive dialecticism." My hope is that the reader will not be negatively influenced by the use of that language. Peng and Nisbett say:

> It is obvious to readers that these laws of formal logic are not congruent with the principles of Eastern naive dialecticism. For instance, the principle of change suggests that life is a constant passing from one stage of being to another, so that to be is not to be, and not to be is to be. The law of identity, on the other hand, assumes cross situational consistency. A must be A regardless of the context.

> According to Chinese belief, the law of noncontradiction of formal logic works only in the realm of concepts and abstraction. Even in these cases, the rejection of conceptual contradiction based on formal logic can be mistaken, because concepts are reflections of things. As S. H. Liu (1974) put it, "It is precisely because the Chinese mind is so rational that it refuses to become rationalistic and... refuses to separate form from content" (p. 325). There is nothing that does not contain contradiction, and therefore, there is no concept that does not contain contradiction. The student, in many ways, is not a student, as illustrated by the experience of many graduate student instructors.

> Finally, if change and contradiction are constant, then real understanding of truth and reality must be relational. Hence, for a dialectical thinker, both A and B may be right, or both be A and B may be equal to a third element C that may not be part of the initial contradiction.

> We believe such fundamental differences in ontology and epistemology lead to substantial cognitive differences. We expected that Western stances for dealing with contradiction would be consistent with Westerners' intuitive understanding of the law of noncontradiction, whereas the Chinese stances for dealing with contradiction would be based on naive dialecticism.

The Chinese stance to which the authors refer is similar to what I am calling near-nonduality. When I speak of nonduality, I would have you see a view tending toward the nondual. It is only from a dualistic perspective that something can be said, and when we are attempting to talk about the nondual, all that can be done is to talk around "it." Let us take a look at that which is so evident that it may not be evident. What is said is offered nondually.

What you are now seeing is ink marks on paper. These ink marks are arranged to have you direct your mental storage to be rearranged in a prescribed way. What I have just said is so obvious that it is infrequently considered. It is so obvious that we are breathing that it is most often useless to mention. That you are now seeing ink marks on paper may be considered useful as we explore some differences between dualistic and nondual ways of being.

Grammar precedes logic. Dualistic thinkers agree with this. The logic used in our communication operates on a grammar which is partly translogical. There are many different grammars. Grammar is similar to axioms of a geometry. There are several different geometries and there can possibly be an infinite number, only a few of which may be presently useful. The axioms of Euclidean geometry are different from the axioms in Einsteinian geometry. Parallel lines do not meet in Euclidian geometry whereas they do in Einsteinian geometry. From where do all these grammars and axioms arise? They arise, say nondualists, from the same "place" where differences and problems arise. If they are contrived, must a contrivor exist or at least "something" out of which they are contrived? That "something," from a nondual perspective, is the spooky nothing which simultaneously includes everything. I will go back to the beginning of Western thought to look for early expressions of duality.

Western society, around the time of Thales of Melitus (585 BC) explained events on the basis of the gods doing this or doing that. Thales, Anaxagoras, Anaxamander, Pythagorus, and a few others, began to explain differences that "arose" on the bases of wind, fire, earth, water, and number. Heraclitus came along and said everything was in flux and is constantly changing, much like the nondual Eastern stance. Parmenides, around the same time, said that nothing changes; nothing is in flux. Socrates, Plato, and Aristotle, shortly thereafter, agreed more with Parmenides than with Heraclitus. They added some notions, and today we have a dualistic society partly because of the "grammar" and "axioms" of thought laid down for us by Plato and Aristotle.

In an age of quantum computers, when artificial intelligence is now predicted by Ray Kurzweil to equal human intelligence by 2019, and to exceed human intelligence a thousand times by the year 2029, and in an age when particles are considered as both waves and particles, might we now be wise to consider that something may exist between zero and one in our digital society?[13] Might we now profitably consider whether dualistic thinking with differences, with subjects and objects, might be a subset of nonduality? If quantum computers are now operating on the principle of things being and not being simultaneously, might we not profitably consider things to be, and not to be, simultaneously, rather than dismissing them as only a contradiction?

How might we become more open to translogical events within and outside of us?

Words relate to experience. I look at the experience of "having nothing to say." This book is an attempt to approach a link between what can be said and the near-ineffable. Since nothing can be said about the ineffable, I will start by saying nothing about the ineffable, but I will return to the topic later. I will also look at absolute multiplicity, an empty set, the educator's equivalent to mathematician's zero, emptiness, the void, and nonsense, in order to talk around, and get a clearer view of what is infrequently considered.

When I say, "what is," I refer to a person's feelings, thoughts, and that unknown which nudges what exists in our unconscious minds toward our consciousness.

Along the way, I will reconsider clarity in thought and expression. I will look at the notions of beyond and between as they relate to a dualistic view-point as well as from a nondual framework. I will give, as an example, the activities of five different teachers in order to move closer to the idea that teachers four and five tend to be more nondual than teachers one and two.

Teacher One: Pay attention, class. The lesson for today is the linking verbs. Repeat after me (said quickly): is, are, was, were, seem, become, appear, feel, look, taste, smell, grow, and sound. Repeat after me again: the linking verbs are: is, are, was, were, seem, become, appear, feel, look, taste, smell, grow, and sound.

Student: I would rather not bother with memorizing the linking verbs. Please tell me something useful by which I may live my life more fully, or more contentedly, or more creatively.

Teacher One: Today's lesson is the linking verbs. Tomorrow we will learn about predicate nominatives.

Student: I have heard that grammar precedes logic. I also learned that there can be many different grammars.

Teacher One: I said that today's lesson is linking verbs. Repeat after me quickly: is are was were seem become appear feel look taste smell grow and sound.

Student: Blah.

Teacher Two: The lesson for today is about the scientific principle, discovered by Isaac Newton, which holds that for every action there is an equal and opposite reaction. If you hold this battery operated fan behind this small sailboat in a small tub of water, while the fan is running, the boat would move forward if the fan is held in your hand behind the sail. If you place the fan on the mount that is attached to the sailboat, when you turn the fan on, you will see the sail fill with wind but the boat will not move. The boat will not move because—ta dah, ta dah, ta dah, etc.

Student: I am now wanting to learn something that will help me live my life more fully, or more contentedly, or more creatively.

Teacher Two: I said that today's lesson was about the scientific principle "for every action there is an equal and opposite reaction."

Student: Blah.

Teacher Three: Today's lesson is to help you to inquire. We will not be dealing with any one concept, but we will be dealing with helping you figure out why the sailboat does not move the second time when the person in this film attaches the fan to a mount that was already attached to the sailboat while the fan is turned on. You have already seen that when the teacher holds the fan, the sailboat moves down the tub of water, and when the fan is attached to the mount that is attached to the boat, the boat does not move. Does anyone have any ideas?

Student: I am wanting to learn how to live more fully, or more contentedly, or more creatively.

Teacher Three: Trying to figure out why the sailboat did not go the second time will be useful for you.

Student: I don't care right now about why the sailboat goes or does not go.

Teacher Three: I suggest you visit the guidance counselor.

Student: Blah.

Teacher Four: After an introduction, and after telling the students his goals of helping the students better notice what is, and to help the students decide for themselves what will secure or endanger their freedom, Teacher Four then says: I am hoping that someone will be willing to react to what I have said or tell me what it is that you want to learn right now.

Student: I am wanting to learn how to live my life more fully or more contentedly or more creatively?

Teacher: What is holding you up from doing that?

Student: I don't know.

Teacher Four: Would you like to find out?

Student: Yes.

Teacher Four: What do you think you could do right now that would best help you find out what you want to find out?

Student: I don't know. I am hoping that you have some ideas.

Teacher Four: Ideas about what?

Student: Ideas about helping me live more fully, more contentedly, or more creatively.

Teacher Four: What would you be doing now if you were living more fully, or more contentedly, or more creatively?

Student: I don't know. I don't think you can tell me exactly how to do that but I do think you have some ideas that would lead me there.

Teacher Four: What leads you to think that I have some ideas that would lead you there?

Student: I don't know.

Teacher Four: What is wrong with not knowing?

Student: I have been trained to want to know things I don't know.

Teacher Four: Would you agree that you do not know trillions and trillions of things? Would you also agree that even if you learned one new thing every second, you would not have enough time in your life to learn trillions and trillions of things? Would you also then agree that your training has been at best incomplete?

Student: I don't know.

Teacher Four: Are you willing to experiment?

Student: Yes but I am not sure how.

Teacher Four: I don't think anyone is ever a hundred percent sure. I would like to suggest that you experiment with thinking about what you might do to help you know how to live more contentedly or creatively of which you are one or two percent sure, and then do those things as experiments, and if and when they do not work, then try another experiment and after trying some of those kinds of experiments, if you want to talk to me again, I will be pleased to do so.

Student: That sounds quite difficult and indefinite.

Teacher Four: Is living more fully, or more contentedly, or more creatively difficult and indefinite?

Student: I guess it is. I cannot even think of an experiment about which I am one or two percent sure.

Teacher Four: You could experiment with doing something of which you are a hundred percent unsure. Are you willing to try that?

The Student sees Teacher Five sitting nearby. The Student goes over and sits next to Teacher Five. Both sit silently as the student wonders when Teacher Five will speak to her. Both are silent for ten minutes.

Student: Are you going to say something?

Teacher Five: What do you want me to say?

Student: Well, you could say that you know I am sitting next to you.

Teacher Five: I know you are sitting next to me.

Student: Is that all you are going to say?

Teacher Five: What more do you want me to say?

Student: I'm wanting you to tell me how to live more fully, or more contentedly, or more creatively.

Teacher Five: What is holding you up from doing that right now?

Student: I don't know.

Teacher Five: Neither do I.

Student: Can you give me some hints?

Teacher Five: What kind of hint are you looking for?

Student: I don't know.
Long period of silence.
Student: Aren't you going to say anything else?
Teacher Five: Not unless you want to me to say something.
Student: What about later?
Teacher Five: I don't know.
Student: What do you know?
Teacher Five: Not much.
Student: I thought you were a teacher.
Teacher Five: Some people say I am.
Student: Well what do you say you are?
Teacher Five: I do not say I am anything.
Student: Well.
Another long pause.
Student: I was hoping you would say more.
Teacher Five: What more are you hoping for?
Student: I don't know.

I hold that Teachers One and Two are more like trainers than educators and more dualistic than nondual. Differences between the two groups of teachers will be clearer as you read on.

Most teachings of nondual sages are for the purpose of breaking through intellectual interpretations and ideas. Ideas develop from the delusion of dualistic thinking.

If you are wondering why Teacher Five did not give any ideas to the student, note what nondual Zen master Yuanwu said, "If you want to obtain intimate realization of Zen, first of all do not seek it. What is attained by seeking has already fallen into intellection."[13] Note that Zen is held, by some Zen teachers, to be the essence of nonduality: Other nondual teachers disagree. Nonduality encompasses "more," and some writers hold that Zen encompasses all.

If you are wondering about what is Zen, Inayat Khan tells a story in answer to that question.[14] The story is about a fish who went to see the queen fish and says she has always heard about the sea, but what is this sea? Where is it? The queen finished replies that we live, move, and have our being in the sea. The sea is within and without us, and we are made of sea, and we will end in sea. The sea surrounds us as our own being.

A connection exists between the above story and a comment by Rollo May, the internationally-known psychologist, who said that you are not neurotic or psychotic simply because you deviate from this or that norm. Instead you are neurotic or psychotic to the degree that you deviate from your own "condition humane." Your "condition humane" relates to mental disturbance that arises when you are doing something that you think and feel you should not be doing, or when you are not doing something that you think and feel you should be doing. When that occurs, you are binding yourself and you are not aware of it.

Yuanwu asks us to become like a dead tree and let go of competitiveness, knowledge about the world, ideas, opinions, images, and intellectualism, and when we have done that, we reach a point where feelings are ended and our views are gone.[15] At this point, our mind is clean, and we can open up to what he calls nondual Zen realization. We, at that point, will not seek liberation because we are already free, independent, and not bound by anything.

While nothing needs explanation, and I do not have any ideas worth mentioning, I want you to know what Yuanwu would say about Teacher Five. He would note that our ability to talk is not just a matter of words, and that speech is not only in the tongue. People who knew this would gain realization and they would know that spoken words are not to be relied on. If Yuanwu were alive today, he might say that racism, sexism, and homophobia are fostered by our excessive socialization/training/reliance on words which are promoted by our closed, out-dated schooling.

Action on opening ourselves acts on reducing racism, sexism, and homophobia, each being fostered by excessive socialization/training, the lack of attention given to promoting self-direction/education, and the lack of paying attention to our present experience. The integration of races, sexes, orientations, as well as the further integration of parts of ourselves, could occur by a recombining to an open, holistic, nondual type of schooling.

We can move toward integrating people by moving toward integrating all things and events. An integrated, highly cooperative world is a nondual world. Nonduality holds that we will have peace in the world, peace among various cultural groups, when we are individually at peace with ourselves. The lack of peace with ourselves manifests itself as an excessive friction with others. Seeing that we are nondual, seeing that we are not separate from the rest of the universe, implies that when we treat ourselves peacefully, and when we are at ease, the world will be peaceful, and the world will be at ease. There is a growing body of evidence to support this nondual perspective in the pages that follow.

It appears that our society is still having racial, gender, and/or sexual orientation battles. These battles will be reduced and/or eliminated when we reduce our delusion. The paradox is that we will be more likely to change more rapidly and conveniently when we are open to our present experience.

We experience dualistically with a sense of self that is separate. We could profitably extend effort to realize what we are looking for is what is looking.

George David Miller states friction is created between facts and wisdom.[16] Miller's comparison between the fact finding approach to teaching and the insight, wisdom-bearing approach to teaching is given below.

The fact-finding approach is given first, then the insight/wisdom-bearing approach is given:

monoperspectivism—multiperspectivism
single body of knowledge—multiple bodies of knowledge
certainty—tentativity
monologue—dialogue
meaning from without—meaning from within
teacherly authority—authority of conscience
consonance/conformity—dissonance/opposition
individuality—collaboration
dicteachership—democracy
generic student memorization—creativity

Present, traditional, closed schooling holds to a monoperspective. That monoperspective is dualistic in that each person and thing is separate from every other. The implication for American schools, from a nondual perspective, is to allow multiple perspectives. This is similar to the wisdom which holds that we can find many ways to the way. Notice that the way is nondual even though it encompasses many ways.

Through seeing from multiple perspectives, and from knowing that infinite bodies of knowledge exist, with creativity and tentative dialogue, including dialogue with various parts of ourselves, we can possibly move toward being wise. Miller believes that through our authority of conscience, by democratically allowing collaboration and dissonance, we can develop the idiosyncratic student who is wise. I extend Miller's view to include that from this wisdom education, the student knows that she or he does not know. She or he does not strive because she or he is already there. The student is empty because she or he is presently full.

The following points will clarify these ideas.

To Shunryu Suzuki, nonduality is not two and not one. He says usually something is either singular or plural, one or two. The nondual is both two and one. Suzuki believes the Western paradigm to understand this is incomplete and, therefore, something being two or not one, or both two and one is not understandable within that paradigm.

According to David Loy, when you realize that the nature of your mind and the universe are nondual, you are enlightened.[17] Noticing what you are experiencing, noticing thoughts and feelings in the present moment, may be a way to enlightenment. Paradoxically, when you are on the way, you are already there from the Zen, nondual perspective. The journey and the destination are one.

Loy believes that all enlightenment comes by accident but he quotes Chogyam Trungpa, who said that the practice of sitting, meditating, and noticing your breathing in the present makes you more accident-prone. We will hear more of Loy's ideas later.

Westerners want closure and definiteness. The freedom of nonduality is not highly desirable to some Western thinkers, since opensure is continuous and ongoing, and as an unnamed sage said, nonduality is terminally unknowable. Our dualistic paradigm has been created so that we can have conceptions. Unless we have conceptions, we think we will not fare well. The nondual paradigm holds nothing exists to attain, and that everything is empty in the sense that everything is already full.

Nondual practice has thought and language as its main interference. The main problem in arriving at nondual practice is language and thought itself.

Some Eastern thinkers hold that silence and the consciousness of silence are nondual, not two different events. To illustrate this point, Simone Weil says that she must tear her thoughts from her body and transport those thoughts to a place that she calls, "outside space." That place is, she says, neither perspective nor point of view. She puts her perception in that place to an infinity to a second or third degree beyond the ordinary expanses of infinite perception. At that point is a silence which she says is not an absence of sound but which is an object.

Within nonduality is nondual action: the action of no action, and the thought of no thought. This is the emptiness phenomenon, and every thing and non-thing is also included. It is a sign of understanding to not understand. Being compassionate to ourselves and our fellow sentient beings may be a purpose of our being, which paradoxically has no purpose. When the compassion is "done" for a purpose, it is not compassion and wisdom.

Being compassionate for me means finding balance, feeding the hungry, giving drink to the thirsty, providing a shelter for the homeless, reducing racism, sexism, homophobia, and helping people notice when they delude themselves. When I do that, I find it convenient for my well-being which is not separate from the well-being of others. This relates to the wise saying, "Treat other people the way you would like to be treated," and we will all be wiser for doing so.

To learn how to be wise, Yuanwu says that nondual Zen work must be done over a long period of time, although enlightenment is often experienced instantaneously.[18] He compares the coming to enlightenment with the experience of a newly hatched bird that is naked and scrawny. The bird eventually grows feathers and flies far and high.

Regarding people becoming enlightened, Yuanwu believes we block ourselves by not emptying ourselves of impurities/delusions. He believes that everything is a gateway to the our becoming free, but if we have ideas of pride or superiority, then that is a disaster.

He also talks about people who view nondual Zen as a concept. Yuanwu says looking for Zen as a concept is like drilling in ice for fire, or like drilling a hole in the ground to look for the sky. To look for nondual Zen as a concept increases our lethargy. He believes that to study Zen by training is like adding mud to dirt and scattering sand in our eyes: that impedes us more and more. He is asking us to give up our former conceptual knowledge and understanding, which is the emptying he is talking about. We can then open our hearts while not keeping anything in our minds so that we may be open to present experience. Our getting rid of all conceptions will help us be calm, selfless, and at ease.

Yuanwu says that beyond cleaning ourselves of concepts is a boundless, fathomless, and measureless more that still can be realized. But as soon as we try to grab or chase nondual Zen, we have already stumbled past nondual Zen. Yuanwu asks us to take away all slogans and intellectual views that cling to us, to empty our minds so that we do not manifest any thoughts on our own, and so that we do not do anything at all.

The implication is that when something is done, the whole of which we are a part is doing what is being done. We are simply parts of a recondite host as I will later amplify. We are not separate selves. If we think nondual Zen is the same as this conceptual stuff about Zen, we are deluded. This conceptual stuff about nondual Zen is not nondual Zen. Yuanwu believes we must transcend those parameters to go to what he calls, "beyond Zen," and magically produce a sanctuary of purity, effortlessness, and coolness, right in the middle of a world of turmoil.

In order to do all of this, Yuanwu is not asking us to abandon our ordinary experience in worldly activities. No difference occurs between ordinary experience and enlightened experience, between worldly activities and enlightening activities. We need to detach ourselves from rejection and clinging, and from both being and non-being, so that we are unburdened and empty, yet calm and peaceful.

No "better" or "worse" exists within nonduality. The experiences we have help or hinder our awareness of nonduality. We find being compassionate difficult when we have not experienced compassion, yet, paradoxically, nonduality contains everything, including all experience.

While nonduality cannot be directly described or explained, additional talking around nonduality can be useful for those who wish to explore more nondual, more quantum-like learning and thinking. Along the way, holism/nonduality and various Gestalt experiences may become clearer.

The roots of dualistic thinking can be seen by relating Robert M. Pirsig's ideas about pre-Socratic philosophers. We will see how Western thinking remains dualistic. Openness and holism are closely allied to nonduality.

Teachers Four and Five, who talk less, may help students become better educated in John Dewey's sense of becoming more self-directing.

Two

ROOTS OF DUALISM AND
GROUNDS FOR HOLISM

To help you wonder why teachers could profitably talk less, consider if all your college classes were strictly lecture classes. I estimate that your teachers, over a four-year undergraduate period, spoke over twenty million words during those classes. What could I possibly say that would make a difference in your life? If you are now making too many differences, the difference I would like to make is to have you make fewer differences. May anything be said here that would undo the differences that were made during your listening to twenty million words? What differences can now be recombined? Must the answer or answers be spelled-out conceptually?

Nondualists believe that silence has value. A part of the value of silence is that silence enables us to clear our minds of dysfunctional fixities and ossifications. Nondualists suggest that a way of countering the effects of being drowned in a sea of words is to set aside five, ten, or more minutes per day to listen to yourself. Listening may be done more conveniently when you are alone and free from distractions. During this listening, you could profitably limit your sense input so that you can pay attention to your thoughts and feelings and simply notice what is. Notice that thoughts and feelings are quite impermanent.

What can you do to facilitate listening to yourself? Could you profitably take a few moments of silence and simply pay attention to what is going on in and around you?

A number of people I interviewed said they had a better sense of what is going on in and around them when they were silent and still. They had a better experience of noticing their present thoughts and feelings, at times, when they had the opportunity to express those thoughts and feelings, although Zen teachers I know do not advocate those expressions, neither do they deny their value.

Some ideas that are expressed in words negate the negative impact of excessive words. The first of these is that you ought not to be bound to any word, any doctrine, any theory, any ideology, or any feeling. The second notion is that it is worthwhile not to mistreat your body or your mind or the body or mind of another person. Perhaps some periods of silence will permit you to see more of the inter-connectedness of all life. When you see the interconnecteness, you may have less of a desire or need to kill animals, or any other sentient being. Such is the way of nonduality.

Some knowledge changes more rapidly than other knowledge. No one truth explains all other truths. Truths, defined as what is natural, derive from culture, which includes a wide variety of forces. These forces are not totally predictable and therefore what may be held as knowledge today or tomorrow may not be totally predictable. We ought not to say things that are not so. Remember that knowledge is socially constructed. We may learn more by being silent more often.

The result of our drowning in words in our colleges and universities as well as in our elementary and secondary schools, is that our consciousness is not permitted to develop. In this atmosphere of excessive verbiage, our thought is domesticated, often to serve the continuation of the *status quo*. The continuation of the *status quo* promotes racism, sexism, homophobia, and non-self-direction.

A problem concerned with drowning in words is that we are often unaware when we are drowning in words because of our need for excessively logical, verbal expression of past experience. We may wish to teach ourselves and our students other forms of expression. From the standpoint of holism/ nondualism, each moment fully lived is an end and purpose in itself and not a means for something else. Each task, then, becomes an awakening of our being and a fulfillment of our life.

Fixed ideas can prevent our noticing what is. Helping students come to know they do not know may be a necessary condition for their noticing what is. Student noticing or awakening may be described as students coming to be aware of what is going on in and around them. Awareness occurs simultaneously with students coming to know that they do not know. Awareness can be paradoxical as emptiness is paradoxical.

Meditative silence may be paradoxical. That silence may be an aspect of an educator's equivalent to the mathematician's zero. Logic may help us go beyond logic. Silence can help us use logic to go beyond logic. Such silence may be the educator's equivalent to the mathematician's zero.

Another possibility for an educator's zero is facilitating the disintegration of students' fixed conceptions. The notion that everything should always be clear, unambiguous, and certain has clouded educators' thinking to the point where we infrequently allow students to become stuck. In order for student stuckness to make more sense, I will view selected similarities between holistic educators and ideas about some pre-Socratic philosophers.

The roots of Western education are often seen in the teachings of Socrates, Plato, and Aristotle. When we explore similarities between holistic/ nondual educators and early Greek thinkers, we find the roots of holistic, open education in pre-Socratic thinkers. I will expand on the roots of holistic, open educators so as to further ground and extend their endeavors. I will do this by first describing some of the basic principles of holistic, open education. I will then briefly restate some views of pre-Socratic philosophers taken mainly from Robert M. Pirsig.[1] Lastly, I will amplify some thoughts and draw some conclusions which tend to promote open, holistic living and teaching.

Holistic, open education may be simply stated with six ideas. The first five ideas are promoted by the Gestalt Institute of Cleveland.

1. A human being is a total organism functioning as a whole.
2. This total organism is born with the capability to cope with people, things, and events in life.
3. Organismic needs determine behavior.
4. The primary tool for effecting change is awareness.
5. These are the three zones of awareness:
   (a) sensory (hearing, seeing, etc.)
   (b) inside body (tension, pain, etc.)
   (c) fantasy (memory, ideas, imagination)
6. Growing awareness generates compassion for others, a sense of being at ease, and not seeing yourself as separate from others. Within nonduality, as you become more compassionate to self and others, you become wise.

Ideas 1, 2, and 3 will not be given more attention here. Idea 4 will be expanded after idea 5. Idea 5 states that of the three zones of awareness, the last is fantasy. Idea 6 will be dealt with later.

Fantasy includes all that we remember, all ideas, all theories, all of what we imagine, and all concepts. Some holistic, open educators conclude that, as a result of our feelings of dissonance, we use reason to manipulate symbols in order to create notions so that we can lower our feelings of dissonance. These notions do not have substance in themselves, yet Western philosophy has given these notions a life of their own.

In idea 4, holistic, open educators hold that the primary tool for effecting change is awareness. This does not mean that reason is abandoned. It means that reason is not a person's primary activity. We can choose to reason as a result of our exercise of free responsible choice. Some people make a distinction between thinking about lived reality and reality lived. Awareness helps us contact the reality lived so that we can abstract to thinking about if we choose to.

An underlying assumption is that if we must have a reason for everything we do and everything we experience, we will cut off our own awareness of those experiences for which we have no good reasons. Holistic awareness may be conceived as a process, with a cyclical movement from confusion and/or anxiety to an excitement stage, where energy mobilizes in a simmering of productive tension, which leads to an action stage. Then, a resistance stage is reached as we approach the next stage of contact with a person, thing, or event. We then move to a withdrawal stage of completion or hanging-on.

The hanging-on may result in an incomplete experience, a part rather than a whole, which leaves a situation unfinished in a way that interferes with other awarenesses which, in turn, can negatively influence intelligent behavior.

Pirsig thinks Plato was the greatest sophist of all and that is why Plato hated the sophists. Pirsig believes that we have great difficulty accepting quality because Socrates influenced Plato to carry on the struggle to capture the minds of people. In that struggle, the good lost and axiological, value concerns became less important than the epistemological/truth concerns. Truth won, and that is why Western people are so enamored with reason.

Greek philosophy failed to see that their society created new myths even though their intention was to provide a conscious search for what was unchanging in the affairs of humanity. The pre-Socratic philosophers wanted to destroy the old Greek myths but failed to see that society created its own myths because, from a nondual perspective, everything changes. Pirsig does not say emptiness is connected to everything changing, but nondualists hold that emptiness is an absence of a separate unchanging substance.

The pre-Socratics held that people, rather than principles were the measure of all things. The object of pre-Socratics' work was the improvement of society, and not to teach any particular truth. The early Greek conceptions about reasoning, matter, subjects, objects, form, and substance are hard to see as creations. The early Greeks could see earlier myths of the Greek gods, but they were not open to seeing their myths as myths. Socrates, Plato, and Aristotle did not see that their "findings" were also artistic creations. They thought that they captured the essence of truth.

The pre-Socratics professed what Plato translated as virtue, but the pre-Socratics used the word *Areté* to mean excellence in all areas of life.

Plato changed reality to an unchanging idea. He rigidified knowing and conceiving because Plato could not conceive of the good that was ever changing, and ultimately unknowable in any kind of fixed way. For Western thinkers, the good became a minor branch of knowledge called ethics. Reason and logic became primary concerns for Aristotle. Excellence in all areas of life is dead, and science, logic, and the university as we know it today, Pirsig says, has been given its founding charter to create a proliferation of artifacts which we call knowledge. The role of the university has become the transmission of these artifacts to future generations as the "system."

Because Plato wanted to fix ideas, Western society has become excessively rational in that what we value is subordinated to what is true, without evidence for either being subordinate.

According to Pirsig, who was relying on H.D.F. Kitto's *The Greeks*, the flavor of *Areté* is lost in the translation to "virtue," since *Areté* should more properly be translated to "excellence." According to Pirsig's view of Kitto, *Areté* comprised a respect for the wholeness, oneness, or nonduality of life, and a consequent dislike for specialization. *Areté* implies a contempt for efficiency, or instead, a much higher idea of efficiency which exists not in one department of life, but in life itself. I will later refer to R. Buckminster Fuller's idea that specialization makes us slaves to the generalist.

Areté, the good, became the highest idea, but still subordinate to reason itself. Some people with power do not want to develop generalists because they fear their power will erode, and they want to keep power so they continue to promote specialization as Fuller says.[2]

Overspecializing and relegating generalization to a subcategory of intellection called "philosophy," whose practice for many years had been to tell other philosophers how language may be used properly and meaningfully, has been the result of that non-quantum specialization. But we continue to slowly move away from that narrowness.

Both the pre-Socratic philosophers and many holistic, open educators are concerned with the superordinality of excellence to reason. Both are concerned with balanced living. Both are concerned with wholeness, openness, and oneness, and are willing to subordinate reason to wholeness and oneness. Socrates, Plato, Aristotle, and the majority of Western thinkers are concerned with balanced lives and the finding of virtue in the golden mean. The balance and virtue, however, are not as golden as reason.

A feeling of balance or total experience of balance in our lives, to Western thought, must be primarily based on reason. Balance, to the holistic educator and to some pre-Socratics, was balance between a person's cognitive and affective sides, between classic and romantic, between Appollonian and Dionysian. Reason was in balance instead of doing the balancing.

Holistic, open educators and the pre-Socratics believe that they can know the whole of a good process or event without striving to define it. To Aristotle, and on to Skinner and the majority of Western thinkers, we cannot know any process or event unless we define it.

Open, holistic educators hold, with some pre-Socratics, that our sense of duty includes a duty to self, others, and the whole of which we are all a part. The notion that we are either selfish or selfless is prompted by our dualistic reasoning. Holistic, open education holds that we can go beyond this dichotomy between selfishness and selflessness to the point where what we do that is good for us, is simultaneously good for those around us. As we meet our higher level needs, group interest and self-interest are recombined. Compassion for others is compassion for yourself.

Neither holistic educators nor pre-Socratics are against the use of reason to order affairs of living. No sane person wants continual chaos, and chaos in the form of continual jungle-type existence would follow, if we did not reason. The problem I see is not whether reason ought to be used in our lives. The problem is that reason has become the value that determines other values for us. Our Western culture has so conditioned us with the notion of the primacy of reason, that questioning the primacy of reason invites alienation from, and conflict with, the majority of Western thinkers.

The holistic, open view includes the notion of permitting stuckness in our lives. The holistic, open view holds that being what we are is okay. We cannot help but become unstuck when we allow ourselves to be stuck. A problem arises when we avoid being what we are. Energy that could profitably energize our growth toward wholeness and quality goes into the process of avoiding our present experience.

Being what we are is essential to the holistic, open educator's notion of good teaching. We cannot learn, change, or move toward quality until we are what we are. Awareness of what we are, and of what we are doing or not doing, is the igniter of change, if we choose to change. To learn something significant is to change. Awareness of avoiding, and choice, removes the behavior from the category of "avoiding" as the term is employed here.

To draw some conclusions and compare holistic, open educators with Pirsig's view of pre-Socratic philosophers, I have concluded that the greater the primacy of reason in our already highly reasonable Western culture, the less we will be concerned with quality. Pirsig reminds us that if we take quality out of pure science or math, it would not make a difference. A corollary to this removal is that we will not know what is good and what is not good, and we will need others to tell us.

The greater the primacy of reason, the more we will be like Alice in Wonderland, when she asked the Cat, "Please, tell me which way I ought to go from here," and the less we will understand the Cat's reply, "Oh, that depends a good deal on where you want to get to." Reason does not tell us what to hypothesize, although it is a useful tool in testing our hypotheses. We need more than reason to do breakthrough research, but not for replicating what has already been found.

For holistic, open educators, and for some pre-Socratics, living reality is superordinate to thinking about lived reality. For holistic, open educators and for pre-Socratics, noticing, awareness of what is going on in and around us, is an activity that is vital to all other conscious activity. What is noticed is a "that." The "why" of the "that" is less crucial than the noticing of the "that." The holistic educator would more likely ask, "How is it to be as you are?" rather than, "Why are you that way?" Strongly desiring a "why" of a "that" can prevent us from noticing a "that."

For the holistic educator, an excellent person, a quality person, a virtuous person, or holistic person is a person who notices well. For the holistic, open person, disinterested noticing is not noticing.

Trying to change and trying to grow, in cases related to personality development, is not change and is not growth. What we often learn by trying is how to try. We learn to change by changing; we learn to grow by growing. "Trying" is sometimes used as an excuse for not changing. We facilitate this change by noticing what is going on in and around us. Some "trying" can be growth-producing. At times, the degree or amount of our change may be barely noticeable.

Excessive intellectualizing can be a way of resisting action and contact with a person, thing, or event. The resisting may interfere with completing experiences. Some experiences that remain unfinished can interfere with new experience. If we do not have new experience, we repeat old experiences. Repeating old experiences, if done in an unaware and unchosen way, can lead to further unbalanced living so that our primary mode of experience is fantasy.

When our primary mode of experience is fantasy, contact with the world is minimized. We primarily think about lived reality, rather than live reality, when our primary mode of experience is fantasy. If I were to ask you to try to hand me your pen, assuming you are only a foot or two away from me, you would probably hand me your pen. Trying and doing would be combined/integrated. This combined/integrated living is quantum living.

If I am trying to change myself without changing myself, holistic, open educators argue that my statement of trying to change indicates my unaware resistance to change. Awareness of the resistance removes it from the category of resistance, and puts the awareness into the category of a root of an individual's free, responsible choice. An individual's free, responsible choice is central to holistic, open, quantum learning as is awareness of present experience.

Using ideas of chaoticians may help us see some unconventional approaches to attending to very large, quantum wholes. For instance, a chaotician named John Briggs said that aesthetics is becoming extremely serious because aesthetics is about a sense of harmony in nature.[3] This implies a recombination of what has been separated.

A holistic, nondual, quantum way is not a way of seeing things not seen before, as an unnamed sage said, but seeing the things we have seen before in a different way. I contend that representations lead us to conclusions which prevent us from seeing in different ways. A representation is a re-presentation, and is impossible, prior to a presentation. We may need to look with an amalgamated, deconstructing, aesthetic lens as well as an epistemological lens if we are to see things in a different, deconstructing way. If we see things in a different way, we may accept ideas about how the use of a holistic, nondual, quantum paradigm may help reduce racism, sexism, and homophobia, improve school practices, possibly reduce the increase of global warming, and help us take care of the environment.

Briggs's idea about aesthetics may be thought of as "fine art," as Ignacio Götz uses the term "fine art."[4] Götz says that Kant remarked that the rules of beauty are nature's rather than ours. Götz believes artists are nature's willing instrument. Götz's ideas capture a holistic, quantum way of being.

The words "holistic," "nondual," "quantum," "deconstructing," "process," "event," "wisdom," "openness," "learning," "insight," and "intuition," seem to include everything, and are by themselves often incomprehensible and indefinable. Holism/nonduality is difficult to gain insight about because holism includes all isms. We can have particular insights, intuitions, and understandings, but the general notion of insight/intuition remains polymorphous, which may be why Western thinkers have shunned the use of those terms.

Educators could profitably pay more attention to "pauses" in the educator's storehouse of thoughtful tools, analagous to the great musician who said that anyone can play the notes, but it was the pauses between the notes that made him excel. Not telling students as much as we now tell so that students may become stuck and unstick themselves may now be helpful for recombining. This way of seeing insights and intuitions is similar to wholes that are not fully defined and which cannot be fully unfolded.

If we are to provide a new education which will help us gain the awareness necessary to live harmoniously in the twenty-first century, we will not only need to change some conventions, we will also need to look for that which will help us notice which conventions to change. We may need to change conventions which keep us dealing with representations while ignoring presentations; conventions which keep us dealing with the past and myth rather than dealing with present experience as we are experiencing it; conventions which keep us dealing with parts rather than wholes.

Educators today could profitably change what they are doing in classrooms within short periods of time. A major concern for open, holistic educators is that we will need to see the concerns themselves from new perspectives. We need that which will help us see presentations, awareness of present experience undeterred by static, fixed representations. These fixed representations prevent us from seeing diverse and rare points of view. Unfixed matters are difficult for Western thinkers to deal with because some newer perspectives lead us not to cognitive understanding but, instead, lead us to experience more fully, more holistically and openly, rather than experience in closed, rigid ways. Some present conceptions may be preventing us from experiencing more fully. General openness helps us experience more fully. Defining general openness is difficult because it is unbounded and to define implies boundaries.

Educators need a tool which helps their students learn how to learn. If a learner may learn that no concept exists to learn, then the learner's mind may be open to experience what is before it. At times, silence can facilitate this openness by making the mind more at ease.

If I am striving to learn some concept, my striving may occupy my mind to the point of interference with openness to what is present but not yet seen. Frequently, our minds are more at ease when our brain waves are in the alpha state. I have heard of research which shows that more creativity occurs when the brain waves are in the alpha state, which is less hurried than our normal thinking/beta state.

Learning, learning to learn, holism, openness, intuition, insight, quantum learning, and nonduality cannot be separately nor extensively defined. We can know them, as we know when one has a puzzled expression, but we cannot describe or explain in detail the facial configurations of puzzlement.

Three

TEACHING AS ART AND SCIENCE

Learning and teaching are part art and part science. I will emphasize the "learning and teaching as art" side of the dichotomy. The science of teaching can be dissembled into techniques, methods, etc. and therefore, can be defined. The art of teaching cannot. When teaching is more art than science, then learning can be more of art than science, especially at the level of learning how to learn. We have also created the fiction that some processes and events are not combined.

We have a need to verbally communicate and we do so by making distinctions. This is not that, that is not the other thing, and so on. Because of our excessive attention given to representations, static, ossified, fixed conceptions, we have not noticed other interconnections. As a result, we forget we have created the fiction that things are separate, disconnected, that one thing can be acted upon without affecting other things. We have created the fiction that each human being is separate from others.

We have forgotten that rewards and punishments are fictions. Activity in the present can be its own reward and/or punishment. Nothing ever happened in the past, and nothing ever will happen in the future. Everything that happens, happens now, or happens not at all. New ecological evidence is showing the interconnectedness between people and everything including processes, events, and people. The path we are on is connected to every path. When we speak of every path or all paths, it is logically equivalent to no path. We are dealing with the path of no path. A nondual sage remarked that a way or path exists but not a traveler. The way, the traveler and the traveling are one.

Western thinkers are often striving to explain, and at times, thinkers explain to the point where they do not live well in the present because they attempt to explain what cannot be explained or adequately defined. General openness cannot be adequately defined from a dualistic point of view and therefore, general openness is not often considered in scholarly circles. The same may be said for criteria of the determination of wisdom stated by Baltes and Staudinger: rich factual and procedural knowledge, life span contextualism, and relativism of life values in life priorities.

The continuity of the whole is what we experience because we are immersed in it. We cannot see that continuity in dualistic terms, and that is similar to not seeing the forest because of the trees. When we attempt to explain a whole, we stop a dynamic process of which we are a part so that the representation of the whole is mistaken for presentation of what is. We forget that explaining is itself a part of a larger whole, and we also forget explanation is capable of infinite refinement. What is, is dynamic. We have, however, made our definitions static in order to be more certain. We can only be certain of logical tautologies such as A is A. Albert Einstein has reminded us that those logical tautologies do not relate to the real world.

The non-notion here is that when we create a concept or set of concepts, we are often preoccupied with conception. We are deluded partly because we are no longer involved with our present experience when we stop present experience through creating conceptions. Conceptions are by definition fixed. Present awareness helps us unoccupy our minds so that we can attend to what is happening, while not holding to any static representation. From Ignacio Götz's point of view, holism/nondualism viewed from a logical/dualistic point of view is even self-contradictory.[1]

Although we have vast knowledge of representations, if we can see the openness, fluidity and impermanence of events and people, including conceptions, we can come to know that we do not know. We may then see that our knowledge is not only incomplete, but incompletable as Kurt Gödel found to be true for proof in mathematics. A friend of mine joked that when a person is deluded, her or his knowing is half vast.

A nondual writer has said that the study of holism is the study of the self. It is not surprising that Götz says true teachers teach because they want being that is intuited and realized in a nondual enlightenment experience, and that only when this unity of teaching/being is intuited will teaching actually take place.[2] Might that experience be called a quantum experience?

Götz further alludes to the notion that a teacher is a person who lets learning happen, who helps the student learn how to learn when he says, "The teacher is the great desire to see into one's own nature."[3] Götz refers to Martin Heidegger who is in agreement with Götz on the point that teaching is letting learning happen.

Becoming open and noticing what is may be viewed as stages of an exceedingly large, unified, quantum whole. The whole will not be talked about directly, but refers to "nonduality" which shares characteristics of whole.

What a holistic/quantum "paradigm" can do for schools and society is to help create a new standard. This new standard would help us see the lack of permanence, and the fluid nature of standards and definitions. This new standard may help educators make sense out of using school time for students, faculty, staff, and administrators to notice what they are experiencing.

No one standard for deconstructing exists, nor does any grand narrative which finally explains other possible narratives. Some school time could become time for general awareness. Ignorance is a lack of general awareness. What can be clearly defined in a dualistic sense is delusion.

Before we can give our attention to what is before us, we need to receive. We need to be open to other unawarenesses. Using the term "nondual" with "paradigm" is misleading in that it implies paradigmness can exist that is apart from nonduality. It cannot, although Shunryu Suzuki holds that nonduality is not two and not one. Nonduality need not be an all or nothing proposition. Nonduality can allow duality so that we may create subjects which have objects when we choose. We need only be aware that subjects and objects are constructions which may need deconstructing. At first glance, nondual/holism implies that no one knows anything. The empty, sunyāta, nature of everything implies that there is nothing to know, but emptiness in the Sanskrit, "sunyāta," sense, implies an emptiness which is fullness. Knowing nothing conceptually is knowing everything. Nothing exists to know. Everything arises from nothing. No separate thing is separate. Everything is connected. Within the nondual/holistic "paradigm," no separate subject does the "knowing." Knowing, as used dualistically, refers to preconceptions and conceptions which are delusions, and which prevent holistic, nondual awareness.

While Plato's ideas do not generally fall within the nondual "paradigm," his notion of our coming to know that we do not know as the beginning of wisdom, resembles elements of a holistic "paradigm." But any separate paradigm is also delusion.

Educators using a nondual "paradigm" may choose to use a dualistic paradigm where and when it may be useful. Educators who operate only within a dualistic paradigm cannot as easily choose a nondual "paradigm." Dualistic paradigms promote external control. A nondual "paradigm" promotes self-control.

The holistic, nondual view holds that the problem we attempt to solve is our own creation and that creations can be uncreated or deconstructed. The realization that life lived in the present is an end in itself and not a means for something else, is "realization." Götz reminds us that nothing exists for us to attain, yet we are astounded when Woody Allen says, "I am astounded by people who want to 'know' the universe when it's hard enough to find your way around Chinatown."[4]

In order to help people become more whole, more self-directing, less ignorant and less self-deceptive, I suggest we change school grading practices. Highly educated people are not necessarily long-schooled. These highly educated people can function well at higher levels of thought, and they can handle paradox and complexity well. An example of a highly educated person is Alfred Korzybski who thinks that whatever he says anything is, he can simultaneously hold that it is not: that it is also something more and something different.

Jean Piaget has written that those who function high on the formal operations stage of cognizing can simultaneously hold conflicting ideas. What is randomness in one context may not be randomness in another context. The contexts for education are as varied as people. Education is a whole that is more than the sum of its parts. Schooling may be one broad context of education. Schooling, at other times, may prevent education from happening. Traditional, closed educators, who still hold to fixed Newtonian principles, have traded uncertainty for a narrow, unreal, and certain context. We have traditional, closed thinkers who hold that being educated is equivalent to being thoroughly schooled. Narrow, traditional schooling can prevent us from being educated. Numerical or letter grading of students is a practice which may contribute to preventing education.

The whole meaning of what is stated is more than the sum of the parts. Unless we are flexible, we will never create new orders. The history of thought demonstrates that some new orders are partly created from previously known orders. Some orders arise serendipitously. An example of a new order partly arising from a known order is an earth-centered view of the "universe," moving to a sun-centered view of our solar system, to an order in which our solar system is seen as a microscopic part of our galaxy, which is only one of billions.

What re-ordering might educators now do to re-structure/re-order schools in ways that reflect a dynamic, non-linear, quantum world, rather than a static, linear, closed world? I am suggesting that widespread experimentation with a long-term moratorium on grading students, for their education, but not necessarily for their training, is one powerful event in school restructuring. Schools more often grade students for business and industry rather than to facilitate the learner's learning. A problem for closed educators is that they think that training is educating, that a student is a learner. Too often, learning how to learn is suffering extreme neglect because Western dualistic thought leads to grading students, under the guise of education.

The basis for newer kinds of orders in natural processes within the sciences would probably be apprehended as, "no order at all" in terms of present traditional conceptions. A subatomic particle having the effect of going through a slit and not going through a slit simultaneously is often seen as no order. Closed, traditional frameworks determine what can be order.

The uncommonly seen quantum order is not order within a traditional Newtonian framework. I am talking here of uncommon orders. We need orders that will help more people better understand life, consciousness, perception, and to generally be wise, but we have great difficulty in studying these with precision because they are complex, vague, chaotic, and so difficult to measure with certainty. New notions of order are needed if scientists and educators are not to be blind to the complex and subtle orders which elude our traditional and conformist ways of thinking. We may need to relax feelings and thoughts of certainty in favor of dealing with what is real and with what is good. We can understand what is real and what is good in ways that are different from only rational thinking. Rational thinking, in a separate cognitive sense, following the epistemological, "What is true?", as the primary determiner of order can reduce awareness.

Newer orders are derived in a variety of ways. One newer order is the order of the configuration of the center of the Milky Way Galaxy. When seen through an outer-space infrared sensor, which has a wavelength different from the human eye, the center of our galaxy looks flatter than when viewed through an optical telescope with a human eye. The Milky Way Galaxy was explored through infrared lenses from outer space where there would not be excess "noise" inhibiting an accurate sensing. When we primarily look at the quality of a student through his or her grades, the grading makes a difference in what is learned as well as how it is learned.

Stars in the center of the Milky Way seem to be more heavily concentrated around the middle when "seeing" through infrared sensors. Within the traditional, Newtonian system of thought, the universe is running down; an increasing disorder within the system. The running-down is the heat loss moving toward stasis between matter and energy, called entropy. But if we look at the notion of order as coming from chaos, an increase in chaos can be understood in a different way.

Heartbeats, for instance, are very ordered during heart attacks and less ordered during normal human functioning. Brain waves are more highly ordered during epileptic seizures, and much less ordered during "normal" functioning, and even less highly ordered during more difficult mental functioning, such as counting backwards from a hundred by sevens. An increase in noticed chaos can be understood in terms of moving toward a possible change of order.

Evaluating students may be useful for training, but student grading has outlived its usefulness for educating. But let us call training "training" and not mistake training for education. Fascists are trained but not educated. When you are self-directing and know you want to be an M.D., you need to deal with the rigors of being trained for practicing medicine, which may include being graded on your progress in clearly defined medical practices. Learning the art of medicine could profitably be ungraded.

Structure, as seen in a traditional, Newtonian world, is constancy. Fixed structure can function as definite known order. In a dynamic, rapidly changing world, an appropriate word for the process of coming into order is "structuring." "Structure" is basically dynamic. Structure changes depending upon its context. In the traditional, Newtonian, unchanging, linear world, structure is always the same regardless of context.

Dark matter is about ten times more common than non-dark matter; ordinary matter which makes up stars, planets and people. The structure of the dark matter is not well known, since astrophysicists only recently have taken indirect looks at dark matter. In order to indirectly look at dark matter, the researchers measure distortions in light from about 145,000 distant galaxies. The galaxies in the study were, on the average, seven billion light years from earth. I mention dark matter because it is only indirectly seen through gravitational lensing which deals with the bending of light. One researcher, who compares cosmologists of today to Christopher Columbus, thinks the maps Columbus used were highly inaccurate, but today, some astrophysicists think that more accurate maps of the known universe can now be made.

The structure of our universe may also be unknown when you note competing views of astrophysicists who think differently about what we are seeing when we look at the sky.

What does all this have to do with quantum learning: beyond duality? Henri Giroux reports that "education" was first used as a noun in 1836. Prior to that education was dynamic and, therefore, was used only as a verb. The rise of public schooling for growing numbers of people contributed to shifting to a static notion of schooling. The shift from developing ability to notice present experience, toward training for socialization is augmented by current grading practices; practices which socialize to maintain the *status quo*; practices which do not assist recombining in a quantum world.

Education equals schooling to many people. Since educators changed education from a verb to a noun, schools have become more involved with "studenting" than with "learning." Students and teachers agree that having a high grade point average is a prime measure of success. I would like to suggest that the closed, traditional, Newtonian conception of a high grade point average implies a very different order in a dynamic, non-linear, quantum universe. A quantum, dynamically ordered universe exalts learning and minimizes studenting. Student grades often become inconsequential in a dynamic framework. A traditional, closed conception of schooling uses student grades to credential students for purposes outside of school, whereas the dynamic concept of schooling leads to learning and exploring for its own sake. Grading of students often serves to oppress learning and exploring.

Oppressing learning may be the epitome of oppression. "Learning," as I am using the term, connotes the primary goal of developing curiosity, and a growing love for learning and exploring. "Studenting" is evinced by questions such as, "How many pages do I have to write?" and, "Is that going to be on the test?" Training is more related to studenting and learning is more related to educating. Training relates more to dualism, and educating/self-direction relates to quantum learning and nonduality.

Notions of right and wrong, good and bad, are different, depending upon the structure in which they are considered. What is good within one order or structure may not be good within another. In complex/chaotic structures, order is more difficult to visualize and measure with certainty. Some writers imply that chaos and complexity are nearly synonymous. If we continue to measure our galaxy with regular telescopes, when we have infrared measures, we will see only limited forms of order. Without other and newer orders, we will be conceiving, measuring, and in other ways ordering our schooling to remain closed, ossified, and static. We will not see possibilities of other and newer orders because the traditional, Newtonian order has already told us what can be seen and how to see it, what to think and how to think it.

As we use newer perceptions and possibly newer sensations, we will be able to create kinds of order that are complex and diverse but still acceptable to those who accept diversity in thought and behavior. Whatever we say structure is, it is simultaneously, in other contexts, not what we say it is. There may be something more than what we say when seeing through a dynamic lens. With a closed, Newtonian lens, we only see what we believe and what fits the Newtonian model. Traditional schools have been involved in a closed, Newtonian framework to the point of our agreed-upon crisis in schools. Grading is a part of that crisis.

Michael Polanyi elaborates on how we can know more than we can tell.[5] We can know when one has a puzzled expression, but we cannot explain or describe in detail the facial configurations that comprise the puzzlement. We can know when the student is learning, but we cannot delineate the learning into letter or numerical grades, and expect that grading to adequately evaluate the learning unless we are training.

A Governors Conference was formed in the mid-1980s by the White House to assist American schooling. This Conference gave high priority in its order of objectives and its order of statements about how the objectives will be accomplished, to what is clear and easily measurable. The objectives speak in terms of performance before invention and creation. The writers of the Conference document hold the essentialist/perennialist philosophies of education of Plato and Aristotle, who dealt with fixities. Some of these early Greek ideas are at variance with newer, dynamically quantum philosophies of education. These words themselves imply a wide variety of orders to a wide variety of people. Other words could profitably be used to describe the kinds of variations, the kinds of orders, and the kinds of structures with which we are concerned when we talk about restructuring schools. Restructuring of schools could easily eliminate grading students for courses which purport to educate. No Governors Conference has come to that conclusion.

A deconstructionist's view of schooling holds that we must change. We must obliterate the nonfunctional to create a more functional school order, an order which will not grade pupils unless the grading is for training purposes. Some deconstruction is needed before reconstruction. In a dynamic view, we would not even use the word "reconstruction," but "reconstructing," which implies continuousness and activity which occurs in the present. This dynamism fits closely with John Dewey's idea of education as a continuous reconstruction of experience. Education, to John Dewey, is what is meaningful as it occurs, and as a result of its occurrence, a person will be able to better direct the course of her or his future experience.

In no Governors Conference report on restructuring of schooling have we seen self-direction as a primary goal of schooling. Citizen development relates only to objectives of big business. The general interest of the country is known, and as Noam Chomsky thinks, no big business special interest group is needed since both Democrat and Republican fit into one big business mode.[6] This mode was derived in a closed, Newtonian universe where inflexible structuring to the definite, the known, and the certain was a primary goal of instruction.

When we address change to teaching more science and mathematics, we are not attempting to follow the view of a dynamic model. It is the certainty of a closed, Newtonian world of mathematics which seems to be rewarding for many politicians, business leaders, teachers, many students, and particularly school administrators.

Certainty has been reduced within mathematics as a whole where Kurt Gödel offered "proof" that we cannot prove anything. Gödel demonstrated incompleteness within any mathematical system. Incompleteness within the closed, Newtonian world is what the rigid, inflexible educators want to eliminate. Closed educators, citizens, and politicians are unaware that elimination of uncertainty is impossible in a real, interactive, quantum universe, and their lack of awareness keeps our society closed.

When we look at the whole as more than the sum of the parts, we see that structure itself is generally considered order, arrangement, connection, and organization of simpler elements. These elements, however, are not necessarily separate physical entities, but are terms introduced for the sake of analysis. One of the leading physicists of our time, John Briggs, supports this view. He believes we tend to think of the whole universe as inherently divided and disconnected.[7]

The distinctions made between race, nation, family, profession, gender, sexual orientation, and age, arise from the way we can see the totality as constructed of independent fragments. Because we see the world constructed of independent fragments, people tend to operate as though they too were independent fragments. Briggs says if we include everything coherently and harmoniously in an overall undivided unbroken whole, then our minds will tend to move in the same way, and from that will flow an orderly action within the whole.

The ossification of categories results from the closed, Newtonian framework in which most of us have been trained. We must now de-ossify, de-fix, deconstruct ourselves if we are to move toward accepting ways of thinking which better mesh with a dynamic, interactive, quantum universe. I suggest that schools experiment with a moratorium on numerical or letter grades, and see students as wholes within larger wholes, so that we may see other breakthroughs. The breakthroughs would open us to an expanded, more holistic, nondual, quantum present. I would not learn how to be open if I were in a school that continued with the fixed, Newtonian framework, the basis of most present-day schools.

1. What I Will Not Learn from Closed Educators

I will not learn that some knowledge may prevent me from knowing. Preconceptions and prejudices prevent certain awarenesses. Fixed conceptions can prevent wisdom from emerging.

I will not learn that I need know nothing, attain nothing, and realize nothing in order to do the good that needs doing. I can do that good now without waiting, especially about racism, sexism, homophobia, the hungry, the homeless, global warming, and other environmental concerns.

I will not learn that I often wait for someone else to tell me what is good, and what is not good.

I will not learn that I am not a separate self.

I will not learn that wisdom is compassion for my fellow beings, and compassion for myself who is connected to my fellow beings.

I will not learn to treat other people the way I would like to be treated.

I will not learn that the way to live that can be said is not the way.

I will not learn that when I look for enlightenment, I have already gone past it.

I will not learn that if I am now not moving toward liberation and openness, I will not know who binds me.

I will not learn to do away with illusory medicines to cure illusory illnesses.

I will not learn to study the self by getting rid of my "separate" self, reducing my ego.

I will not learn that my habitual, fixed conceptions of self, others, right and wrong, prevent me from studying myself.

I will not learn to pay attention now, and I will not learn to be at ease.

I will not learn not to look for teachers, mysteries, shortcuts, principles, secrets, and ways of being.

I will not learn that I too often cling to a rule, principle, or way of life as something ultimate.

I will not learn that a 10,000-mile journey begins with the first step.

I will not learn that to be patient is to be wise.

I will not experience, deep down in my bones, that it is better to give than to receive.

I will not learn that the future is no more than a present anticipation.

I will not learn that the past is no more than a present remembrance.

I will not learn that people learn as birds learn to fly.

I will not learn that to understand is to forgive.

I will not learn to understand that each of us is interconnected with everyone and everything.

I will not learn to understand that when we experience interconnections, we are generous and helpful, naturally virtuous, energetic and persevering, and mindful that it is best to use wisdom for the benefit of others.

I will not learn that wisdom comes from desiring less and less until we are free.

I will not understand that it takes noticeable effort to arrive at an effortless state.

I will not learn that none of us arrives until each of us arrives.

I will not learn that suffering can be reduced by the acceptance of suffering.

I will not learn that a way to suffer more is to desire to suffer less.

I will not learn to sing the following to the tune of Betty Boop's "Poop Poop De Do":

One couldn't aspire,
To anything higher,
Than to get rid of desire,
To make me not my own.
Poop poop de do.

From open educators, I learn that to be mindful, I need to be unminding in the sense of not preconceiving. An Eastern sage said the Tao is mindless of union with humanity; when people are unminding, they unite with the Tao. Although I do not know how to connect that unminding to self-directing activities in great detail, I do believe our preconceptions and prejudices contribute to non-self-direction. The unminding I am talking about is doing away with prejudices.

A story about a social system several hundred years into the future, which continued evolving to where people rarely desired anything, may illustrate a point. The social planners talked about production and consumption, and some people thought there would be no production, and therefore no earnings, without consumers. If people desired very little they would consume very little. The story had a happy ending where people were feeding each other.

This story also included a vignette where a number of people would each get two other people to discuss white racism and go through activities mentioned in Judy Katz's book, *White Awareness*.[8] In the vignette two people discussed racism with two people, who would discuss it with two more people, etc. This took place around the year 2005, and it did not take long for society to rid itself of white racism/institutional racism, sexism, homophobia, and other fears.

The attitude expressed by Meister Eckhart who said, "The eye with which I see God is the same eye with which God sees me," helps move us toward nonduality.[9] Nonduality may help bring about this near state of contentedness, wisdom and general well-being. Almost everyone in this make-believe society was at ease, and almost everyone believed that they were passing by this way but once, so that they would, therefore, do immediately any kindness that they might do, or any kindness that they might show to any human being. They would not defer nor neglect it, for they would not pass this way again.

This story includes a university teacher who discusses Sheldon Kopp's "Eschatological Laundry List."[10] The first item on the list is, "This is it." Because of the students' past, closed schooling, many students do not believe "this is it." They think that they need more than "this." The students are looking for shortcuts, rules, secrets, principles, ways of life, and mysteries. Perhaps the biggest mystery of all is the quantum statement, "This is it."

"This is it," and ideas about balance between content and process, and ideas about an evolving society are included in the story that follows:

2. Woody the Student

Woody wanted to be told what was going to be on the test. He wanted his degree so he could get on with his life. Schooling, at this point in his life, was an interference with what he wanted to do. He did not want to be a student. He was a learner. He noticed that being a student frequently interfered with his learning. He was sick of school.

He really liked Woody Allen. He remembered chuckling when Woody Allen said, "What if everything is an illusion and nothing exists? In that case, I definitely overpaid for my carpet." While Woody was only in the sixth grade, he was enthralled with the possibilities of quantum computers. He was not sure exactly what "quantum effects are instantaneous" meant, but he was enthralled by the idea. He thought that change would rapidly accelerate as a result of the development of quantum computers.

Woody knew that widespread use of intelligent robots was just around the corner, and that neural implants were not far behind, but his teacher was asking him to memorize the capitals of the fifty states and other trivia. His teacher was asking him to use his brain at its lowest conscious level. He was rarely asked to do anything creative or surprising.

He knew that technology was rapidly changing, but he noticed schools and many of his teachers were not keeping pace with the change that was going on. "Why," he asked, "do I have to know the capitals of the fifty states? I mind my teacher forcing me to memorize trivial information. I know when

I memorize trivial information, I have less time to be curious about matters that would help me meet my immediate and long-range needs." He thought that many teachers in schools were overly concerned about following orders, being excessively rational, and conforming. He read that Max Planck said something about science cannot solve the ultimate mystery of nature because we are part of the mystery we are trying to solve. He connected that to Meister Eckhart's saying about the eye with which he sees God is the same eye with which God sees him. He knew, at a young age, that he was trying to see his own eyeballs without the aid of a mirror.

Many of his classmates were not interested in Woody's interests, but he knew that many more of them were interested in greatly expanded contexts, a much larger picture than what was being presented by his teachers. His teachers were presenting the capitals of the states; a very narrow context relative to the expanded contexts with which he and many other students were concerned.

He wondered about large contexts. He wondered what could be the largest possible context. He thought of that largest of all contexts as the container that contained all containers. He thought that a container was a lot like a definition in that containers and definitions both had binding functions. He would frequently get back to "This is it." What contains more than "this"? He wondered why it was necessary to put this in quotes. Why is this different from "this"? He was unsure about the answers to these questions, nor was he sure about the answers to any question.

Being uncertain, and allowing that uncertainty to be a part of him, was Woody and something he cherished. His teachers, however, did not cherish that uncertainty. They so highly cherished certainty that they "taught" the capitals of the states, because they could be certain that Columbus is the capital of Ohio, and that Springfield is the capital of Illinois. His teachers could not be as clear and certain about what was or was not a creative way of being, and how they should teach in a quantum society. In a quantum society, machines will do most of the trivial and some high-powered work, and people can have tremendous amounts of leisure time if they notice well.

Woody knew that when you are farther-out than far-out, you are farther-in than far-in. He would rarely say those ideas because he did not want to be thought of as weird. He would rarely say, "This is it," because most of his teachers thought there was more than "this." The "it" and the "this" were both largely undefined, and he knew that most people thought others were stupid about something unless that something was defined. He knew that the past was no more than a present memory and that the future was no more than a present anticipation. Both present memories and present anticipations, when noticed, are part of "this" in the statement, "This is it." When his friends and teachers heard Woody speaking about "this" and "it," some of them thought, "this" and "it" were inconsequential. Woody thought they were highly consequential in a karmic sense.

At times he thought he was overly concerned about what was of consequence. He knew that for every cause was an effect. He experienced that for every unifying thing he did, a unifying consequence would occur for him, and for every disunifying thing he did, a disunifying consequence would occur for him. It was as though the cause and the effect were simultaneous. If they were simultaneous, he thought they were like the workings of a quantum computer.

He heard a definition of time which said that time was nature's way of preventing everything from happening all at once. It was said as a joke. Woody changed it to read, "Conceptions of time are ways of conceiving everything to be in sequence." The roots of consequence means, "with sequence." From this nondual point of view, no sequence could exist because nothing existed to be sequential. When the subject and predicate are one, nothing can be said. Perhaps, he thought, that is why the way that can be said is not the way. What was so consequential about "this" and "it" was because "this is it" is self-evident. The unusual part of Woody's thinking is, "this is it" can include, "and this is not it," from Woody's near-nondual frame of reference.

Woody cautions us not to fixate on anything. Remember, to fixate on something is a fixation and fixities are nonrealities. About this, Woody tells about a Chinese, nondual sage named Foyan, who tells a story of fixating ideas, which he says is like making a boat and outfitting it for a long journey, then tying the boat to the shore before you start on the journey.[11] He says, you can row or sail forever and still be near the beach, even though you see the boat waving this way and that. You think you are on the move, but you never move a yard. When you set limits on boundless openness, says Foyan, you have set up limitlessness as boundless openness and you have trapped yourself.

Foyan was talking from a nondual frame of reference and he was talking about being aware of that which is non-conceptual.

Woody thought about difficulties of a nondual frame of reference because nothing could be said about problems, such as the inconsequentiality of closed schooling where grades are more important than learning. But, he thought, we have said too much and have done too little. We need to do more and talk less about grades. Woody believed, at this stage of societal development, closed people need to be told closedness is limiting, but maybe, he thought, closed people need to find that out by themselves. Again, it seemed that balance was needed, but closedness was previously more prominent than openness in the age of pre-quantum learning.

The second item on Kopp's list is, "There are no hidden meanings."[12] Woody thought that traditional, linear, dualistic schooling, with its focus on the there and then, taught most of us to believe in hidden meanings. When meanings are hidden, shortcuts, rules, secrets, principles, and ways of life can help us find those hidden meanings. Those hidden meanings provide a condition for us to focus on the past and future rather than the present. So if we wonder why so few people seem to know what is going on, we need only look at the emphasis in our schools and society, which focuses primarily on what has gone on, or what will go on. What is going on is of little consequence to traditional educators who may be mentally ossified and closed rather than holistic and open. "This is it" is a whole, and wholes are not given attention by closed people. Holism is nondual and transcends subject and object. No mysterious principle exists: nonduality transcends subject and object.

Woody was glad that he contributed to social planning which arrived at a society where people rarely desired anything. Woody thought greatly reducing desires was near paradise. He thought we were taught that one person can hardly do anything in our society, and he wanted to encourage everyone that they could do much, if they concentrated on it. Woody would frequently quote the poem by Jefferson L. Humphrey and Frank L. Nasca, "I Am Only One Person."

The poem begins by saying Rosa Parks is only one person and then asks what one person can do. In poetic form, the authors then say what Rosa Parks did almost by herself.

While Woody did not consider it a mistake, he was not highly tuned into the present moment although he wanted to be. He remembered that B. Alan Wallace said we often completely miss the crisp simplicity of the moment. Instead, we are too often consumed with anxious feelings and desires. Wallace thought that whatever we are doing (standing, sitting, walking, etc.), our minds are frequently disengaged from the present reality and instead, our minds are absorbed in compulsive conceptualization. Compulsive conceptualizations are about the future or past. When we eat, we often think about doing the dishes, and then as we do the dishes, we often think about what we will be doing next. Wallace believes that is a weird way to run a mind because we are not connected with the present experience, but are frequently thinking about something else.

Woody was more involved with concepts like those B. Alan Wallace talked about rather than paying attention to the present moment. Woody thought most of his education and training allowed him to conveniently disengage himself from the immediate reality. His education and training helped him become absorbed in compulsive conceptualization about future or past. Woody's present frequently dealt with present remembrances or present anticipations, and as a result, past and future seemed to be more important than the present. Woody frequently wanted to know what was going to happen next.

Woody wanted to be a teacher and, at times, he was perplexed about his primary goal of education: the development of the student's ability to inquire as well as love of learning, growing curiosity, and noticing what is. Academic inquiry often relates to conceptualization about the future or past. He thought he possibly needed to go through some of that academic inquiry before he could inquire into himself, so as to forget himself, but he was uncertain about that too. He partly projected that belief onto others. He projected that less as he became more aware.

The Woody story ends here.

Some differences between open, holistic education and closed, dualistic education are cultural. The Western dualistic framework more easily allows us to put people on the moon. The Eastern, open, near nondual, holistic stance aids awareness of what is happening in the present moment, and as a result, one can better know what to do or what not to do, and how to be, and how not to be, at any given moment.

Although George Bernard Shaw was not an Eastern writer, what he said about education has an Eastern flavor: Shaw described himself as a fellow traveller who pointed ahead of himself as well as ahead of us. Surrounding the traditional, Western, more linear approach to education, plans made by the teacher relate to arranging, so that students arrive at a point at which the teacher has already arrived.

Thomas Groome says the opposite of what most Western educators would say: He describes a great educator as one who can lead students out to new places where even the educator has never been.

Classrooms ideologically grounded in Western thought strive to avoid surprise. Malcolm Campbell believes that avoiding surprise derives partly from our Cartesian Legacy. Learning places, usually not classrooms, cherish surprise. Some postmodern thinkers believe that an infinite number of orders exists, and known order no longer explains what may be known. When something is said or done, that something's order can be conceived in various ways. If you were to begin to do something you have never done before, that new something would be a new order for you. Surprise, therefore, implies new ordering. Spontaneity implies newness of ordering.

When was the last time you noticed something surprising happening in a classroom? When was a last time you noticed a teacher or school administrator being spontaneous, or creating a new order? In order to get a feel for, and thoughts about, creating a new order, I invite you to surprise yourself now. I invite you, during the next fifteen minutes, to do something you have never thought of doing before. It does not have to be great, just do it. Thinking a bit before you act is okay, but do not think too much. Excessive thought puts the brakes on spontaneity and surprise.

Four

OPENING WIDE THE DOOR: NONDUALITY

To expand on nonduality, notice that philosophers do not know what truth is, mathematicians do not know what proof is, and biologists do not know what life is. Is it not true that the behavior of atoms does not allow us to accurately predict the behavior of molecules, and the behavior of molecules does not allow us to accurately predict the behavior of cells? The behavior of cells does not allow us to accurately predict the behavior of human organs, and the behavior of human organs does not allow us to accurately predict the behavior of human beings. The behavior of human beings does not allow us to accurately predict the behavior of groups of people. Each unit is, at times, a whole, yet when the context is expanded, each unit is a part of a larger whole.

The process of integrating sub-units into larger wholes moves to the point where discussion about very large wholes becomes cloudy, because very large wholes can become larger than conventional experience and conceptions account for. Quantum experiences include uncertainty and lack clear definitions. Quantum learning is about moving in the direction of recombining unknowns. Balance or moderation is central, but the result of balance is quite different from the absence of balancing of fifty years ago, yet schools have not changed much in fifty years.

When we attempt to speak about exceedingly large wholes, conventional language loses usefulness and we need to make allusions to that which is rather unconventional. Nonlinearities arise when exceedingly large wholes are given our attention. "Quantum" is a useful word for these exceedingly large, recombined wholes.

The most nonlinear nonlinearity is nonduality. Nonduality is simultaneously singularly linear. Nonduality is singularity. In order to begin to gain insight into what cannot be described or explained: nonduality, I will use many of David Loy's ideas. Loy asks us to look at a cup in space which is separate from the cup itself. Loy asks us to note that when the cup and this space are separate, we are looking with a dualistic perspective. When we see the cup as what space is doing in that place, we have an analogy to a nondual perspective. The cup and the space are one as the wave and the ocean are one.

Talk of nonduality within a dual paradigm is awkward. Nonduality is a most abstract notion because nonduality includes everyone and everything. Nonduality is also most concrete because it includes all concretions as well as all abstractions. Nonduality is not a notion and because nonduality is not a notion, concept, or idea, nonduality cannot be described or explained. Some of these abstract notions appear to be abstract only because they are so concrete and continuous in the present moment.

The Western, dualistic paradigm may refer to these abstractions as "non-notions." The nondual paradigm about which Loy writes includes a dualistic paradigm, plus adds that which goes beyond a dualistic paradigm. What transcends the dualistic paradigm is similar to the "more" in the notion, "the whole is more than the sum of the parts."

When Loy speaks of nondual practice, he is speaking within a paradigm which cannot be measured in terms of the dualistic paradigm. For instance, in the dualistic paradigm, immutability is different from impermanence. "This" is different from "that." Self is different from an object outside of self, and substance is different from mode, and emptiness has no form. Within the nondual "paradigm," emptiness is not other than form and immutability is not different from impermanence. This is not different from that . The self is not different from an object. There is no object outside the whole.

Loy, in referring to Western thinking, states that the idea of self, what Loy calls the most hypostatized thing, "me," is why causal relations form a hierarchy.[1] Nothing is more important than the self which craves other objects in order to manipulate people, things, and circumstances to get what that self desires. Loy also believes that a separate self is not satisfied with each particular thing, and the separate self then desires the next thing. That desiring and obtaining of what is conceived as separate is essential to the maintenance of that sense of self and, according to Loy, that notion is why causality is the root category of thought.

Loy elaborates by asking the very interesting question, what if the object the self desires can never be an effect, because it is always unconditioned? What if that object of desire can never be gained, because it is unattainable? That, Loy says, is the dilemma because it seems if you make no effort to do anything, the result will also be nothing, and there will be no progress toward the desired end. All effort appears to be self-defeating, and that is what Loy believes is the paradox of spiritual practice. The paradox exists because the goal is no separate goal because they are nondual. The object the self desires is unoriginated because it is beyond causal and temporal relations.

How, Loy asks, can we escape this double bind?[2] The path of no path is a path, for Sankara, a Vedantist, while for the nondual Dogen, a Zen Buddhist, no path is very much no path. Loy is saying that nondual experience transcends both temporal and causal relations. An important conclusion for Loy is that all possible means are severed from any ends. Within the framework of nonduality, Loy asks, could nonduality be any other way? Loy elaborates that within the nondual paradigm, language and rational thought are the problem rather than means to solve problems. Loy believes that because causality is the root category of thought, it is the category most in need of deconstruction.

Loy elaborates that any method or technique understood to lead to an enlightenment experience maintains the very present-future, cause-effect dualism that the method or technique is trying to escape.[3]

An interesting inclusion of nonduality is that we can continue to use a dual paradigm if we choose. We must be aware of nonduality in order to choose it. Can we legitimately say that we are not aware of a dual paradigm unless we are aware of nonduality? Nonduality helps us see that the dual paradigm is but another aspect of the nondual, and not totally separate from the whole of which it is a part.

When operating nondually, we need to be aware that our use of words, such as talking about dualities, is re-presentation which, at times, keeps us from being aware of presentation. Presentation equals noticing present experience. We may also be aware that we re-present to avoid the struggling before a potential release from a self-imposed struggle. Release from struggle may arise from presentation. Awareness of what is may include being at-one with what is. Self-imposition of a struggle arises from imposing a separate self according to the nondual "paradigm." Creating a problem arises by not accepting what is, when nothing can be done about, "what is," at that time.

If we would deconstruct our deconstructing, as Loy claims Jacques Derrida did not do, language/thought would no longer be the problem.[4] We could then go about living ordinary lives. Ordinary living itself would be extraordinary since we now do not know something unless that something is defined. Definitions are necessary for reasoning. We cannot reason without them. From a nondual viewpoint, definitions are part of the problem. The probable efficacy of nonduality in schools and society will become more evident when educators become more open to experimenting nondually.

I will describe some differences between the nondual and the dual, and offer ideas that are more consistent with the books *Tao of Pooh* and the *Te of Piglet* than with mainstream Western thought. As teachers and students become more involved in higher levels of technical and social complexity, I think looking into the present, chaotic implications of a nondual paradigm, for longer-than-usual time periods, may reap benefits. I project that a benefit will be noticing rare kinds of order, a quantum order, which are now frequently experienced as randomness or disorder. Disorder is not noticed because dual frameworks only permit noticing of what has been ordered.

Some process philosophers hold that a major danger to philosophy is narrowness in the selection of evidence. A presupposition of Western philosophy, since Aristotle, has been subject-object duality, in its broad sense, and since René Descartes, in a narrower sense. When the seer and the seen are one, what might be said? I suggest that faintly formulated social problems, including aspects of racism, sexism, homophobia, and other blind following, arise because of our sole use of a dualistic paradigm.

I suggest the use of a near-nondual paradigm may help society and educators become open to possibilities which are now rarely seen. I project that an opening to new possibilities may arise as a result of unlearning some preconceptions to which our dualistic process of conceptioning gave rise. Dichotomization, which dualists carry as baggage, may prevent the occurrence of educational experience. An anonymous author reminds us that the quarrel between poets and philosophers, elaborated on by Plato, did not occur in China and, as a result, no great distinction is made in Eastern thought between the practices of philosophy and art.

Nonduality is so radically different from mainstream Western, dualistic thinking that you may wonder whether the consideration of nonduality and its implications is worth your time. In my discussions with mainstream Western thinkers, I find that rarely is it considered that psychologists do not know what "normal" is, or that educators do not know what "learning" is. What is evident to the mainstream Western intellectual may not be evident to the nondual mind, and vice versa. What a mainstream Western intellectual experiences is often different from what a nondual practitioner experiences. Loy believes that a mainstream Western intellectual might experience the world as a collection of discrete objects which interact causally in space and time.

The nondual practitioner's way does not completely deny the existence of a dualistic relative world. She or he does, however, often base her or his experience nondually. Mainstream Western intellectuals claim that it is self-evident that an object is different from a subject. Nondual experiencers say the subject and object are one, and Loy thinks some deny there is a subject.

Nonduality can be experienced by those who discipline themselves, claim nondualists. To nondual thinkers, objective reality itself is called into question, and they say they need no objective criteria by which to judge. To mainstream Western intellectuals, nondual experience is a delusion. To nondual experiencers, mainstream Western intellectual dualistic thinking is a delusion. The nonduality relates to nonduality not only between subject and object, but also between seer and seen.

To the mainstream Western intellectual, Loy says, "It is evident that an I that does an action exists separate from the I itself."[5] To the nondual experiencer, such is not the case. Modes of experience can be dissected in a variety of ways. One way to dissemble experience is to dissect it into perception, action, and thought. To the nondual experiencer, there is no need for such dissection. The mainstream Western intellectual, says Loy, "separates the I from the action which the I does in order to gain a desired end."[6] Some nondual experiencers move to fully eliminate desires.

Again, Loy believes that concepts and intentions are dualistic because thinking is preoccupied with perceptions and actions rather than experiencing nondually, which springs up creatively. Loy believes nondual action is spontaneous, and effortless, and empty because one wholly is the action.

There is not a dualistic awareness of an action separate from what is being done. That is similar to the notion of the way that can be said is not the eternal way, as Lao Tzu said.

Paradoxically, Loy elaborates on four nondualities, the last of which is the nonduality of duality and nonduality. According to Loy, we can interpolate from nondual experience to explain duality. We cannot interpolate from dualistic experience to explain nonduality. This nonduality of duality and nonduality is similar to the equation of Samsãra, ordinary experience, and Nirvana, enlightened experience. Enlightenment is found in ordinary experience. Loy says that by asking what kind of thing is of pure experience, we run into difficulties.[7]

This pure experience of which Loy speaks seems to occur at a time before conceptions of subject and object, and at that time no separation into intellect, emotion, and will yet exists. There is only independent, self contained, pure activity before we have added complexities of thought, such as conceptions which are myth creation. Myth making is fine but myth making leads to delusion when we are not aware.

When processes or events change rapidly, we can easily communicate about them because other processes or events remain constant. When some processes and events remain constant, we have a basis for relating change. When everything changes very rapidly, difficulties in communication arise. The bases, the constants for knowing and relating the change, also may change exceedingly rapidly. The constants may then be no longer constant. Saying A is not B, with highly rapid change of all processes and events, may not hold an instant later since within the time span that you say, A is not B, B could become A.

Dualistic and nondual experiencers have different views of the rapidity of change and of what is changing. Thomas Kuhn, Joel Barker, and others have shown paradigms have shifted and they are continuing to shift. What has been little noticed through our mainstream dualistic, Western intellectual lenses, are rapidly shifting paradigms, which frequently result in social change, including change in what counts as knowledge.

Mainstream Western intellectual lenses capture more of an epistemological flavor, while a nondual type lens captures a flavor that is an amalgam of epistemology, axiology and metaphysics, plus something intuitively and quantumly more. Logical differentiations and extensions are more fittingly made when we look through an epistemological lens. We see unity more easily with an amalgamated, quantum lens. Lenses, as I am using the term, vary as paradigms shift, and as the culture of the person using the lens changes.

What is seen through an epistemological lens may shift if we look with the primary emphasis on an amalgamated lens. I use the words "primary emphasis" to allow for the possibility of a shift so far in degree, that we may consider the shift to be a shift in kind. Substances shift for dualistic experiences. No separate substance exists for nondual experience. Loy asked us to look at a cup using different lenses. The first, epistemological, lens helps us see a cup in space which is separate from the cup itself. The second lens; an amalgamated, intuited, quantum, near-nondual lens, may help us see that a cup is what space is doing in that place. We may say, when we operate in a nondual, amalgamated manner, we are using a different paradigm from most mainstream Western intellectuals.

Dualistic philosophies tend to place experience in categories. Near-nondual philosophy/non-philosophy breaks the categories, recombines differences, and, as a result, deals with more of what can possibly be experienced; a broader selection of evidence. For Western philosophers, if no category has been established for something, that something cannot be experienced in a way that can be communicated.

Within mainstream dualistic philosophies, what is real is the concept or the thought that is represented by the concept. In nondual philosophies, the ineffable does not tend to be stated. Meditation, aimless awakening, awakening for the sake of awakening with no other aim, is practiced. Such a nondual practitioner can be aware of what is, and be free from fantasies, unless fantasies are chosen.

If experiments in quantum mechanics show that particles can be in two places at once, dissolve into waves when no one is looking, and communicate faster than the speed of light, then perhaps nonduality could profitably be given some serious attention, since those experiments in quantum mechanics demonstrate weaknesses in dualistic paradigms.

When we know that we know nothing in a fixed sense, we cannot be prejudiced against skin color, gender, sexual orientation, or anything else. A continuous reconstruction of experience may prevent one from knowing anything in a fixed sense. Conversely, knowing anything in a fixed sense is evidence of a narrow selection of what is evident.

An implication of nonduality, applied to schooling, is to provide teachers and teachers-to-be with models of openness and creative behavior, and with experiences designed to help teachers be aware of their present experience. Once we are aware of present experience, we may be more inclined to be more open, and to see more interrelatedness. We may be more inclined to be caring and compassionate because interconnectedness implies that what we do for others, we do for ourselves.

The dualistic philosophies, which have been ingrained and programmed in us during our many years of schooling, have led us to a dualistic form of thinking where the ego is central. Albert Einstein thought that a human being is a part of the whole, called by us "universe." He thought that our task must be to widen our circle of compassion to embrace all living creatures and the whole of nature in its beauty.

Aristotle said that wonder is the feeling of a philosopher and all philosophy begins in wonder. According to Abraham Kaplan, Zen, a nondual experience, ends with awe and wonder. The way things are is wondrous enough without trying to explain it, says the nondual mind. Kaplan believes that we imprison ourselves in our own conceptions, and then we think that if we make those conceptions more subtle and complex, we will escape, but that we cannot live our lives with these abstractions even though we can manage elaborate abstractions such as those of Immanuel Kant.[8]

Kaplan believes that conceptions of academicians have nothing to do with our lives, yet those abstractions deal coldly with science, art, religion, politics, or interpersonal relations. Kaplan cannot find much significance in philosophy that only deals with abstractions.

Nondual experience seems to hold the opposite view of most mainstream Western intellectual thought. Nonduality holds that rationality, regardless of how far it is carried, is not the solution to the great problems of human existence.

Kaplan says that nondual Zen has no sacred book or symbols, adheres to no special dogmas, and performs no characteristic ceremonies or rituals. Nondual Zen is one of the most vitally significant philosophies known to Kaplan because most of our living is not abstract.[9] Kaplan believes that we are not in bondage, struggling for freedom. We are already free, and if a bondage exists, it is something like the human bondage which consists only in ignorance as Baruch Spinoza thought.[10]

Dewey's notion that education is the continuous reconstruction of experience to reduce ignorance, thereby making the learner free, roughly finds sympathy with a nondual Zen view, except Zen followers believe we are already free. Dewey's notion implies a future, whereas nondual Zen holds only now; past, present, and future are one.

Awareness, with its concomitant attending to what is, will not as readily occur without noticing that "receiving" is a stage preceding "attending" in the affective domain. We must be open to receive what is before we allow ourselves to receive it. When what is to be noticed is received, we can then give it attention. While nonduality can appear to bring with it a variety of uncertainties, nonduality may bring us closer to notice what is inherent in Dewey's notion, process is reality, and in Alfred North Whitehead's notion, reality is process.

Reality and process can be one as the cup is what space is doing in a given place. Process is what reality is doing. Ignoring nonduality or dismissing it without looking for longer than usual time periods may be a form of ignorance. Looking for longer than usual time periods and/or presently being open to other possibilities may increase the chances of seeing awe and wonder in ordinary, non-abstract reality. Would we be less burdened if we felt less of a need to explain as much as many of us feel we ought to explain?

Nondual education and quantum learning, with focus on ordinary present experience, hearing what you hear, seeing what you see, can help students see that life is no longer a problem to be solved but is just to be lived. Kaplan believes that the wisdom that Faust comes to in the end is where nondual Zen starts.[11] The nondual Zen experiencers never abandoned fixed representations. According to Zen, fixed representations never existed. To Zen experiencers, living life fully each moment is an end in itself and not a means for something else.

Kaplan believes that philosophy is itself the disease for which it pretends to be the cure, and as a result, the wise person does not pursue wisdom, but rather lives life, and therein exercises wisdom.[12]

Beginning to live in a nondual way would not start with words. In one sense, I have been deluding the reader by using words. Some words may help us free ourselves from the chains of excessive and prolonged conceptioning which scholars tend to cherish. Since nonduality is impossible to contain, I will need to use more words to be clearer about nonduality. Some words may lead you to avoid the trap of being too wordy by being aware that some processes and events cannot be verbalized.

Alan Watts, a nondual teacher, promotes contrived laughing for several minutes which generates real laughing for several minutes thereafter. He thinks laughing is more worthwhile than several hours of silent meditation. Nondual teachers think this effect of laughing is to be experienced. You are now invited to start laughing for thirty seconds, and if you do not continue genuinely laughing on your own thereafter, then you will note that the contrived laughing does not work for you. However, you will never know whether continued laughing occurs unless you try it. So go ahead and try it now. Just fake a laugh for thirty seconds and make it loud and hard. See what happens. If you are trying contrived laughing for the first time, try it alone unless you have a high tolerance for embarrassment. You will not feel shame if you are alone. Incidentally, evidence of the existence of the subjective "other" is found in experiences of shame and fame.

Within nonduality, and remember nothing is without nonduality, no mind does not think no thought about no things. A separate self is a delusion that desires. A separate self is a delusion because all is one. The creation of subsets makes one subset separate from another. Such a creation is fine, and this is how duality is an element of nonduality, if you realize that duality is a myth. All words are myths, including the word "nonduality." Non-awareness is also okay since what is not to be okay? Such logical creations may be manufactured, as in a game we play as a part of the levity of living. As we notice the delusion of a separate self, we take ourselves less seriously.

No one way to live exists, nor any one way to do anything creative. Each of us is a part of this larger whole which does the same thing, but we each do the whole differently. We are not two and not one. Nonduality is.

The lack of levity in schools is evidence of the lack of freedom of teachers, school administrators, students, and society. The lack of freedom in schools reduces levity. If we learn by doing, then we learn to be free by being free, we learn to have more levity by having more levity, and we learn to be more compassionate by being more compassionate. So when we lay ourselves down to sleep tonight, let us ask ourselves to allow ourselves to be more compassionate, to be more free, and to increase the levity in our lives.

Five

THE CONVENIENCE OF BALANCE
AND BALANCING CONVENIENCES

Think of everything you have, everything you do, everything you will do, everything you will have, everything you are now conceiving, everything you will conceive, everything you imagine, everything you will imagine, almost everything you can possibly imagine, what you are now afraid of, that which you will be afraid of, what you now use to resist your fears, what you will use to resist your fears, all of your present deceptions, all of your future deceptions, all of the stores you now frequent, all of the television programs you watch, all of the cars you drive, all of the places you go to now, all the clothes your are now wearing, and all the toothpaste you use. Obviously, you cannot think and/or do all of those things simultaneously. All of the above are thought and /or "done" because they are convenient.

All of those things were conceived and/or are done or because we believe they add or will add quality to our lives. Instead of convenience or quality, let us say because they are creative, growth-producing, or add to our self-directedness and openness.

In the end, what we do is done for someone, something, or some event that is an end-in-itself. We usually drive a car so that we may go, for example, to a movie. We go to a movie often to laugh, or to learn, or for our health and well-being, or so that we may be at peace or at ease, or be in harmony with the universe, or to better live a balanced life.

Convenience, quality living, openness, creative living, growth-producing living, laughing, learning, educating, harmonious living, being at ease and being self-directing are ends-in-themselves. Other ends-in-themselves exist. May we have a meta-end for which we have those other "ends in themselves"?

What the teacher in the classroom is doing could profitably be connected, in a subordinate way, to an end in itself, something that cannot be explained in terms of a simpler idea, something that is self-evident to the teacher as having a purpose in itself, rather than being done for something other than itself. Let us take a look at balance as an end-in-itself. You may see that balance and freedom are meta-ends-in-themselves for the previously mentioned sub-ends. Freedom and balance are the least contained ends, and are the end of other ends. When we are free, we are balanced, and we notice what is.

Everyone wants a balanced life if the price is not too high. It is difficult to know how and where we have become unbalanced, but our history of balancing various processes and events is a factor in seeing how we best balance forces at this moment.

Before we grow and develop, taking risks and allowing ourselves to be more uncertain are helpful. Since around the year 400 BC, Western society has been unbalanced on the side of wanting too much clarity, wanting content, products, and excessive certainty. Our desire for certainty opposes processes which make ideas flexible and fluid. Both the substance/content side and the process/openness side of the dichotomy want clarity. The substance/content/ permanently-fixing-ideas side attains clarity by narrowing contexts and closing processes and events.

The process/openness side achieves clarity by expanding contexts; opening things up. The substance/content side gains clarity in the short run, and the process/openness side gains clarity in the long run. Western society still follows many lessons of Plato and Aristotle who closed processes and events. In order for our society to be more balanced, society may find wisdom in taking a look at what is said by people who open processes and events.

People on the process side, tending toward nonduality, think that Plato was very uncomfortable with the fluctuating notion of what is good, as Robert M. Pirsig has noted. Plato narrowed the context of what is good by making the good the highest virtue which we know through reason. Some people in favor of rebalancing, recontextualizing to a larger context, claim that Plato made the good a static thing, which became subservient to reason. This had the effect of making reason higher than the highest virtue, so that today we frequently think we need to have a reason for everything all the time.

Much of our playing is done without having reasons. Play, levity, is good in itself. Reason is a tool to be used at appropriate times when problems need solutions. Imbalance in our lives creates problems which would not otherwise exist.

People on the process/openness side, tending toward the nondual, think that we can know what is good without defining it. Such "knowing" is similar to noticing that Julia Roberts and Brad Pitt are attractive people without defining in advance what is "attractive." Their attractiveness is self-evident and known without using reason alone. As a result of that knowing, we will, when appropriate and when we choose to, use reason to become wise and notice what is. The people on the substance/product side think that we will not know what is good or attractive unless they are defined.

Those on the substance/product side are more comfortable with using definitions almost all the time. They know that we cannot reason without definitions, but they often forget that political factors help us arrive at agreements concerning the definitions of various processes and events. Definitions arise from more than reason. Undefined political elements are involved in any human agreement, including the agreement concerning what definition is given to a process or event. In Western society, we do not frequently consider how processes and events are defined, or where definitions come from, yet definitions affect our behavior and well-being.

In order to bring about more balance, we may need to be open to what is before us without preconceptions, without fixed notions. As a result of this greater openness, we may have a greater likelihood of relating in new and more growth-producing ways with each other, and with processes and events. Everything and everyone is changing all the time. Western society since Aristotle has had a cultural bias to keep things as they are. Providing additional openness may be a condition which fosters societal and individual growth, as well as long-range harmony, and wisdom.

Societies need to balance concerns for society as a whole with concerns for individuals. Society has given schools the charge to socialize youth, and to teach independent thinking so that students may decide for themselves, as Thomas Jefferson said, what will secure or endanger their freedom. No exact scientific measures can determine the balance needed for society and individuals within society to function most effectively. Judgment determines appropriate balance.

Since schools rarely teach how to use judgement, the imbalance has gone to the side of socialization, so that an individual's deciding for herself or himself what will secure or endanger freedom, has been greatly neglected. We too often look to authorities for answers rather than doing the good that needs to be done. The great frequency with which our students look to authorities for answers is evidence of this imbalance toward socialization. Our students do not know what is good and what is not good until somebody else tells them.

Students are not given time in schools to think for themselves because teachers are giving the students answers before the students have questions. When the students do not have questions, that is an indication the students are not wondering. When students are not wondering, the students are not thinking at the analysis, synthesis and evaluation levels of thought. What experiences would help our students to use judgment, to decide for themselves what will secure or endanger their freedom, to think at the analysis, synthesis and evaluation levels of thought, to wonder and become more curious, to love learning more, and notice what is?

Using judgment, deciding for yourself what will secure or endanger your freedom, thinking at the analysis, synthesis and evaluation levels of thought, wonder, curiosity, and love of learning allude to ends in themselves, and are learned by judging, deciding, analyzing, synthesizing, evaluating, wondering, becoming more curious, loving learning more, and noticing what is going on. We learn by doing. We learn to be free by being free, and we learn to balance by balancing.

Higher-level thinking will occur if teachers provide the three conditions: a freer environment, a responsive environment, and discrepant events. Discrepant events are what the students see or hear that is at variance with their expectations. When the student wants to find a powerful answer to a discrepancy, the teacher will answer any student question, unless the questions are designed to get the teacher to agree or disagree with the student's theory which explains the discrepancy. The teacher almost never tells the student the correct answer. The teacher will ask the student to experiment until the student knows he or she knows without somebody else authorizing the knowledge. Inquiry regarding external processes and events, may lead to helping us examine ourselves so that we may forget our separate selves.

For those interested in examples of teacher/student dialogues regarding open inquiry, please refer to the J. Richard Suchman's Science Research Associates' Inquiry Development Program.[1] This open inquiry, using conceptions and theories, may be needed for some people before we come to realize that we do not need concepts and theories in order to be intelligent and wise.

When openness is the goal of our instruction, Sharon Salzberg's idea about what we can change and what we cannot change, concerning our degree of openness, and the amount of loving-kindness we have for ourselves and others, can be useful.[2] Salzberg asks us to visualize ourselves putting a teaspoon of salt in a half ounce of water. We would then notice that the salt made a tremendous impact in the half ounce of water. She is asking us to notice that we cannot control the amount of salt, uncontrollable hardships that come into our lives, but we can make ourselves into a container so large, like an ocean, that no amount of salt and tribulation would have an effect on our openness and loving kindness regardless of how much salt were dumped toward us. She is asking, if we want to be open and have loving-kindness to ourselves and others, to provide conditions for ourselves where we may become this very large container.

I have made some partial attempts at increasing the size of my container, but to date, I experience my container to be about the same size as it has been. What is different is that I am noticing more often that my container is still the same size, but I am noticing that more rapidly. I am also noticing that I, and everyone else, would be better off if I pushed back the boundaries of my container.

Creating a container so immense may be considered moving toward emptiness, emptiness of a self, of ego. Emptiness of all the boundaries is freedom, nonduality. Freedom arises through balancing processes and events. Moderation in all things may be the epitome of balancing. Both arise when noticing what is. Balancing arises through being free and being free arises through balancing. Awareness that the "I" of which we speak is a delusion, is awareness that each of us is not a separate "I." The delusion arises when we are not paying attention to the present moment.

As you notice you are less of a self, you have less of an ego. All this is done while you are accepting yourself as you are and is done effortlessly. The paradox is that paying attention requires some effort to arrive at effortlessness. As numerous sages have said, "it" is what you cannot hear when you listen for "it." "It" is what cannot be seen when you look for "it," and "it" is what cannot be found when you search for "it."

What is so convenient about that which cannot be said? Am I suggesting that we reach a better balance by allowing ourselves to be unbalanced? We reach a better balance by allowing ourselves to move toward unbalance, when we do not rigidly hold ourselves in any fixed position, mentally or physically. Before we notice a change in ourselves, it is useful to accept ourselves as we are. Silence, at times, can be convenient for noticing and accepting. The silence, in the short run, is often inconvenient. When we notice what is going on, we can better accept ourselves as we are and find long range convenience through silence.

Balance and convenience make us free. Freedom and balance are the meta-ends of learning and living. Those ends in themselves: growth, creativity, openness, laughing, convenience, etc., could be seen to have their purpose in creating conditions whereby we may become free and/or balanced. Those ends in themselves have the end of freeing us. We are only not free when we are bound and constrained. When you are bound and constrained, who binds you? When you become aware that you are binding yourself, then you can work on stopping the binding. Unbinding is convenient. Nothing is more convenient than freedom and balance which is tantamount to wisdom and patience.

Stretch your imagination for a moment. Imagine nothing as something, somewhat as Robert S. Kaplan does in his book, *The Nothing That Is*.[3] Take your time and stretch the imagination. Logically, with this stretching (keep in mind that the stretching is more than logical), knowing nothing will help us become free, if nothing is more convenient than freedom, and if convenience is evidence of freedom. Limits of language are seen with the paradox that we are not separate selves but we do not often realize that we are not.

The paradox of doing whatever you are doing so that you can become free is that, when you are free, you are free of yourself. "Yourself" is your ego. Within the nondual frame of reference, separate selfhood is a delusion. Nondualists believe that nothing exists outside of the nondual frame of reference. Dualistic frames of reference are contained in a nondual container. When you awake, you are no longer deluding yourself, and you notice that you are not a separate self. When you notice that you are not a separate self, you are free; free from the delusion of being a separate self. Reality is not that at one time you were a separate self, and once you are awake you are no longer a separate self.

Realizing you are not a separate self, and never were, releases the binding. You unbind yourself when you realize you are not a separate self, so you were never bound other than by yourself with your conception of a separate self. Only a separate self can be bound, and a separate self is bound by the delusion of separation. Only a separate self pays attention to past and future. When we rid ourselves of the delusion of a separate self, we also rid ourselves of the delusion that present, future, and past are separate.

"This is it." This "this" needs to be experienced. "This" only exists in the present and awareness of the present is the key to experiencing the present. It is now and here that we can be aware of nothing to say and why, in one sense, saying anything is a delusion. Nothing needs balance because no self is separate. No individual growing exists because there is nothing separate to grow. No creating exists because nothing is separate to create. Remember all of those activities you were doing to be free.

Both constraint and freedom are delusions. If freedom exists only in relation to constraint, then no separate freedom exists either. Freedom and delusion are words. We need balancing in our lives. "Balancing" is also a word. Perhaps Lao Tzu is now clearer when he said, "The way that can be said is not the eternal way."[4] Nothing can be said because there is nothing to be said. As Abraham Kaplan said, "The wise man does not pursue wisdom, but lives his life, and therein does his wisdom lie."[5] The wise person goes about living his or her life; not pursuing wisdom, because he or she is already wise. About a wise person living his or her life, what may be said?

When you notice someone near you threatening a baby's life, you do not write a letter to the editor stating why babies should not be killed. You go to the potential baby-killer and do what you can to stop him or her from hurting the baby. When you see a hungry person, you provide food. When you see a person who needs shelter, you give shelter. When you see people in need of clothing, you give clothing. When you see people who need rest, you help them find rest. When you do this for them, you do this for you. You and they are one, as the wave and the ocean are one. That is nonduality which has no separate parts.

The delusion of separateness is what causes hunger, thirst, and homelessness. Hunger, thirst, homelessness, create a lack-of-ease. This lack-of-ease is dis-ease, disease. Delusion causes lack-of-ease, racism, sexism, homophobia, and poor care of the environment. The cycle seems endless until we are awake. The awakening goes south when you look for awakening in the north. The awakening cannot be heard when you listen for awakening and cannot be found when you seek awakening, yet things may be done to increase our chances of becoming awakened. As a nondual sage has said, "seek without seeking."

Say, "Notice" to a dualistic person, and he or she asks, "Notice what?" as though something separate exists to notice. What about noticing your noticing and/or consider noticing that nothing separate exists to notice?

By accepting yourself as a person who is aware that you do not feed the hungry, you have a greater chance of being at ease. You may become aware of hungry people. When you give food to the hungry and drink to the thirsty you are compassionate. When you are compassionate, you are wise. When you are wise you are not a separate self so you do not think of yourself as wise, and you simply go on living your life as Abraham Kaplan said. When you are not a separate self, you are a container so immense that, "even a truckload of salt dumped into it" will not be too much for you.[6]

What may teachers do in schools tomorrow to help students see they are not separate selves so they can be this immense, empty container? It may help to notice that people are hungry and thirsty, and then it may help to give teachers and school administrators and students time to notice what is going on in the present. Thousands of people die every day from starvation. We will not notice the hungry, the thirsty and the homeless until we notice what is going on in the present. Only in the present can we be nondual.

Let us now look at reconsidering clarity in thought and expression from a near-nondualistic viewpoint. I will use subjects and predicates, but the flavor and tone will be toward the nondual end of the spectrum.

Part Two

RECONSIDERING CLARITY
IN THOUGHT AND EXPRESSION

Six

CONSEQUENCES OF THE BOILED FROG SYNDROME

We are surrounded by a Boiled Frog Syndrome. Robert Ornstein found that by placing a live frog in a pot of room temperature water, and slowly heating the water until it boiled, the frog would die because the frog would not notice the gradually increasing temperature.

Robert Kunzig spoke about new discoveries by Roberto Mendez, an astronomer at the Munich University Observatory.[1] Mendez found that "space between galaxies is not as dark and empty as we thought."[2] Fifty to a hundred percent more stars may occupy the space between galaxies than was previously thought. Mendez thinks a lot of blank space exists between galaxy clusters. He said, "astronomers have no terribly good reason to think it should be full of stars, but the truth is no one has ever really looked."[3] Astronomer Robin Ciardullo says he "wouldn't like to go to a telescope time-assignment committee and say, 'I want four nights to look in the middle of nowhere. I don't think I'm going to find anything but.'"[4] Kunzig concludes, "Maybe it wouldn't be such a dumb idea."[5]

The Mendez findings support the idea that our thoughts may become clearer by noticing the murky and dark nature of what is now beyond what we know. As the telescope time-assignment committee has difficulty in supporting the request for four nights, to look into the middle of nowhere, by a researcher who does not think he or she will find anything, so would any grant committee have difficulty in supporting research that wanted to take a look at general murkiness. The Mendez conclusion: "Maybe it wouldn't be such a dumb idea," to look between galaxies, suggests that focusing on apparent voids and discontinuities between what we know may help us be clearer about what is now murky.[6]

Arthur Fisher stated that the discovery that neutrinos have mass could undo the laws of physics.[7] Referring to neutrino research, the author states that further research will deepen our understanding of the universe and will yield what John Milton called, "no light, but rather darkness visible."[8] Physicists' questions often deal with the amount of matter in the universe. If too much matter exists, the universe will end in a big crunch. If not enough, the universe will continue expanding. If neutrinos have mass, we might be moving toward a big crunch.

Fisher notes that as much as ninety percent of the required mass of the universe may be "missing." Physicists know that mass may be missing through observations from astronomers regarding the velocity of rotating galaxies. Indirect evidence of dark matter has now been found. Ordinary matter is now extraordinary.

Tim Folger cites unusual findings from physicists, astronomers, and mathematicians which show how weird our universe is. Reporting on these weird aspects of our world might make the notion of quantum learning and nonduality seem less strange.

Folger talks about secrets of the universe, including how it will end.[9] He said that a region of space smaller than a proton is thought to have ballooned into the size of earth within a billionth of a billionth of a billionth of a second after the big bang. His research shows that these vacuum spawned particles are constantly moving in and out of existence, which, he says, are arising from and sinking back into the void. Folger's calculations show that the visible universe, such as stars and galaxies, accounts for less than ten percent of the required gravity. Folger believes that an unknown entity, called dark matter, makes up the remaining ninety percent. Dark matter has now been indirectly found. A space mission launched near the end of 2000 was intended to discover not only the total amount of matter, but also how much of it is in the form of dark matter.

David Spergel, a scientist, asserts that a truly infinite universe is strange, but that a finite universe is also strange. Some scientists think that our universe, filled with hundreds of billions of different galaxies, is an illusion, and that we may be seeing that the universe has the hall of mirrors effect: we see our galaxy at different stages of development as it revolves around at different time periods.

We can create the illusion of infinite space although it is a finite shape, a doughnut, and the only way people would discover they were on the doughnut would be to travel all the way around it, or look at the light that had traveled around it.

The Boiled Frog Syndrome is an example of "what is," a hole in our awareness of which we are ignorant. If ninety percent of the physical universe may now not be visible, perhaps ten percent of the ahas! about the universe are now known. If we are to look at new evidence of what is clear and what is murky before we get to light on this topic, we may need to see "darkness visible."

When speaking of murkiness and conceptual clarity, I point to ideas of prominent thinkers who look at intervals between events. Looking at those intervals between events is done by chaoticians, Nobel Prize-winners, and poets, and now may be the time for more of us to look in these murky, infrequently looked at places. The Nec experiment, which recently showed the speed of light in a vacuum, 186,000 plus miles per second, is one three-hundredth of what it was under experimental conditions, would not have been done if the experimenters had held to fixed notions.

A strong desire for excessive conceptual clarity may be a part of the murkiness. Overly clear concepts may prevent us from noticing what is yet to be noticed. The frog did not notice the gradual increase in temperature. We have difficulty in noticing some subtleties of living in the present, where experiences become more confusing, when new experiences are permitted to remain uncategorized for longer than "usual" time periods.

Definitions are grist for the reasoning mill. We cannot reason without definitions. Do we use reason alone to arrive at definitions? Without definitions we would have no standards. A standard is a type of definition. It is obvious today that civilized societies prefer reason, standards, and definitions over random thoughts and behavior. How, beside reason, do we arrive at definitions, and particularly, a definition of definition? Do we reason in a circle when we (1) reason only with definitions, and (2) allow reason to determine definitions? How do various grammars and axioms of geometries relate to how definitions arise?

A feeling of dissonance often arises when we experience something we do not understand. We want to integrate unexplained experience into our conceptual framework. We wish to make ourselves whole and to close gaps. When an experience seems to open a gap between what we know and our awareness, what is experienced is not integrated/understood adequately. The inadequate integration causes feelings of uncertainty, and as a result, we often create a definition. When we create a definition or fit an experience into a known definition, we are often holding to the maxim, "if we can name it, we know it."

An example is an event in an elementary school where an eraser drops from the teacher's desk and a student asks, "Why does the eraser fall?" The teacher's reply is, "Gravity." Both the teacher and the student assume that the student and teacher have "covered" the material. The notion of gravity is still not well understood by physicists, yet the teacher gave the impression that both teacher and student know why the eraser fell. We may be more productive to think that all we know is the name for a complex and not well understood process.

Whenever one expounds upon various explanations, except in training for specific skills such as how to fix a refrigerator, all explanations are held to be expedients. They primarily serve the purpose of breaking through various intellectual interpretations, doubts, uncertainties, obsessions, and ideas. Plato said that the wise person knows that he or she does not know.

What events or processes may help us refrain from interfering with our openness to our experience? The word "gravity" is such an incomplete answer to the child's question, yet the answer, "gravity," gives the impression of a complete answer. We think we know why the eraser goes down rather than up when it leaves the desk, when we use the word "gravity." Knowing some names, when we are unaware that our knowledge is highly incomplete, may prevent us from coming to be aware of other ahas!.

Interconnections between people, other sentient beings, and other processes and events are difficult to perceive. The experience of interconnectedness, nonduality, has not been experienced on a wide scale. Nondual holism helps us be tentative about what we know, even though our knowledge may be doubling every year and a half. Tentativity will help us better notice what is yet to be seen in a Quantum Age. An example of an old story about a farmer whose horse runs away may help.

The farmer's neighbors come to him and say, "Oh, poor farmer, your horse ran away. We are very sorry to hear this. That is unfortunate for you," say his neighbors. The farmer says, "That may be." The next day, the farmer's horse returns with five other horses and the neighbors say, "Oh, how fortunate you are to have your horse bring back these five other horses." And the farmer then says, "That may be." The next day, the farmer's son takes a ride on one of the wild horses and breaks his leg. The neighbors say, "Oh, too bad that your son broke his leg." And the farmer responds, "That may be." The next day, the government sends people around to conscript young people into the army, but because the farmer's son's leg is broken, he cannot go into the army and fight in the upcoming battle. The neighbors again say, "Oh, how fortunate you are that your son broke his leg so that he won't have to go to battle where he might die." And the old farmer says, "That may be."

I mention this story because having extensive knowledge of many things is often highly valued. Extensive knowledge can prevent us from uniting various knowledges to the point where we become untentative, excessively certain, and unaware of trouble, such as the Boiled Frog Syndrome. Then hidden trouble arises, and various problems such as racism, sexism, homophobia, and other moves toward excessive societal control continue.

The widespread lack of awareness of global warming and its consequences may further support the need to avoid a variety of Boiled Frog Syndromes. I contend that the knowledge of a wide variety of lower-level skills, when unconnected to higher-level notions and experiences of what these skills can do, is only moderately useful, and may contribute to the continuation of a variety of social ills.

We may benefit by looking at the assumptions behind our ideas, and for this I would like to explore interconnections using a story told by an unknown author. The story is set many years ago. A son comes to his father and says, "Father, you are aging. Teach me the trade so that I will be able to provide for our family after your demise." The father happens to be a burglar. The father says, "Fine, Son, come with me this evening."

After dark, the son goes with the father to a house where they break through a fence, quietly break into the home of the people who are sleeping, and the father then opens a very large chest where all of the valuables are kept. The father instructs the son to get in the chest and pick out the valuables. As the son is getting in the chest, the father closes the lid of the chest and locks it. The father then makes a loud noise so as to awaken all of the people in the home, and then the father sneaks out of the house, and goes home. The sleeping people arise to look for what made the sound. The son, inside the chest, hears them nearby so he makes the noise of a rat. The woman of the house gives the chest key to the maid, along with the candle. The maid opens the chest to see whether a rat is in the chest. The burglar's son pops up, blows out the candle, and runs out of the house, followed by the members of the household. He hears them coming as he passes by a well so he throws a large rock down the well. The members of the household stop to see whether the thief is drowning in the well. The burglar's son sneaks away and when he gets home he says, "Father, how could you do this to me?" The father says, "Tell me what happened, Son." The son then narrates the story of what happened and the father says, "There, you have learned the trade."

Another child and parent, several years later, are together by the parent's deathbed, and the child says to her parent, "Please tell me some things that you think might be useful to me in my life when you are gone." The parent says, "The way to live that can be said is not the way. My guess is that each person must discover this for themselves." The child then says, "But please, tell me something that you think may be useful." And then the parent says, "Well, there is really not much to know. Just notice well what you are and what is going on in and around you. Some people make differences because making some differences happens to serve their conveniences at times. Considering very long-range conveniences, you may be more useful to yourself and your family if you make fewer distinctions."

The child says, "Well, that may be of some use to somebody at some time, but you are near your death, and I wish to have you tell me something that could be useful to me very soon." And the parent then says, "A poster your mother has reads, 'Bad spellers of the world, untie!' I was talking to a friend the other day and I asked her if she took a shower, and she said, 'No, I didn't know one was missing.' What I'm trying to say, Child, is that if you pay attention to the present moment and don't take everything too seriously, you will demonstrate more intelligence than the highly schooled person who is taking everything seriously all the time. Let me give you an example. At one time, people would explain things on the basis of the gods doing this or doing that, and later, people began to see that they could explain various phenomena on the basis of observation and logical reasoning. People began to note events that they thought were either true or false. People developed categories from true to somewhat true, to somewhat false, to false. They then extended those further, adding more distinctions. And today it might be better if we would just use logic as the tool rather than as the be-all and end-all of our lives. We could benefit from seeing connections between the many separations we have made. In other words, if we have to be only rational all the time, we will miss out on a lot of 'ahas!' because 'ahas!' are not always arrived at using reason alone. Ahas! occur serendipitously sometimes. Ahas! can be optimized by openness to experience."

The parent told the child other things and then shortly after, died. The child had many children and the offspring continued to flourish and be happy, and around the year 2000, their distant offspring were found to be in a similar situation where the child was asking his parent, an educator on her death bed, for some secrets by which to live. And the parent said, "Well, perhaps, Child, some people seek too much and, as a result, they miss out on what is immediately before them." "Please, Mother," the child said, "Tell me more of what you mean." So the parent quoted the great philosopher, John Dewey, who in 1920 said,

> The great systems of Western philosophy have all seen themselves as dealing with something which has variously been termed Being, Nature, or the Universe, the Cosmos at large, Reality, the Truth. Into this state of affairs there recently entered the discovery that natural science is forced by its own development to abandon the assumption of fixity and to recognize that what for it is actually 'universal' is process; but this fact of recent science still remains in philosophy, as in popular opinion up to the present time, a technical matter rather than what it is: namely, the most revolutionary discovery yet made.[10]

The story ends here, but the idea of deossifying ossifications and abandoning fixity is expanded below.

Speech-givers rarely speak about what they are presently experiencing during their speech. They speak on what they previously experienced or previously thought. The thinking they do during their speaking concerns how to best deliver their material. During the course of speaking, the speaker will draw some conclusions and make statements about what he or she will think about at some future time. I will clarify the malevolent effects of excessive talk about what happened in the past.

Dewey said, "We only live at the time we live and not at some other time, and only by extracting the full meaning of each present experience are we prepared for doing the same thing in the future."[11] Ashley Montagu held that the danger people face is not that our intelligence, purely cognitive cleverness, will be drastically lowered as a result of forces moving human beings to evolve, but that our intellectual side will be so highly favored that our cognitive intelligence will increase at the expense of other valuable traits. Older, more closed views of intelligence, cognitive cleverness/logical-mathematical form of intelligence, have favored our attention to the more easily verified statements of John Dewey rather than to his more comprehensive ideas, embodied in his two previously-mentioned quotations.

The useful and long-cherished aspects of ossified thinking are evident. We would not be able to know, predict, and control without some fixity. However, that excessive ossification of thinking helps create more long-term problems than it solves. Abandoning fixity, as Dewey used the term, does not mean doing away with that which assists us in our conscious, productive, dualistic knowing, predicting, and controlling. Dewey used the notion of abandoning fixity to avoid excesses such as those which paralyze most of the social sciences with positivistic structures. Behaviorism has been detouring educators from productive paths.

We now could profitably take another look at some negative effects of excessive fixity so that a better balance of knowing, predicting, and controlling can lead toward the type of exploration needed during our new century which may be thought of as a Quantum Age.

Although thinkers are gradually paying more attention to such notions as "caring," "kindness," "compassion," "intimacy," "wisdom," "anxiety," "loneliness," "deception," "suffering," "spirituality," and "death," we still have been excessively clever, narrowly intelligent, at the expense of broad intelligence, as Howard Gardner uses the term.[12] Gardner's view of intelligence includes the following factors: (1) linguistic, (2) logical-mathematical, (3) spatial, (4) body kinesthetic, (5) musical, (6) interpersonal, and (7) intrapersonal. Dewey spoke about social intelligence, alluding to the idea that leaning on fixed authority is what education as process would eliminate. Perhaps if we would widely accept Gardner's view of intelligence, we would become more aware of the problem of fixed notions.

A closed, Newtonian view of science holds that canons of scientific investigation imply we should not observe the way we observe because we will find contradictions. Those canons imply we must not look at murky areas which, for now, may simply be called, "between between/beyond between," elements of nonduality. If we abandon the notion of fixity, and if we see what Dewey said about process as the most revolutionary discovery yet made, we would then be more inclined to look at our experience as we are experiencing it; observe our observing as we are observing. If we did notice present, continuous experience in an open, nonjudgmental way, we could then more legitimately allow the experience to continue, rather than cut it off, as we frequently do, by prematurely giving it a name.

Naming an experience frequently stops it before we extract a fuller meaning. We often give an experience a name to allow our feeling of security to remain highly stable. Allowing an experience to continue while we are having the experience allows more awareness of our present experience to emerge. Some Eastern thinkers have known this for centuries.

Dewey implied that excessive fixity could return us to the logic of ultimate first principles expressed in the logic of Aristotelian and Thomistic thought. He further implies that such a return would be folly. Dewey believed that knowing and predicting are hypotheses and that they must be continually tested and revised.

If we abandon fixity, we see that process implies relations between events, and that these relations are continuous, ongoing, and impermanent. In order to feel more secure, we often cut off the process of integrating, the process of allowing ourselves to experience what we are experiencing. We wish to reduce feelings of dissonance by turning present experience into a particular past experience.

If we control what people think, we will not have to keep them in chains. "They will seek the chains themselves," said an unknown sage. The primary idea educators have long cherished is that education makes us free. We have engraved that in stone above many school and university entrances. I suggest that security, rather than constraint, is the opposite of freedom. I suggest that as a result of our excessively high needs for security, we too often cut off/limit present experience. We establish fixity in order to feel secure.

Too often it is thought that when we name it, we know it. For many students who have gone through our schools, the notion of "gravity" is not conceived as "the stuff" which holds the physical universe together through curving space. As a result of excessive reliance on a variety of fixities, we have unconsciously duped students into thinking that they understand processes which are very complex, when all they know are names.

Fixed notions have played their negative role when students know only names. For example, I have heard of research which shows that students know the names of the three ships led by Christopher Columbus, but many of those students tested did not know why Columbus was sailing west. When our citizens know only names for complex events and processes, it is not surprising that we have serious problems of racism, sexism, homophobia, population explosion, pollution, threats of the use of nuclear weapons, and global warming.

Our failure to deossify ossifications, our lack of seeing that what is universal is process, has allowed us to know in an overly certain way. It is better not to know than to know wrongly. I suggest that we give up some certainty/security so that we will be more free and more open to experience. When we are open to experience, we can allow our experience to continue.

When we allow experience to continue, we can extract from each present experience more meaning. When we cling to fixity, we intensify specialization. "Specialization" as R. Buckminster Fuller has stated, "is only a fancy form of slavery wherein the 'expert' is fooled into accepting his slavery by making him feel that in return he is in a socially culturally preferred, *ergo*, highly-secure, life-long position."[13]

The process of abandoning fixity may need to include abandoning some symbols and notions that are tantamount to sacred. Abandoning fixity, we would no longer adhere to any special dogmas, nor would we perform particular characteristic ceremonies or rituals common to philosophy and education. Fixity, a non-process, is a sacred notion to many Western thinkers.

Many of us are looking for ways to bring growth-producing change to our schools and society. We need not abandon logic and rationality. If we are on our way to abandoning fixity, it may be useful to note that logic itself has shifted from the early Greeks through today. It is changing even more rapidly than in earlier times and as a result, we can now more legitimately abandon fixity than when Dewey wrote *Reconstruction in Philosophy*. If we do not provide for our students and citizens the wherewithal to eliminate a variety of Boiled Frog Syndromes, we will be doing them a disservice.

The disservice arises from the love of fixity, and as a result of our failure to see process as revolutionary, some researchers continue to use the more fixed versions of older models of science in their attempts to analyze analysis, education, and learning. These older models of science are full of fixed notions, and treat the process of teaching as though it were a technical practice disconnected from values, interests, and norms.

Richard P. Iano has said that the chief characteristic of technical knowledge is that it can be precisely formulated and articulated, whereas practical knowledge, which is not reflective, cannot be formulated as rules that exist only in its use.[14] He refers to Michael Polanyi's ideas about articulate and inarticulate forms of knowledge. Iano quotes Polanyi when he says that skill, craft, and art, including scientific skill, is achieved by the observation of set of rules not known as such by the person following them, and the articulate technical knowledge serves as a guide only to those who can integrate that knowledge into their already existing practical knowledge. While the integration is logical, the integration is not only logical. A part of the integration is translogical.

As William James thought, the greatest enemy of any one of our truths may be the rest of our truths. That idea is similar to the holistic, nondual notion of the value of having an empty mind. An empty mind is always ready for anything. It is open to everything. It is like a beginner's mind containing many possibilities. Shunryu Suzuki says, "In a beginner's mind are many possibilities; in an expert's mind are few."[15]

Openness to experience is a continual process. When we view and express experience as we experience, we may reduce our chances of drowning in a sea of words. When we abandon fixity, we will provide an open condition. Because we have largely failed to abandon fixity, we have given constructs a life of their own. As Albert Camus thought, we have made constructs more real than the constructors and we have waged war and killed people because of these fixed constructs. Perhaps thoughts such as these brought Lao Tzu to think that as soon as we have made a thought, laugh at it. Fixity has kept us from realizing that, as Mark Strand said, "Each moment is a place you've never been."[16] By abandoning fixity, we will think with Gustave Flaubert that everything we invent is true, and we may be sure, as Flaubert suggested, that poetry is as precise as geometry.

Consider that by abandoning fixity we will have a fuller understanding of what Alan Watts said, the word "water" is itself undrinkable, and the formula H_2O will not float a ship. Because we have not abandoned fixity, many of us do not agree with Einstein's idea that the mysterious is the most beautiful thing we can experience, that the mysterious is the source of our creations. Emptiness which nondual Zen masters describe is similar to the mysterious of which Einstein speaks. Our eyes are closed because we have a fixed view of a dynamic, continually changing world. Chaos researchers estimate that most of our universe is nonlinear. Fixity breeds linear thinking.

As Robert Anton Wilson reminds us, we are all much better at believing than seeing. Wilson believes we are seeing what we believe nearly all the time and only occasionally seeing what we do not believe.

Seven

SPECIALIZATION AND GENERALIZATION

As students move through the elementary grades, junior high, high school and college, the concepts we teach frequently become more specialized. One reason we specialize is for greater clarity. We want greater clarity to further remove ourselves from confusion and chaos. Too much clarity too often, however, can keep us in a dogmatic slumber.

I am reminded of the old saying, "If you give a person a fish, you will feed him or her for a day. If you teach him or her how to fish, he or she can be fed for a lifetime." If we consider a concept to be like the fish, and the process of recombining separations to be learning how to fish, we have an analogy which implies that learning to recombine what was made different may better serve us than the learning of any particular concept or set of concepts.

We need to learn wholes and parts, and to learn how to involve ourselves in the process by which wholes and parts are related. General thinking may serve us many times and in many places, whereas some specialized thoughts are rarely used. Some specialized thinking may have great value even though it may be rarely used, but we have neglected open-ended general thinking. Evidence of this neglect of general thinking was recently shown by a United States Supreme Court Justice who was against the standard of counting ballots by reasonable and prudent people determining the intent of the voters by the careful personal examination of ballots.

We now have an excessive emphasis in schools on specialized concepts. This emphasis may have occurred because the complexity of generalized thinking has forced teachers and students to be excessively uncertain about the existence of complexities/what the generalized thinking is about. Recently, behaviorists had many of us believing that only if something could be directly sensed, did it exist. This implied that mind, beauty, intent, wisdom, and goodness did not exist in any public sense. If this complex thinking did exist with reasonable certainty, its function may have been unclear; therefore, complex thinking beyond mathematics was infrequently considered because it is difficult to verify and define.

During the past quarter century, the notion of "chaos" has emerged in a variety of disciplines. Chaos is a tool to help us understand much as a stethoscope, electroencephalography, sonograms, or magnetic resonance imaging help medical doctors understand and solve health problems, or how weather patterns can predict storms, or how neural nets and genetic algorithms can be efficiently used in developing artificial intelligence.

A use of chaos for educators is to help students better learn how to learn by harnessing complexity, which includes more connections between more events.   Along the way, students discover a sort of regularity to some irregularities, a kind of order to what was previously seen as disorder. Students can find a kind of pattern to what was previously seen as random, a reasonably certain unity to what was previously not seen. Scientists generally agree that their understandings of most basic and general concepts such as "space" and "time" are not yet complete. It is also generally agreed one way of measuring space and time is no more true than any other. Our concepts of space and time are agreed-upon definitions, as Robert Pirsig reminds us, based on their convenience in handling the facts. "Facts are what we absorb. We do not have time to absorb all the facts, so we need to be selective," says Pirsig.[1] Pirsig relates some ideas of the French mathematician, Henri Poincaré, and these ideas that may help us to be optimally selective.

Poincaré thought that by moving into the micro and macro-levels in our observation, we are more likely to find facts that are at variance with our rules. These facts overturn rules. The rule of the geocentric view of the universe did not fit the observations. Those observations helped create a heliocentric view. These observations at the micro and macro level then better allow us to see what may be occurring nearer to us.

A heliocentric universe, at one time, was considered chaotic. Chaos researchers are saying that we should not simply try to find what is the same or different in convergences, the same dull observations; instead, we could profitably observe likenesses, order, or pattern behind what appear to be divergences. I gave the example of fractal geometry and measuring coastlines from near and far. Fractal geometry is a set of mathematical ideas that help us see order in what was previously seen as chaos/disorder.

Pirsig reminds us of Poincaré's statement that mathematics is not only a matter of applying rules.[2] For Poincaré, to state the rules that guide the mathematician's choices was impossible. Those rules must be felt rather than formulated. A hierarchy of facts exists; and Pirsig reminds us that the simple facts are likely to reappear when we choose them because simple, interesting facts are often new in some way.

We begin with facts from which we may generalize to create rules. What Pirsig finds interesting is that facts, in conformity with the rule that has been established beyond all doubt, become dull because they teach us nothing new. Pirsig notes that the sun rises every day, and this effect is not frequently of interest because it is so common, but if the sun did not rise one day, that would be a very interesting event.

Poincaré believed that these choices are made by what he called "the subliminal self" and what Pirsig calls "pre-intellectual awareness." Only the interesting solutions to problems break into awareness. Educators and scientists pooh-poohed this kind of language, but in a Quantum Age, more people are dismissing preconceptual, semi-conscious, transrational thinking less quickly.

This process is partly precognitive and it may be likened to Michael Polanyi's example of tacit knowing.[3] Tacit knowing is demonstrated when we can tell that a person has a puzzled expression but we cannot, simultaneously, describe or explain in detail the facial configurations that comprise the puzzlement. The whole puzzled expression is more than the sum of the parts that comprise it. The arrangement of the parts is itself an element that cannot be seen apart from the whole. Likewise, Poincaré is talking about a problem's solution which cannot be described or explained in detail: the arrangement of the parts of the solution is itself an element in the solution. The solution is the whole, and its parts, when detached from the solution, are less than the solution.

Pirsig repeats Poincaré's statement that mathematical beauty is the center of solutions, which are creations he describes in discussing the problems expressed in mathematical language. A sense of harmony and beauty makes people choose the facts that best fit in the arrangement of that harmony or beauty. Pirsig says the relation of things is the sole objective of reality. That relation could extend to nonduality. Nothing is important nondually, because all relation has the effect of no relation, but let us not try to conceive that.

"Chaos" is a word which seems to describe the disordered or disconnected elements of reality. The early Greeks believed the goddess Gaia brought the earth out of uncertainty and disorder. Western thinkers had previously excluded chaos from their framework of thought because chaos, they thought, was random, unpredictable, and did not fit with the highly predictable, Newtonian universe which most Western thinkers desired.

Disharmony and ugliness are words which allude to what has not yet been connected or related to ordered aspects of our experience. We could not make complex connections when a scientific canon was that the whole equals the sum of the parts.

The science of chaos is interdisciplinary and major questions of this field relate to how complexity arises and evolves. Furthermore, complexity is often seen as a thing with a life of its own. Turbulence is a form of complexity. Many physicists believe that most of the known universe appears to be turbulent. Chaos pioneers are studying turbulence in space, air, water, and human and artificial brain functioning. Some scholars think that the twentieth century will be remembered for relativity, quantum mechanics, the computer-Internet, and the use of chaos.

Turbulence in waterfalls, long-range weather patterns, our nation's or the world's economic fluctuations, how snowflakes become different, or how students act and react in classrooms, are examples of complexity with which chaos researchers concern themselves. One pioneer in chaos research observed changing cloud patterns for days and days at a time. Classical physics, for instance, would not deal with questions about how order arises in a universe ruled by entropy, the movement of matter and energy toward equilibrium.   What is turbulence? and How does life begin? are other questions that classical thinkers would not investigate.

The basic concepts of space and time in chaos research show that some chemical reactions display order in terms of time but are disorderly in terms of space and others are orderly in space but disorderly in time.   Chaos researchers have found something different from what we learned in elementary and high schools.   That is, "sensitive dependence on initial conditions" shows that very small differences in input can quickly become overwhelming differences in output.   The "Butterfly Effect" is an example.   The Butterfly Effect implies that a butterfly stirring the air in Beijing, China, today can later transform into a storm system in New York City.

We grew up in a world which believed that arbitrarily small differences do not blow up to have arbitrarily large effects, but chaos researchers are finding that they can.   This affects teachers.   Most high school physics teachers teach that the pendulum is a model of measurable regularity.   Galileo theorized that a pendulum of a given length not only keeps precise time, but keeps the same time no matter how wide or narrow the angle of its sway.   This is taught in most high schools, but it is wrong, say chaos researchers, because the changing angle of the bob's motion creates a slight nonlinearity in the equations.

A commonly accepted view of an educated person is someone who knows tentatively, and who knows that it is better not to know than to know wrongly.   I posit that our societal slowness to accept cultural diversity, including acceptance of other races, ethnic groups, the handicapped, and those with a sexual orientation which differs from the majority, arises from our being taught things which were highly incomplete.   This excessive slowness may arise from not paying more attention to chaos.

Society has not wanted many of its students or its citizens to be creative. Order is order because "things" stay as they are.   Unknown variations are often considered to be disorder.   Disorder is the hallmark of older notions of chaos.   Many of us have not yet learned of the rewarding kinds of order which emerge when we accept what was formerly thought of as unwanted variations.

Accepting other races, genders, and sexual orientations can bring to society a freshness and vitality.   This acceptance of diversity can provide a different and more complex form of order which may be more rewarding to society.   An exciting newness springs from acceptance of unity within diversity.   Some societal members, however, because of their excessive need to know in advance what will happen before it happens, remain in an unevolved state of unconsciously promoting disorder by clinging, again excessively, to notions such as Galileo's pendulum theory, or Newtonian views of a static universe.   White supremacist ideas seem to fall into that category, as do some older notions about teaching and learning, which tend to rigidify and fix thought and behavior.

Those who study complex states, beyond those that are easily measured, see their slices of nature, their disciplines, differently. This newer seeing will continue to have far-reaching effects in our teaching and learning. We profit from looking at different ways of teaching so that we and our students can experience some slow kinds of change which are not immediately evident.

One slow kind of change is the evolution of the relative importance of theory and practice. Practice has always guided theory and since the early Greeks, theory has guided practice. Practitioners in classrooms have slowly allowed school practices to become unglued from powerful, general theory. Wholesome general goals such as developing our students' love for learning, and helping our students become more inquisitive, and becoming more aware of what is, have greatly diminished in importance, partly because they are so general and difficult to measure. The very highly general is empty.

Some teachers find that general student questioning cuts down on teacher's time to present "required material." With more American states requiring proficiency tests on content that students "must know," we are giving students fish without teaching them how to fish.

Behind the differences between theory and practice are now seen glimpses of a unity between theory and practice. Nonduality is a word which expresses that unity, and quantum is a word which expresses the process of recombining theory and practice.

Regarding proficiency tests, students will be tested on what is taught mainly because state tests are determining what is taught. Since the love of learning and becoming more inquisitive and more aware are complex, chaotic, and difficult to measure, those general goals may not be tested and they will not be taught.

Specialization, which in earlier and more balanced days was for generalizing and *vice versa*, has now taken on a life of its own. In schools, we are surrounded by chaos under the guise of short-term order. Short, right answers are too often the goal of much school instruction. The primary present order seeks to develop students to fit the needs of big business which, except at the highest levels, does not cherish independent, creative thinking. We are like frogs being boiled and we do not even notice the heat. The earth is warming and little is being done. The water feels warm and we like it.

Because we usually are not involved with generalizing beyond rudimentary levels, we cannot see the consequences of the growing control that goes on in our schools and society. We have been controlled so much that we seek additional control. Creative thinking in schools, since it is difficult to measure and difficult to order, is not taught. America has become an uncreative nation as a result. Our needs for certainty have led us to know things that are not accurate. Newton's laws, which imply a static universe, are the bases on which many schools are grounding their operations. Much of the universe appears to be quantumly dynamic and nonlinear, yet schools and society usually operate as though most of the universe were linear. Many believe that mathematics is certain. Mathematics is certain only if we do not connect it to the real world.

One result of being "warmed like the frog" is that we rarely consider generalizations to be of value. Life, love, happiness, wisdom, caring, compassion, general learning, education, and self-direction are all generalizations, and they have multiple meanings and often appear to be chaotic. Those general processes are shunned as lacking clarity and are, therefore, not to be investigated or cherished.

In order to further develop and accept complexity, we could involve students in the process by which differences may be recombined. Involving students at the analysis, synthesis, and evaluation levels of thought, where cognitive evaluations are recombined with affectivity, may now be helpful. That students may decide for themselves what will secure or endanger their freedom, and awareness of what is, is the center of holistic, open, near-nondual education.

Analysis without re-integrating, without synthesizing what has been taken apart, leads to prevention of citizenship and self-government under the guise of thoughtfulness. Analysis without synthesis promotes excessive specialization and technocracy. A technocracy is a society run by relatively few persons and powerful machines.

John I. Goodlad and his researchers visited more than a thousand secondary and elementary schools and found that less than one percent of the instructional time was devoted to discussions requiring some kind of open response involving reasoning or perhaps an opinion from students.[4] Goodlad found excessive student passivity and teachers who rarely went beyond possession of information, to understanding the implications of the information, in their teaching.

I wonder whether our minds are partly crippled from the intellectual and emotional pillaging and subtle raping done to us as a result of school over-specializing and focusing on short, right answers. Schools often stifle wonder, and rarely encourage a sense of awe and love of learning. Is it any wonder that our students are not highly self-directing. Is it any wonder that our students do not know what is good and what is not good without others telling them? Is it any wonder that our students are allowing themselves to be subtly controlled? Is it any wonder that the percentage of eligible voters who vote is relatively low?

Teachers need to provide certain conditions for students before students will use chaos to learn more complex/unified thinking. Teachers who provide these conditions involve students in the process of simplifying and unifying thinking, teach the students to fish instead of simply feeding them fish. This process is both chaotic and ordered. Regularities are found in what was once viewed as irregular when this open, holistic, process is followed.

One condition for open-ended inquiry is that a teacher must have a reasonably good rapport with students. The students must believe that the teacher believes what he or she is saying, and that the teacher must believe that the students believe what the students are saying. A reasonable amount of trust must be established between student and teacher. A second condition is that students must be willing to honestly respond to each other and to the teacher. This approach works best when the teacher responds to students after condition three is provided.

The third condition is that something must be puzzling for the student. The student must see, hear, or otherwise think of something that is at variance with his or her expectations. In a word, they must experience some chaos. Experiencing a discrepancy, "being stuck," is an example of experiencing discontinuity which can function.

The environment must be relatively free in that a student may choose not to be concerned with puzzling situations which the teacher has posed. The student is free to choose his or her own puzzlements, events or processes in which he or she is stuck. The student is not free to do work for another required course during an open inquiry session. The freedom is in no way absolute. The freedom is a relation between people. How freely a teacher wishes to relate with her or his students reflects the degree of openness in their relationship.

Students will ideally be increasingly free not to relate with their teacher and fellow students. It is only then that students will be free to relate with teachers. If we "have to" relate, deceptive relations emerge. The students are free to the degree that they can act on what they perceive to be sufficiently interesting pieces of chaos, discontinuities, which help cause wonder.

As Albert Einstein said, "It is, in fact, nothing short of a miracle that the modern methods of instruction have not yet entirely strangled the holy curiosity of inquiry; for this delicate little plant, aside from stimulation, stands mainly in need of freedom; without this it goes to wrack and ruin without fail."[5]

Students are invited to explore something that is chaotic or puzzling if a discrepancy the teacher provides is not puzzling. What is puzzling a student need not be limited to the subject or course title. If nothing is puzzling to a given student, the teacher attempts to focus on that lack of puzzlement so that the student may become puzzled about why nothing is puzzling. Lack of curiosity is evidence of schools not fostering curiosity. When a student is not wondering, and not noticing what is going on in and around himself or herself, then that student does not know that he or she does not know.

The school's previous emphasis on having students primarily recall information leads them to not know that they do not know. Teachers can provide conditions that facilitate inquiry. Inquiry goes on within the student and inquiry cannot be forced. Experience of chaos, of functional discontinuity, is an important element of inquiry and learning how to learn.

A teacher may show how a concept may prod the student, but this prodding is not necessary and is only done after the student has been stuck for a long time. When the primary goal of teachers' instructional efforts is to involve students more deeply in the process of exploring, then the teacher's dispensing knowledge is secondary or tertiary, and only to be done if it will facilitate the primary goal of developing inquisitive students, who love learning and who are aware of what is.

What basic field does not include learned Ph.D.s with differing views of how knowledge of the field is or ought to be structured? The process of structuring, rather than any particular structure, is of paramount importance when your primary goal is to involve students in the process of exploring. Involving them in this process is tantamount to increasing their general intelligence/wisdom.

This stage of providing a discrepancy is what Alfred North Whitehead calls the adventure or romance stage of the learning process. This discrepancy stage is also advocated by John Dewey as a problem to be explored. Pirsig advocates the use of discrepant events by his elaboration of the positive features of stuckness. I will refer to this process of stuckness as functional discontinuity.

Providing the three conditions of discrepancy, responsive environment, and freer atmosphere, brings about initial chaos and more long-term order. The "how" of involving students in the process by which what has been separated is related/recombined, is the teachers allow themselves and their students to experience this chaos, the unknown. Involve students in the murky thinking that precedes illumination, let them be stuck for more than a short while. A student cannot help but get unstuck if the student pays attention to the stuckness for longer than usual time periods. Students will think their way through the stuckness and another stuckness emerges. Then the students will think their way through that stuckness, etc. What is chaotic often becomes ordered. Regularities are found in what was previously experienced as irregular. Order is found by noticing disorder.

Encouraging students to pay attention to their present experience is an excellent way of helping students experience chaos that may help generate more order and well-being.   The students' present experience includes students' feelings as well as their thinking. Students find difficulty in being aware of their present feeling because most of their past schooling had not focused on attention to their feelings. Past schooling prevented students from exploring. Those who desire high degrees of socialization kept many of us socialized and in their control by providing conditions which relegated our present feelings and interests to an unimportant place in our lives.

After the students have focused on their present experience, and permitted themselves to experience chaos, the teacher asks how whatever subject she or he may be teaching: biology, English, math, psychology, etc., relates to ordering that chaos. More chaos may be experienced, but hypotheses may be provoked and formed for later testing. This provocation helps awaken us from our dogmatic slumbers.

I suggest that teachers start the open inquiry process by taking risks. If we allow ourselves to fail, we will have gone a long way toward more openness. I also suggest that teachers wait, in silence, between the presentation of a discrepancy and aborting the attempt of student inquiry. Our students have been conditioned not to be inquisitive. They have not been rewarded for inquiring. Involving his or her students in the process of open inquiry requires that the teacher defy the students' unconscious attempts to manipulate the teacher into telling the students "the answer." Teacher silence helps the students loosen their holds on being "students" and to become "learners." The teacher may compassionately tell the students why he or she is not giving them "the correct answer."

Students have been dull, docile, and passive. Teachers need to take risks in order to help students become learners who decide for themselves what would secure or endanger their freedom and notice more of what is.

A teacher's first attempt to involve students in the process of open-ended inquiry may be difficult. Most students have not learned to inquire or think for themselves. They must learn that nothing productive will happen unless they ask a question or make a comment. If a student's question or comment relates to his or her being a student instead of a learner, the teacher points out the distinction between being a student and being a learner. Student questions such as, "Will this be on the test?", "Should I write a paper about it?", or "How will you know that I did this assignment?" have little to do with learning but have much to do with studenting.

Some goals of some courses keep us in the dark. Specializing in this or that has led us away from generalizing about this or that. Alfred North Whitehead's view of solving the over-specialization problem is to generalize as part of each "bout" with specializing. We need to specialize somewhat. A problem arises when generalizing is not done. Generalizing is something similar to simplifying by complexifying and *vice versa*. Generalizing includes some experience of chaos, some experience with uncertainty, both of which may profitably grow in a Quantum Age.

Modern science has aimed to give the impression of objectivity so that political elements are posited away. The human sciences want to follow the respectable nature of hard sciences, particularly physics. Math has been obviously value-laden because of a variety of positings that are useful to mathematicians. Mathematicians have never hidden this, yet they have never found it useful to call their axiom generation "political." Politics may be seen as what people do when they exhaust agreed-upon criteria for doing whatever they are doing together.

Mathematics makes sense when you view it as a language that helps people, particularly mathematicians, scientists, and engineers, meet their needs. Some of the unstated needs of mathematicians are their needs to explore and create. Their exploration and creation is facilitated by their ability to control their environment. When they teach math, their control sometimes becomes excessive and the control is, at times, exercised primarily so that they may have more and better control. Control in schools is frequently exercised by administrators and teachers. Excessive control contributes to the development of racists, sexists and homophobes. Students, at times, also control teachers and administrators, and, at times, that controlling is done in an unaware way.

Language is an artifact; what people make to help predict, control, and explore so that needs can be met. Some people have not met low-level needs and they have high needs for food, clothing, shelter, and rest, and/or high needs for that which they have little of, namely, feelings of protection, safety, and security.

Those who have not met their needs for protection, safety, and security find that they get temporary feelings of belonging, and mistaken feelings of respect, when they join groups such as the Ku Klux Klan and other white supremacist groups. This temporary meeting of their needs is similar to the temporary satisfaction which a masochist receives when he or she allows himself or herself to be hurt.

As the language we use is an artifact, so are some non-linear images that derive from attention to the chaotic. Mathematicians create geometries for non-existent space, such as Riemann's geometry, until someone like Einstein used Riemann's ideas to create Einsteinian geometry. Euclid's geometry is useful for common "ordinary" scale reckoning, but for space travel, we need Einsteinian geometry founded on different axioms.

I mention this because the human sciences, including education, have often attempted to emulate physics and math. Newtonian physics of certainty and determinacy has given way to indeterminate quantum physics, yet the human sciences have barely begun to accept indeterminacy and uncertainty as modern physicists and interdisciplinary chaoticians have. That is why little research, until recently, has been done about assisting people in becoming wise.

Because many experts in the human sciences are still operating excessively in overly-determinate modes and have excessive needs to eliminate chaos, we have allowed institutional racism, sexism, homophobia, and other evidence of a lack of self-direction to continue. By not taking steps to eliminate these social ills, we have condoned them. By avoiding chaos too much, we have helped to create chaos.

It would be painful for white American society to admit that it continues to be racist by condoning the existence of ghettos and by condoning conditions that lead to African-Americans and women earning seventy-five percent of what white men earn in the United States. Whites infrequently consider their racism or the racism of other whites. Racism seems to rarely affect white people in the short-run. That is changing. By the year 2025, it is projected that only one-twelfth of the world's population will be white.

Gradualism, gradually giving African-Americans and other people of color what is rightfully theirs as human beings, is a part of institutional racism. Recently, gradualism has not only slowed, some gains made earlier have been lost. White people do not often see that drug problems, school drop-out problems, and much crime is directly related to how white society has treated African-Americans, Hispanics, American Indians, and Asian-Americans recently and in the distant past. Our present competitive societal order nourishes racism, sexism, homophobia, global warming, homelessness, and hunger.

To bring about the freedom guaranteed by our constitution, we need a form of schooling that does not avoid complexity, uncertainty, and some chaos. Note Goodlad's findings which indicate that most teachers do not know how to teach for higher levels of thinking. If we do not think at higher levels, and do not become more aware of what we are doing, we may be racist, sexist, and homophobic. Bigotry and institutionalized racism can only exist when schools contribute by subtly teaching that learning to follow orders is more important than thinking for oneself and noticing what is.

If we thought for ourselves, we might not follow orders because we would notice that we were partly enslaving ourselves. Following orders is done so subtly that many people are not aware of it. If America's early citizens only followed orders, we might still have taxation without representation. The tacit order we receive from our schooling is to maintain the *status quo*. The *status quo* means acceptance of racism, sexism, and homophobia, the avoidance of chaos, and continued specialization to avoid the development of powerful, inventive generalists.

School curricula at most levels, including much of undergraduate teacher education, often focuses on short, right answers which are highly ordered. Short, right answers can be easily measured, and allow authorities to easily determine if a citizen knows what a citizen is "supposed to know." Accountability becomes easy. States promoting these short, right answers with their proficiency tests do not attempt to measure students' love of learning, or the level of students' curiosity, or awareness of what is.

We are often unaware that the heavy focus on short, right answers leads to what Theodore Sizer found: many high school students are without initiative and are docile and compliant.[6] This, some authors say, is not a failure;

instead, it is a subtle success for big business which schools promote, often unconsciously.

Because training in specialized areas to meet the needs of big business has been the primary goal in most American schools, education in a broad Jeffersonian sense of enabling each student to decide for herself or himself what will secure or endanger her or his freedom has been dismissed. It has been dismissed because big business, mostly white males, benefit from closed schooling.

As Walter Karp has indicated, schools do not do what they profess: teach for self-government and citizenship; instead, with remorseless proficiency, schools prevent citizenship and self-government. This prevention simultaneously promotes racism, sexism and homophobia.

I use the notion of promoting racism to show that deeper understanding is not taught. It is not taught because our fear of chaos has continued for such a long time that many of our teachers have not learned to be inquisitive. They have not learned to handle holistic, open understanding and broad awareness. We are now finding that some of these fears are ungrounded because more order is created by the productive experience of chaos. Let us develop teachers who are not afraid of uncertainty and chaos.

Eight

DETERMINING READINESS
TO ACCEPT UNCERTAINTY

Determining which teachers are less fearful of uncertainty and chaos demands a different "testing" procedure. A teacher who is unafraid of uncertainty and chaos can be a quality teacher who is often open to new experience.

The following is an example of a procedure suggested by Don Conable to help in the hiring of quality employees. This "test" is an interview procedure to be used in conjunction with other procedures. The prospective teacher is asked to, during the interview, attempt to steal the interviewer's pen, to catch some flies, and generally show both spontaneity and willingness to be open to new experience. I must add that reverence for all life prevents me from recommending the killing of flies; however, an interview procedure of this type could improve the acquisition of quality teachers.

Most of our formal schooling has not concentrated on those experiences which would help a student score high on this interview procedure. The opposite is probably true. The more important reason becomes, in our highly reasonable Western-type lives, the greater the probability of a lower score. If we are too reasonable too often, our silly side will not emerge. Fun arises, at times, from silliness. One who has learned the art of teaching, while not neglecting the science of teaching, would probably attain a high score on this test.

What "being open" is will become clearer as we move on. Our openness can be noticed much the same way we can know what quality is without defining it. The topic of quality education is like the blind men who go to experience the elephant. These blind men dispute loud and long because of their limited experience with the elephant. Each of us has limited experience with quality and each of us is partly blind regarding open, wise, quality living.

Pirsig demonstrates the existence of quality without defining it by using a realist's definition of whether something exists: the world would not be the same, the world would be abnormal, if quality were subtracted.

Pirsig shows how neither fine arts nor poetry would exist without quality. We would not place pictures on walls because the bare wall would be as good to look at as a wall with a beautiful painting, if quality did not exist. When we listen to scratchy CDs, we would not be able to distinguish those scratches from a Beethoven symphony but for quality. He also demonstrates how comedy, humor, or sports would not exist without quality. He then says the only areas where a lack of quality does not matter are pure science, math, and logic.

We need to occasionally "fix" in order to abandon fixities. One way of getting a better fix on abandoning fixity would be to look at Gilles Deleuze's rhizomatic model of knowing.[1] We might be able to find a process of looking at "process" in a more than technical way when a rhizomatic, flat, non-heirarchical model of knowledge supplements the frequently employed arboreal, heirarchical model.

A peony plant, which arises from a rhizome, is a useful example. From a rhizome grows a number of peonies. Each shoot has a life of its own, can be broken off from the main plant, and still grow full sets of peonies. In a rhizomatic model, each whole is just another part, and each rhizomatic system is more closely allied to holographic systems than are arboreal systems. Each rhizome contains the entirety of whatever is present in the whole.

An interchange may occur between different parts. In a rhizome exists other potential rhizomes connected to each other. The whole is in the part. The part is the whole as the wave and the ocean are one. Quantum learning focuses on such recombinations similar to what a holograph includes.

Elsewhere Gilles Deleuze and Felix Guattari state that rhizomes connect any point with any other point and they are unlike trees with their roots.[2] The rhizome, they believe, is made only of lines, lines of segmentation and strati-fication as dimensions, but also lines of flight or of deterritorialization. This allows for multiplicity of change in nature and of metamorphoses.

Deleuze and Guattari elaborate on the notion that rhizomatic lines should not be confused with arboreal type lines. They state that a rhizomatic system is uncentered, nonhierarchical, and nonsignifying with no one part at the top of a hierarchy of parts. A rhizome is not, in their judgment, an object of reproduction. I read into their exposition that a rhizome is itself more like a process than a product.

As we have heard from Edward DeBono and others, sometimes we need to be "wrong" within a system in order to update the system. The "updating" of the arboreal model may mean its abandonment since fixity is so central to the functioning of that model.

Approximately thirty years ago, mathematicians developed what is called fuzzy logic. This type of logic is less fixed than older forms of logic. Howard Gardner's seven types of intelligence may be seen as an unfixing of older, narrow views of intelligence. Western societies have tended to focus primarily on the logical/mathematical type of intelligence.

Linguistic, numerical, and spatial factors of intelligence have been focal points while society and its schools have neglected the other four factors because they were not as fixed. The body kinesthetic, the musical, the interpersonal and the intrapersonal forms of intelligence have been avoided perhaps because of difficulties in measuring, fixing or clearly defining those four forms of intelligence. I believe these last four forms are among those which Ashley Montagu called other valuable traits which may not be developed as a result of over emphasis on the linguistic, numerical, and spatial factors of intelligence.

Lao Tzu relates, in the *Tao Te Ching*, that a good leader, who talks little, when his work is done, his aim fulfilled, says that those being lead will say, we did it ourselves. Ossified thinking has prevented us from developing such leaders; in fact, it has contributed to the development of fascist dictators and of excessively dominant white males who are generally unaware of their privileges in our society. Fixity continues to contribute to fascism, sexism, racism, homophobia, and other social problems. Overly fixed school systems train us to stand by and allow fixity to continue its promotion of the same, contributing to an ossified society in which women and people of color earn twenty-five percent less than white men.

Many of us want our students to say to themselves, "We did it ourselves." Rethinking of our foundational models is in order if we are to move to that point. The Western arboreal model of knowledge structures places the teacher in a central position. Deleuze's rhizomatic model can be the model in which the student is central.

The following is a brief list of ideas that do not clearly fall into the old fixities to which we are accustomed: Quentin Crisp states that his function in life was to render clear what was already blindingly conspicuous.[3] Robert Goheen believes that if you have both feet planted on level ground, then the university has failed you. H. L. Mencken thinks that we are here and this is now, and beyond that, all knowledge is moonshine. Nikki Giovanni thinks that if this is not a good time for the truth, she does not know when we will get to it.

Researchers in nonverbal communication tell us that about eighty percent of our communication is nonverbal. I believe that those who hold that intelligence is only logical-mathematical would prefer that we communicate one hundred percent verbally or numerically. Their desire emanates from the fixed arboreal model which maintains power mainly in the grasp of white men. Deleuze is uncovering the rhizomatic model as a production of the unconscious. We can allow our present experience to come into awareness when our model of knowledge structuring is more rhizomatic than arboreal. The rhizomatic model allows us to be aware of our present experience and to more legitimately express our present experience.

Each individual's present experience may come to awareness more fully within a more open, rhizomatic model. The arboreal model does not allow experience to come to awareness. Again, it is easy for us to see what we believe and very difficult for us to see what we do not believe.

The following is an example of one who has abandoned fixity. Harold Clurman said, "My happiest experience in reading plays occurred during the Group Theatre days. A script had been submitted which began:

Act I: Ten thousand years before the creation of man.
Act II: Two weeks later."[4]

Nine

ATTENTION AND ATTENTION TRAPS

Syntheses are not your syntheses unless you make them. Explanations are often others' syntheses, and are rarely taken as hypotheses to be continually tested and revised. Syntheses, in a broad sense, are intuitions rather than fixed concepts. Concepts only contribute to delusion, and if you are deluded, ten thousand books of explanations may not be enough. When you become a nondual synthesizer, one word may already be too much.

My experience leads me to believe that we do not pay attention to what is going on in and around us, because we are often avoiding attention by excessive, unaware attempts to figure out another's synthesis rather than to create our own. Inattention to present experience is why ten thousand books is not enough for some, and why one word is already too much for others.

Since schools are places where inattention is learned, schools are where change may be most urgent. Attention, and the process of focusing attention, in schools and universities, is a phase in a self-directing experience cycle.

To view paying attention holistically, I give a context of attention which includes what students do to diffuse attention. Diffusing attention can lead to incomplete, nonproductive experience. The assumption is that one experience is not as productive to learning as another. Productive student learning is more likely to occur if a student is open to what is.

Student growth is more likely to occur when a student's energy is focused on what is happening. As a result of focusing on the present, energy can heighten into higher excitement which mobilizes us to act. The action may be no more than the movement toward non-movement and silence. Some action can be for itself, yet action designed to help us make contact with people, things, and events may, at times, help us have a fuller and more growth-producing experience.

At other times, being alone quietly may be more growth-producing. Many of us believe that we are interconnected social beings. When we are compassionate to ourselves and others, we make a kind of contact. When we notice that we are the opposite of compassionate, we are also opening our eyes. Noticing what is happening is the key.

The last phase in an educational experience cycle, before a new sensation restarts the process, is a completion-withdrawal stage where withdrawing from the contact with a person, thing, or event completes the cycle, and allows a synthesis or fusion to occur. When the withdrawal stage is skipped, a hanging-on can prevent synthesis. Preventing synthesis can leave our attention frozen to a contact. This frozenness results in unfinished experience.

Without withdrawal and completion, we prevent ourselves from having new experience, and instead, we repeat old experience. The roots of boredom, *malaise*, and alienation are often found in the unconscious repetition of the same experience. That murky unknown which nudges unconsciousness toward consciousness helps us to stop repeating the same unconscious experience. Paying attention to murkiness, at times, can help generate greater clarity.

Productive student learning, although not fully defined, implies an adventure. Adventure implies newness and freshness. The newness permits reception of new stimuli, new sensation. You may chose to focus on and continue new sensations so that another energy rise, action, contact, and withdrawal may further the possibilities of your continuous reconstruction of experience.

When you do not pay attention to some sensations, you may jump the attention and energy rise stages and move directly to an action stage. The action that often results from such a jump is unaware action. Psychotic behavior often includes actions of which we are not aware. The legal definition of insanity includes the idea that the insane person is one who does not know the nature and quality of his or her acts and their probable consequences.

Conversely, we may say that we are educated, have grown and developed or are self-directing, to the degree that we are aware of, and choose, the nature and quality of our acts and their probable consequences. If we view education as involving aware choice regarding the nature and quality of our acts and their probable consequences, we can see that by paying attention, optimally focusing attention, and allowing the focusing to continue, we gain focused energy, action, contact, and withdrawal. These are at the roots of holistic, open education where murky attitudinal factors in a free, responsive, quantum, environment are as much included as the specific behaviors which citizens "must be trained to do."

Inattention implies an avoidance of focus on what potentially could be figural, and clearly distinguished, from the ground out of which the figure emerges. If we look at previous unfinished experience, getting stuck somewhere between the sensation and withdrawal stages is a common occurrence, and we all have pet ways of getting stuck, pet ways of not completing an experience. For example: How are you now not free? Who is binding you? A clue to your answer may be your incomplete experience.

Within the holistic, open view, if we take responsibility for the stuckness, we can do something about stuckness. The first and most difficult step occurs when we believe, "I am getting myself stuck," then we can move on to paying attention, and focusing on the sensations which lead us to believe, "I find that I am sticking myself." As we energize ourselves from the focusing of attention, we can move and act in ways that can lead to contact with people, things, and events. We can, through contact, nourish ourselves in ways which we cannot often nourish ourselves. We can withdraw from a contact and rest before we choose to pay attention to another sensation which can lead us to another nourishing experience. The cycle is open and continues.

Avoidance implies an unawareness, and therefore, there is no choice and no responsibility for its consequences. If we are focusing attention on what was avoided, if we are choosing to avoid, and if we are responsible for the consequences of the avoiding, then we are simultaneously permitting ourselves to better direct the course of our present and future experience.

The three elements, (1) focused attention and awareness, (2) choice, and (3) responsibility for the consequences of the choice, are foundational ideas within this holistic, open, integrating/recombining framework.

Processes exist which cannot be explained in terms of simpler thoughts. Within this framework, sensing, focused attention, energy rise, action, contact, and completion-withdrawal are outgrowths of aware responsible choice, and simultaneously, the catalysts in the further development of aware open, responsible choice. The part is the whole and the whole is in the part.

Choice implies a sense of freedom to select among alternatives. Within the holistic, open framework, education as the continuous reconstruction of experience arises from aware, responsible choice, and enables the continuation of aware, responsible choice. Education is for more education in a way that carrots, for example, are not simply for more carrots. Inattention, or unfocused unawareness, is then the germ of our devolution. When we do not pay attention, we cause our own enslavement.

Student attention in school is commonly assumed to relate to paying attention to either what the teacher is saying, or to the subject under study. The holistic, open framework does not make this assumption. Students should not pay attention to teachers and subjects if that is the student's choice, and pay attention to teachers and subjects when they choose. Students should be encouraged to focus attention, much more often than is now the case, on the assumptions, feelings, and thoughts that arise and stand out for the student. In so doing, we help students avoid waiting for some power external to themselves to do what each individual is responsible for doing.

John Dewey said that people do not fully use the power they possess to advance the good in life because of this waiting for some power external to themselves.[1]

The holistic framework also includes the Deweyian notion that to find the meaning of something, one must see how it is presented in experience. Focused attention can be a part of a more complete and growth-producing experience. To Dewey and to thinkers within this holistic, open framework, things are what they are experienced to be. My experience leads me to believe that each of us experiences selectively, and this selective experiencing arises from our individual needs and wants which are unique as well as common.

I read an article about a teacher who helped some black children significantly improve their achievement in selected basic skills. She said that an assumption behind her efforts is that some students need a more active learning environment than that provided in most American classrooms. That author believed that African-Americans need it more than whites, and boys more than girls. This article referred to research which found African-American infants had more advanced motor skills than white infants. The African-American infants were found to crawl, stand, and walk earlier.

A part of this teacher's success was attributed to her permitting her students to move around the classroom in ways that our more conventional teachers would consider unruly. I mention this teacher's success to support the idea that a teacher's and students' paying attention to their sensing, and the consequent energy rise, action-movement, and contact with things and events, can result in learning basic skills of reading, writing, and arithmetic. Had this teacher behaved in a more conventional manner, the students would not have been as free to pay attention to what they were sensing.

It is difficult to pay attention to sensations that can lead to movement, etc., when the student would be criticized or even punished for moving. If students are conditioned not to move out of their seats during lessons, they learn to turn off body signals which may reap dividends if they are given attention. Junior and senior high school students would need to move less than elementary students.

We turn off body signals with attention traps. We trap ourselves in many ways. I will briefly describe six common attention traps about how we get ourselves stuck, how we prevent ourselves from growth-producing experience, how we stop ourselves from completing experiences, how we stop ourselves from focusing our attention so that we do not get needed nourishment from our environment, how we avoid meeting our higher level needs; and how we avoid being whole, open, and aware.

The first trap is everything in our minds that we have not chosen to put there. I expect that most people have some "I shoulds," or "I oughts," or "I musts," about various ways of being that they acquired as a result of growing up in a particular culture. As children, we were not supposed to question or wonder about "certain things." We were to do "the good things" and avoid "the bad things."

The carryover of these through our youth and into our adult years remains in varying degrees. If we pay attention to them, and decide for ourselves whether we, and those around us, will be better off with those "shoulds," then those "shoulds" become congruent with "I choose to," and the result is integrated, open, balanced, holistic, wise, and harmonious living. Attention, in this case, obviously pays off since this case relates to free, responsible, aware choice as the means to and end of our living. The ultimate "I should" within this holistic framework is that I should be aware. From this awareness we move to "I should freely and responsibly choose to do what I do and to be what I am." As a sage said, "We are what we think." Choosing not to choose is itself a choice.

The trap is lack of attention to these "I shoulds," which disintegrate our living and our behavior. The disintegrations which result from avoiding attention in these matters can lead to immature behavior and a variety of social ills, as well as behavior that comes back to us in kind. Hateful behavior returns in hate, and kind behavior returns with kindness.

The second trap relates to our projecting onto others experience we have to which we do not pay attention. If we do not pay attention to this experience, we do not take responsibility. An unattended to "I should" is then perceived as being apart of someone else. This happens because we find difficulty in acting or non-acting in a way that we believe we should act or not act.

If we take responsibility for what we are and for what we do, we will minimize the projection of our unexamined attributes onto other people. An example of an extreme case of this is the paranoid who is continuously thinking, "they are out to get me." In reality, he or she may be out to get himself or herself, but he or she has not paid attention to that possibility, and as a result, the paranoid is getting himself or herself, and is unaware of it.

The third trap is the deflecting of attention: diffusing or defocusing of attention to something inconsequential when the energy rise is uncomfortable. Newer and higher energy levels are often interpreted as "bad feelings." If we allow them to be present and continue to focus on them, we can become more familiar with them. As we stay with the energy rise, we naturally move into action which can lead to contact with a person, thing, or event which, in turn, may result in a complete, growth-producing experience.

Deflecting is avoiding paying attention to what we fear. This holistic, open view holds that not only is fear okay; it can be beautiful in that fear can help us grow. What is not beautiful is our excessive fear of our fear.

The fourth attention trap is an unaware continuation of a contact with a person, thing, or event. It is the loss of our identity in that person, thing, or event so that the person, thing, or event is choosing for us rather than our mutually agreeing to choose together. Attention is not paid to our sense of completeness. Completeness is not felt because this trap has sucked us in; our attention is elsewhere in a way that inhibits free, responsible choice and awareness. When avoidance of attention occurs, we are afraid to let go of the contact because of the uncertainty involved in not knowing what will happen next.

The fifth and last attention trap is almost an occupational hazard for many thinkers. This trap is an easy way for us to avoid growth-producing experience. We trap ourselves so subtly that we do not even recognize the trap. The trap is called retroflection. It is a non-chosen reflection of whose consequences we are not aware, unlike chosen reflection which is a source of much of our growth-producing, self-directing behavior.

When we retroflect, we are not aware, and retroflection is a source of some of our incompleteness, imbalance, disharmony, and further lack of awareness. Excessive thought without action may be debilitating in that a hanging on to avoid present experience may result in delusion. Retroflection is what we do when we want to be excessively certain. We block ourselves from action and contact by retroflecting in an unaware way. If we do not pay attention, we cannot choose.

If we do not choose, we lose control of ourselves. An excessively compulsive person exercises little or no choice during his compulsive activity. The paradox of self-control is that we get more self-control by not over-controlling. Unattended to retroflection is a result of over-controlling which results in less control. Living with some uncertainty can help us become more certain and aware.

Retroflection is an attempt to give to ourselves what we need to get from our environment. If we retroflect, it is like attempting to breathe without atmosphere. We diminish ourselves when we reflect without choice. When we are unaware of what we are doing, or when we are unaware of what is going on in and around us, we are probably not attending to our retroflecting. Being aware of what is pays off. We must be interconnected/interdependent if we are to be mature, open, holistic people.

The scale in schools is unbalanced on the side of student dependence. Many educators, parents, and students opt for external control. I believe this choice is the result of avoiding paying attention to much of what counts.

My experience leads me to believe that we could profit from paying attention to the uneasy feelings we sometimes have as we notice racism, sexism, homophobia, looking to be told what to do, and a general lack of independent thinking. These feelings, if focused on, can lead to an energy rise, action, and contact that often result in increased individual and group openness, awareness, and self-direction.

This holistic, open experience cycle, to which focused attention is central, can be a form of experimenting with ourselves and our transactions with our environment. If we have to know the exact result of the contact before we have it, we will stop our energy flow, and not act or move toward contact that can promote self-direction. When this happens, we are not paying attention to what counts. Lack of attention leads us to have the experience in our heads before we have the experience, before any transaction or contact with another person, thing, or event. This results in our not completing the experience; consequently, we do the avoiding again and again. We do old experience over and over. As a result, we avoid life-enhancing spontaneity and surprise. Schools are notorious for an absence of spontaneity and surprise.

If we are open, not having an excessively high need to know exactly what will happen at all times before it happens, we can pay attention to what we are experiencing at each stage of our experience cycle. As we choose to know exactly what will happen before it happens, we are paying a kind of attention. The consequences of such a choice are that we are choosing not to explore the world, but rather, our fantasy life about the world. This holistic, open view holds that we can only pay attention within the three zones of awareness.

If you have a toothache, for example, you would probably experience an energy rise that would move you to make contact with the expertise of a competent dentist. The completion of such a contact allows you to pay attention to matters other than the aching tooth. If, however, we experience frequent boredom, depression, frequent tiredness, and alienation, we find it more difficult to pinpoint the decay and eliminate it.

Schools have not been paying attention to these kinds of experiences and, as a result, we usually push this kind of experience—the boredom, etc.—aside rather than complete it. This kind of experience returns when it is not completed. At times, lack of attention returns in various forms of illness. Unaware pushing experience aside is unaware avoidance of attention to the completion stage of the experience cycle.

We have not been schooled in paying attention to these kinds of experiences probably because schools do not pay attention to them. These kinds of experiences can be signs that some need is not being met. Older, more closed notions about schooling can prevent needs from being met. They prevent the noticing of what is.

I do not believe that schools can meet all of our needs. Schools, however, can help us learn about how we can meet our needs. If we cannot meet our own needs, I suggest that we are not self-directing. The "back to the basics" movement seems to have avoided what is most basic within this holistic, open framework.

Focus on the learning of basic skills of reading, writing, and arithmetic is a necessary element in this structure, but openness, creativity, recombining separated elements are also needed since reading, writing, and arithmetic were created by openness, and recombining elements. Openness, creativity, and recombining elements are more basic than the skills that the back-to-the-basics group thinks are basic.

Those basic skills are but a part of a larger whole. The part makes sense in terms of the larger whole. If we demand that our students pay attention to only a part, we do not intend holistic experience. We do not intend the whole because we do not attend to the whole. When we do not attend to the whole, we "pre-tend." This pre-tending is a pretension; pre-tension. The pretension is often done to avoid tension. We do not complete our experience of tension so we remain tense. The tension, if attended to, could become productive tension that can lead to increased self-direction, openness, and awareness. We do not pay attention to that stage of the experience cycle, and as a result, schools too often remain tense places that lack openness, adventure, and surprise.

Schools are tense places largely because we do not attend to the tension in attention zones other than fantasy. The holistic, open, nondual view holds that our minds and bodies are a unit, but not a separate unit. Too often we are trained to believe that we are primarily minds who unfortunately have a subordinate appendage called a body. As a result, we do not pay attention to much of our experience which, in turn, causes us to remain unaware.

Schools which better serve a democratic society may eventually blossom more fully. These schools shift curricular emphasis from socialization as the primary goal of instruction, to development of independent, inventive thinkers/doers as a temporary primary goal of instruction. I say "temporary" because eventually, our democratic society will need to balance the socializing and the development of independent thinkers-doers and other newly-discovered factors.

We need balance between training and educating. Today, American schools are unbalanced on the side of training, and we do the training under the guise of education. I say "guise" even though we are not generally aware it is a guise.

The "doer" is added, after independent thinker, as a primary purpose of instruction, to emphasize that the thinker who does not act on his thought, with compassion to self and others, is as dangerous to a free society as one who acts without thinking. In an excessively controlled society, compassion to self and others is not encouraged. Robotic, docile servants are cherished in fascist societies. In externally controlled societies, the citizens act, but the action is unaware maintenance of the status quo.

Schooling today is largely maintain-the-*status-quo* closed schooling, and is focused mainly on socializing students. As a result, schooling has neglected the development of the students' ability to decide for themselves what will secure or endanger their freedom. Walter Karp refers to a national study which shows that fifty-eight percent of America's thirteen-year-olds believe it is against the law to form a third political party.[2] Karp believes that such thinking is a sign, not of school failure, but of subtle school success. Is that a result of deception?

I support the idea that some self-deception saves us from high degrees of anxiety. High degrees of anxiety are unconsciously interpreted as excessively destructive of well-being, and we, at times, lack awareness in a self-deceptive way to avoid anxiety. Some anxiety probably should be avoided. Other anxiety, if received without an excessive need to know in advance what will happen before it happens, can produce contact with others which may help us grow and meet our higher-level needs. No one is perfect and each of us must decide for ourselves what is balance.

Accepting some potentially anxiety-producing events, along with general receptivity to experience, is what is frequently referred to with the use of the terms "open," "being open," and "being open to experience." When we are closed to experience, we prevent ourselves from making contact and, therefore, prevent ourselves from growing. When we do not grow, we keep ourselves from becoming self-directing.

Some school administrators and teachers are not aware of the stifling of independent thought, and the prevention of the development of citizenship. If they were aware of this stifling and prevention, they would foster more independence/freedom in schools and society. This lack of awareness of independence and freedom may be evidence of growing excessive external control. Hard line leaders do not want mature, open citizens.

The creeping nature of fascism, like the Boiled Frog Syndrome and global warming, includes within it the conscious thinking that independent, inventive thought is to be guarded against, lest "things" change too much, too fast. Rapid change to a full-blown democracy causes too much anxiety so we unconsciously exclude it from awareness. I believe that the United States is closer to excessive external control than many think.

The bases upon which holistic, open teachers operate are: First, that a holistic classroom is a learning environment where education is viewed as a life-long process in which the learner is guided to the learner's outer limits; second, creative, free, responsible choice is maximized to enhance the learner's ability and desire to invent the learner's present and future; and third, learning is viewed as a process in which the primary emphasis is on learning how to learn and awareness of what is.

The priority in this learning environment is on the learner's self-knowledge, enhanced through fusing cognition and feeling. The learner's self-image is a condition for his or her achievement. The learner's growing awareness is an often unstated goal.

Because the learning process has not yet been fully conceptualized, and cannot be totally conceptualized, the open, holistic learning environment is a flexible structure. Were the learning process fully conceptualized, the concept would be a delusion. I will later amplify on how conception is a delusion from a nondual perspective. Inherent in the open, holistic view is the notion that there are many ways to teach. The learner's inner experience is regarded as a context for learning and coordinate with what is external as a context for learning. As integration and recombining continue, external and internal do not remain separate.

The open, holistic learning environment promotes whole-self education in which nonlinear, intuitive, holistic, open strategies augment linear, analytical rationality. The learner is viewed as transrational. The learning environment stresses that relationships between teachers and learners are of primary importance. Technology is seen as a tool to be used by people for the humanization and opening of minds.

The open, holistic learning environment views the learner as an open system who continually reconstructs his/her experience, so that the learner can notice what is and invent the learner's present. Inherent in this is the belief that prior to a major reconstructing of experience, a feeling of discontinuity emerges. This discontinuity may be viewed as a productive stress whose intensity ranges from wonder, puzzlement, excitement, uneasiness, creative tension, and confusion to, at times, anxiety. Deconstructing is regarded as an aspect of reconstructing.

This learning environment is seen as safe enough to explore. The learning environment encourages exploratory and experimental effort within the framework of safe emergencies which teachers help promote. The open, holistic environment shows that dealing with disequilibrium can help foster greater equilibrium, as greater order arises from paying attention to disorder.

Teaching in open, holistic, responsive learning environments fosters openness to new possibilities, some of which may be strange. In this open, holistic environment, the teacher is seen as a midwife of ahas! and a facilitator of learner whole-self integration and awareness. The teacher believes that not only does the learner cause learning, but also learning can be assisted by providing appropriate conditions.

A part of this open, holistic, responsive, learning environment is activity to increase trust in teacher-learner relations. This responsive, open learning environment encourages each learner's uniqueness. Teachers, as well as learners, need to deal with ambiguity, puzzlement, conflict, paradox, and general murkiness, if noticeable reconstructing or transformation of experience is to occur. Awareness is a major key in this transforming process. Awareness allows greater access to unconscious anxieties which may stand in the way of the process of reconstructing experience.

This whole-self, open, holistic development creates a common sense and this common sense helps teachers generate, on the spot, the various skills and knowledge they need when faced with unique situations. Common sense generates inventive resourcefulness.

The holistic, open educator has always believed that not only is each student unique, but so is each day, hour or minute. Individualizing instruction, consequently, has been, and continues to be, prized by holistic, open educators. There is no fusion, no integration/synthesis which amounts to an aha!, without grappling with some confusion. Fusion does not occur without confusion.

To find what is worthy of the name "education," I look for an educator's equivalent to the mathematician's zero.

Robert S. Kaplan shows that the Sumerians, before early Greek thinkers, had the idea of zero, although it may not have been used in mathematics operations until around the year 800 AD.[3] Before I read Kaplan's book, *The Nothing That Is*, I found a book which said that Leonardo Pisaro introduced zero into Western mathematics in 1202 AD. This introduction of zero—a place holder, an empty set—permitted mathematicians to solve problems which were previously unsolvable. Society is groping for solutions to numerous problems.

A fertile area for further investigation lies in formulating the roots of these problems. Educators today often feel a need for tools and processes that will allow them, in their work of educating, what the use of zero does for mathematicians. Zero is the notation for a missing position. Zero permitted mathematicians to take a quantum leap. Many educators want to take this leap if they knew how. Antonio Porchia's idea applies here.[4] "Set out from any point. They are all alike. They all lead to a point of departure."

From what direction may we take this leap? The direction relates to a tool that, like zero, denotes nothing by itself, but when used in relation to other thinking, may function to better clarify what is worthy of the name "education." The parameters of the educator's equivalent of the mathematician's zero are highly polymorphous. Such a concept, process, thing, or event may now be nonexistent.

At first glance, the idea of an educator's zero is not a logical impossibility. The terms "mathematicians" and "educators" are used, instead of the terms "mathematics" and "education," to include the human, translogical elements inherent in the use of such a tool.

These dualistic, translogical elements include a thinker as well as thought. As has been alluded to, some continuous processes are incapable of definition since they are ongoing. The highly polymorphous is tantamount to the amorphous. That is one reason why it is so difficult to define time. Nondualists hold that everything is involved in a continuous process and continuous processes change as you are talking about them. The change that keeps everything changing remains constant, unchanging. That may be considered a reason for the centrality of impermanence to nonduality. Beware, however, of rationalizing regarding nonduality, for nothing exists to rationalize.

From a near-nondual perspective, education may be thought of as a clear fuzzy. Although educators have questions about what they are doing when they educate, they frequently believe that they know what they are doing when they teach. Time is another clear fuzzy. We all know what time is, yet when we are asked to define time, we have great difficulty in doing so. We all know what quality is, yet defining quality is difficult.

A fuzzy fuzzy, this educator's equivalent to the mathematician's zero, will be used to help explain the clear fuzzy "education." We know little about that fuzzy fuzzy. To illuminate the clear fuzzy of what is worthy of the name "education," I will use an educator's equivalent to the mathematician's zero. This educator's equivalent to the mathematician's zero might be that which nudges clear fuzzies into the fuzzy fuzzy category.

I posit that we mainly wonder about fuzzy fuzzies. Clear fuzzies seem to be sufficiently clear so that we do not frequently wonder about them. If we do not wonder, we probably will not involve ourselves in the process of opening our experience. Without open experience, we will not involve ourselves in extracting a fuller meaning from experience.

The educator's equivalent to the mathematician's zero may be, among other things, "that" which helps us become curious. A Western sage implied that some closed educators are carrying a medicine for which no one has found the disease, hoping they would make it on time.

The educator who primarily trains, primarily dispenses information, remains in abundance. Thirty-some years ago, an unknown researcher found that teachers rated inquisitiveness on the part of students as their tenth most troublesome characteristic in their classrooms. Developing students' curiosity, love of learning, and awareness of what is, are not frequently on teachers' minds as they "train."

Since we are usually only curious about those matters which we desire to explore, I will shift our focus to the space between what we know and what is yet to be known. I suggest that the major focus of educators' attention is on what is known. What is known is frequently clear, unless we are wondering about it. We usually do not wonder about clear ideas. Clear fuzzies are often thought to be clear and precise ideas unless we ponder them. Clear fuzzies have degrees also. We do not have technical questions about the functioning and uses of our feet, for instance, unless we are podiatrists or their like.

Educators more frequently have questions about what to do in their classrooms tomorrow, yet some educators occasionally grapple with coming to a deeper understanding of education as process. Relatively few teachers define education as, for instance, "the continuous reconstruction of experience," partially because relatively few teachers delve into considering process. Such a definition is capable of infinite refinement and elaboration. "Continuous" is largely unbounded, as are "reconstruction" and "experience," yet when we are in the process of defining, we are engaged in a binding activity. We are, in a sense, attempting to bind the unbound.

Belief can inhibit wonder when belief, or any of its facets, is held to be certain, held unquestioningly. When I asked a few people "what is gravity?" most of them indicated that they knew. In a sense, many of them do know, but few know that they know little about gravity. The same idea may be said for time, education, learning, knowing, believing, being wise and other ideas shrouded in polymorphicity. Undergraduate students are relatively certain about those matters. They believe they know what they are talking about when they use those terms, and they usually do not wonder about them.

Knowing gives us a reasonable certainty. Knowing reduces polymorphicity. Knowing something implies creating a separate unimorphicity. When context is highly limited, knowing can provide us with even greater certainty and less polymorphicity, if there is little concern to expand contexts and open minds. Contexts expanded indefinitely approach pure polymorphicity, as contexts narrowed indefinitely approach pure, separate unimorphicity. Approaching pure polymorphicity, and its productive use, may well surround the educator's equivalent to the mathematician's zero.

Such an educator's zero could assist us in coming to know that we do not know. The awareness of our knowing that we do not know can literally do wonders. Holding a separate unimorphicity can stifle wonder, in that we usually do not wonder about things we know. Gravity, to many students, is a separate unimorphicity.

When Kurt Gödel wondered whether he could prove that he could not prove "something," he was not bound by the current constants of his day. When Werner Heisenberg elucidated his indeterminacy/uncertainty principle, he was not bound by the constants of earlier physics. I mention Hubble's Constant because astronomers have found flaws in Hubble's Constant. Hubble's Constant is a formula which enables astronomers to calculate distances by measuring a "red shift." As a result of some new evidence that points to flaws in Hubble's Constant, the universe may not be expanding after all, said one unidentified astronomer.

I mentioned Hubble to illustrate the shifting of belief about fundamental concerns. Gödel and Heisenberg provided ideas that shifted mathmaticians' and physicists' beliefs about math and physics in a quantum world, which may help others open their minds to the possibility of additional mental shifting about teaching, learning, educating, and being wise.

Evidence continues to mount that we need some shifts in beliefs of educators. I conclude that we need those shifts so that we can be more open to experience. This openness to experience is stifled by perceptual filters that are fogged with beliefs about the impossibility of certain experience. Can we experience nothing? Can we be aware of emptiness and nothingness? Is the absence of something capable of being experienced? Can we possibly have the educator's equivalent to the mathematician's zero?

The field of mathematics, as frequently taught below graduate school level, is often considered a closed system. Educators deal with an open system. Trying to find an educator's equivalent to the mathematician's zero is doomed, some say, because of this difference between open and closed systems. Mathematical discoveries over the years have demonstrated that openness exists in mathematics. A totally closed mathematics implies that mathematics is simply a big tautology. Is Einsteinian geometry more true than Euclidian geometry? One works better for given problems in space than the other.

Perhaps the first way that a possible educator's equivalent to the mathematician's zero may aid educators is to help shift constants, fixities, and ossifications of long duration. This shifting may be difficult to do since some constants prevent others from emerging.

If we temporarily forgot all constants, we would probably be asking too much of ourselves, for then we would know nothing. We can, however, wonder about and question some constants, especially those for which we have strong feelings, the ones about which we are certain. Such wondering and questioning would permit us to deal with more paradox and ambiguity. As educators deal with more paradox and ambiguity, so will students. As a result, we may all wonder more and become more self-directing which can lead to more compassion and wisdom.

When we perceive a short, vertical line on a blackboard, we often conceive of number one. A short horizontal line becomes a minus sign. Signs are everywhere. Some signs prevent us from seeing other signs. What signs now prevent us from using that educator's equivalent to the mathematician's zero in relation to that which helps us continuously reconstruct experience?

We use some metaphors that prevent us from seeing aspects of reality; they allow us to see only aspects of reality that they themselves help constitute. What are some of these metaphors? What contexts inhibit decontextualizing so that recontextualizing can occur? What constructs prevent reconstructing? When we examine reconstructing, an element of deconstructing emerges shortly before reconstructing. Perhaps the educator's equivalent to the mathematician's zero functions more vigorously in the deconstructing phase of the reconstructing process. I say reconstructing instead of reconstruction to treat it as a present activity.

The process of exploring is that of relating what we know to that which is unknown. We will not find relations unless we look. We will not look where we "know" nothing can be seen. Looking at nothing is the purpose of the "not knowing" element of wisdom. Getting our students to look at polymorphous events and processes includes some looking at nothing. We may synthesize better when we do. Prior to a synthesis is a void, an absence, a lack. Without this void, absence, lack, an experience of nothingness, or emptiness, no synthesis can occur. Awareness of present experience is the only experience that results in synthesizing, creating ahas!

Syntheses can be both meaningful and truthful. John Dewey chose to use the term "meaningful" in that truth can be relative, as a truth in Euclidian geometry can be a falsehood in Einsteinian geometry, but meaning can only be had in the present, and meaning can only be had by a person who may or may not share the meaning with other persons. Truth, in a dualistic Newtonian sense, is generally held to be timeless even though we always remember truth in the present. We do not guess that $2 + 2 = 4$ will be true tomorrow. We know it will. As a result of that knowing, we inhibit wonder regarding the conditions and events under which $2 + 2 = 4$ may not be true.

The continuous reconstruction of experience can only go on in the present. The deconstructing element of reconstructing can also only go on in the present. Dewey was implying that synthesizing can only happen in the present.

"Knowing" does not fit the previously quoted Deweyian statements as well as the term "awareness." Awareness subsumes knowing; we can be aware without "knowing." We can be aware of confusion, yet we only "know" without being aware, in some unconscious sense that I wish not to deal with here. Where "knowing" can prevent other "knowing," awareness facilitates other awareness. "Knowing" can prevent some awareness. Awareness expands contexts; "knowing" can prevent expanding contexts. With different contexts, what we know changes. Our knowing that we do not know may be an element of experiencing nothingness/emptiness.

That which we are looking for is that which is looking. Such looking applies whether we are looking to make "precise concept" a more precise concept, or whether we are looking for an educator's zero. We are involved in the problem of attempting to see our own eyeballs. When we are aware of this, we can see our own seeing.

Many psychologists, but definitely not behaviorists, experience themselves and their clients as selectively perceiving. Selective perception allows us to easily see what we already believe, and causes difficulty in seeing what we do not believe.

As Pirsig talks about Poincaré's subliminal pre-conceptioning regarding his intuiting of solutions to mathematical problems, some nondual Zen masters hold that we must be enlightened before we are enlightened. Intuitive kinds of knowing may be at the basis of selective perception. Our needs and desires are the heart of our selective perception.

Nel Noddings and Paul J. Shore view intuition as an experience-enabling function in that intuition precedes, and makes possible, the experience from which knowledge is constructed.[5] Noddings and Shore believe that intuition, as a source of truth, has been discarded by modern thinkers. I have been indirectly contending that the educator's equivalent to the mathematician's zero may help educators recontextualize intuition as a resource in extracting full meaning from present experience.

Most of us would rather avoid looking, which probably will not result in "a seeing." I suggest that the educator's zero be narrowed to primarily function at the stage of the intuitive process which precedes the first clear intuition. Noddings and Shore argue that intuitions form when there is subjective certainty and objective uncertainty. The educator's zero helps us allow ourselves to live with higher degrees of uncertainty. Paradoxically, we can be more certain when we accept higher degrees of uncertainty.

Because of increased receptivity, we can be more aware of what we are experiencing as we are experiencing. If intuition is an experience-enabling function, intuition is the ground from which knowledge is constructed. The educator's zero could be viewed as that which enables us to begin or continue intuiting.

We want to provide conditions which enable our students. Students can be enabled by helping them notice their indecisiveness and need for certainty, and by fostering awareness that students are creating their agony which helps generate unaware avoidance of their present experience. If the students, with their teacher's assistance, notice that they are agonizing themselves by deciding not to decide, then they have the opportunity to refrain from agonizing themselves.

Sensing the concrete world is essential to a build-up of awareness. An excessive need to know in advance what will happen before it happens is a major way of avoiding experience. Unaware avoidance of some experience leads us to have experience only in our heads. This prevents us from making contact with the real world of things and people.

We cannot have awareness at any time other than the present. Our students are often unaware that memories are present remembrances, and the future is present anticipation. The excessive need for certainty results in our use of precision in our statements as a tranquilizer to delude ourselves into thinking we know what we are talking about, when we use terms such as gravity, education, democracy, learning, motivation, science, and poetry. This educator's zero can spark the insight that it is frequently wise to know tentatively, openly, and receptively.

Such tentativity, openness, and receptivity can lead us to agree with Jean Piaget's highest form of cognitive functioning. This is the ability to hypothetically consider any state along a continuum of possibility as potentially equal to any other state, and then to return to the operation's state.

Knowledge of what will happen before it happens is, at times, quite useful. Knowledge is power in the sense that we can control ourselves and more of our environment with knowledge. When we have an excessive need to know what will happen before it happens, that need can greatly reduce receptivity to what is happening. Awareness of what is happening is reduced when receptivity is reduced. Without awareness, most of our knowledge is useless. We cannot extract any meaning from an experience we do not have. Inquiry is not value-free. We see and hear what we want to see and hear. We perceive selectively, and our inquiry relies on what we perceive. The affective elements of our sensations, perceptions, and constructions are often shunned because they cannot be described or explained in detail. The educator's zero may be likened to a French writer's connection to the word "understanding," which implies that a person who understands, forgives.

Concepts are formed in many ways. "Science" has taught us to test hypotheses but it has not taught us to form hypotheses. Forming hypotheses includes an affective or value element. The testing of what is formed attempts to minimize and perhaps deny value statements. Value elements are frequently connected to the political. Political power is enhanced by education. Education of the powerful has always been the goal of general education for rich people.

General education, since the days of Thomas Jefferson, has been intended to help us to judge for ourselves what will secure or endanger our freedom. For most people, education has been a training to follow the orders of the rich and powerful. Creating concepts is relating concepts in infrequently related ways. Judging for ourselves which infrequently related sets of concepts may help us secure or endanger our freedom is part of the creating of concepts. Is there a conceptual limit to concept creation and what is the role of present awareness?

Judging for oneself is crucial. Modern schooling not only does not promote judging for ourselves, but actively attempts to control minds so that we will not openly judge for ourselves. We can more easily forgive those rapers and pillagers of minds when we understand that their unenlightened ways of being do not permit them to judge for themselves. The notion of understanding and forgiving is quite similar to an Eastern view which holds that when we do something "wrong," we do the wrong because we are deluded. The nondual way does not contain "wrong," partly because only awareness of what is and delusion exist. When we are aware of the delusion, it is no longer delusion. Also "wrong" is a concept as is "right," and concepts are delusions.

Ten

DISCONTINUOUSLY CONTINUOUS LEARNING IN A QUANTUM AGE

Students will not learn to judge for themselves unless the students deal with discontinuities. Without choice, the need to judge is superfluous. No need to choose exists if everything is always continuous.

To learn how to use discontinuous elements of experience, I will start by giving the example of counting by ones to a hundred. If we counted to a hundred, we would probably not have an educational experience. We know we can generate "the next number" when we are counting. In fact, we are sure of it. A young person who is learning to count by ones to a hundred is not nearly so sure. In all probability, this young learner is quite uncertain. Once this young person is reasonably sure that she or he can generate "the next number," we often say that she or he has "learned" to count. We are no longer learning to count. We use this process that we have "learned" to learn other events or processes.

If we learn to count at an early age, and we are uncertain of our counting then, and if we are reasonably certain of it now, could we conclude that the process of learning an event or process involves some uncertainty? When the uncertainty is noticeably reduced, could we conclude that the event or process has been learned? I contend that the uncertainty/certainty notion, as it applies to learning simpler processes such as the process of counting, also applies to learning complex processes, such as how to avoid Boiled Frog Syndromes, how to be just, how to be aware of what is, how to be wise, how to be whole, and how to reduce racism, sexism, and homophobia.

Quantum learning now may recombine those "other" events and processes to learn larger events and processes, then larger ones yet, etc. Ludwig Wittgenstein's idea to use his ideas as a ladder, then kick over the ladder after it had been used, applies here. When we are afraid to take risks of recom-bining, we are refraining from kicking over the ladder.

Counting often functions in the solution of problems. Both individuals and machines count, and there is little dispute that machines count much more efficiently than human beings. There is little discourse about machine democracy, machine justice, machine consciousness, or machine wholeness although Ray Kurzweil and Watts Wacker have recently alluded to that likelihood.

We can safely conclude that democracy, justice, and wholeness are relations between and among people. Most of us posit that relations between and among people are more growth-producing when we are wise.

I am more concerned with uncertainty/certainty, being-learned/been-learned notions than with answering the question of whether these notions apply to learning complex as well as simpler processes and events. I have concluded that it does. How I have come to such conclusion will not be dealt with directly. If we are concerned with providing conditions which will enable minds to learn and become whole, I suggest we should also be involved in the process of assisting minds to be more uncertain. I suggest we comfort the afflicted and afflict the comfortable on certain occasions. I am also suggesting that when in doubt, try recombining. Try recombining again, and again, and again, until all is combined: nondual.

If we want to expand and open our minds, make more connections, relate more sets of phenomena to each other, become more whole, and notice what is, and if we want our students to do the same, then I propose that we take what is uncertain to us and our students and use the uncertainty rather than run from it. The uncertain is that which disconnects or discontinues what we know. I will label the uncertain, "discontinuity."

We would have great difficulty using something that does not exist. The placebo effect will not be dealt with here. Discontinuity, when used, is functional discontinuity. Functional discontinuity will be partly described and explained in terms of how a teacher may use it with his or her students.

Alfred North Whitehead believed we can never reach the interval between events, yet functional discontinuity can assist us in moving in that direction. To get "more between" two events or processes does not make much sense; however, moving toward "more between" may be an adventure. Moving toward "more between" may eventually have the effect of recombining separate elements. Although Whitehead has used the terms "romance" or "adventure" as stages in the learning process, I suggest that what is romantic or adventurous about the romance or adventure stages of learning is the functionally discontinuous state of our knowing.

When functional discontinuity operates, we come to know that we do not know. Plato effectively used this process. With functional discontinuity, we can make more sense out of the process of getting between what we know. We will not get between the dichotomies we have created unless we feel a need to get between them. Functional discontinuity can be a tool to help us to feel the need. This need is similar to a need to integrate what has been productively disintegrated in order to recombine separations of a pre-quantum age.

Functional discontinuity provides an internal mental signal to restabilize what the teacher or environment has made unstable. Functional discontinuity is analogous to an interference; it provides a challenge so that a mind will not too quickly avoid discontinuity and puzzlement. Functional discontinuity leads students to know that they no longer know what they once thought they knew.

Dissonance, a partial mental vacuum, the partial experience of emptiness, provides internal motivation for mentally processing, which contributes to opening minds. The temporary result of the mind-opening takes into account the former, narrower conceptions plus the event or process that caused the student to feel/think that a set of phenomena contains more meaning than existed in his or her "old and narrower" view.

Closed, narrow, more conservative schools have curricula which purport to teach by telling. Even when the teacher attempts to have the student "discover," the "discovery" the teacher has in mind is frequently what the book or teacher predetermines is the "right answer." Jean Piaget reminds us that by giving the right answer, a teacher often prevents students from learning many new right answers themselves.

Functional discontinuity disconnects a student's conception. A concept is continuous, closed: fixed. The closedness is the conceptual boundary. The conceptual boundary or conceptual limit is what differentiates the concept from other concepts that are also closed or limited.

The closedness of a concept continues until awareness of an event or process makes it discontinuous. The discontinuity is functional when the fascination/positive dissonance of the student motivates her or him to take into account the event or process that rendered the previous view noticeably incomplete and somewhat insufficient. This process may continue until we unite everything: nonduality. Some people become nondual without going through the excessive intellection stage.

When you are aware that your view is closed or fixed, that awareness is tantamount to saying that you know that you do not know. Until the event or process created a feeling of puzzlement, conflict, surprise, fascination, or lack of wholeness, the student thought he or she knew. After a student is functionally discontinued, processing by the student is intensified so that the feeling/thought imbalances are brought into a new balance by the creation of a tentative more open view. A more open view may lead toward the non-view which is tanramount to emptiness. That kind of processing reduces as we move closer to nonduality. Quantum learning provides the conditions which increase our chances for moving closer to nonduality.

Functional discontinuity as a mind-opening catalyst may be used by a teacher as the zero is used by mathematicians. It has no value in itself, but may be used to make possible operations that would otherwise be impossible. If we view it as a product, it makes no sense. If we view it as a subprocess within the process of the continuous reconstruction of experience, it may be a useful tool. The koan may be seen as an instance of functional discontinuity.

Until the recent past, ideas or myths outlived people. Today this is no longer the case. The restructuring of ideas which occurred in the past often arose from random discontentment with the then popular views of phenomena. Perhaps the new view of no view will increase chances for openness, peace, and harmony.

Today, the interferences needed to tilt students from their preconceptions and narrow conceptions can be brought about, in part, with tools such as functional discontinuity. Functional discontinuity may be viewed as an element or a process that is the common denominator of conflict, surprise, doubt, perplexity, puzzlement, interference, paradox, bafflement, wonder, dissonance, lack-of-at-one-ment, discrepancy, and lack of wholeness.

I view functional discontinuity in its similarity to zero. Functional discontinuity is capable of facilitating excitement and a need to learn when used as an educational zero. Functional discontinuity enhances the continuousness of the restructuring of experience, or enhances the restructuring of the continuous structuring of experience. Deconstructing is involved in reconstructing. As we become more nondual, our deconstructing is also deconstructed. That deconstructing of our deconstructing occurs as we empty ourselves of our separate egos. We become empty instead of having a concept of empty.

The field of education uses concepts such as "wholes" and "parts," "stimulus" and "response," "fact" and "value," "being" and "becoming," "objective" and "subjective," and "content" and "process." We don't seem to have a process, like the function zero, between concepts to change their value by restructuring, expanding or narrowing these and other processes and events.

Functional discontinuity can help us get between these processes and events, using functionality discontinuity as a relational invariant. Functional discontinuity is an invariant in that it is always the same, as a zero is always zero. Functional discontinuity functions only in relation to other events and processes. Functional discontinuity may help us to eradicate our egos as delusional conceptioning.

Continuities or concepts are already organized. Students organize only that which is discontinuous or disorganized for them. What makes "the known" known, is the particular organization or structuring which we give to some aspect of what was previously unknown. The unknown is uncertain, and is discontinuous from what we know. The known is continuous, at least temporarily.

It is the "temporarily" that we forget and our needs for certainty too often make the known permanent/fixed. These fixities prevent open exploration and move us away from quantum learning. Temporarily, from a nondual perspective, may be less than a few milliseconds, but temporarily could also include years.

The classroom where functional discontinuity is employed could be any grade with any subject, excluding classes where training, instead of educating, is the primary goal. The process, according to my experience, works best in grades four and up. It takes somewhat longer to work in grades above six due to the present greater student rigidity at higher grade-levels. It would not be useful where the primary goal of instruction is training or memorization, such as a keyboard class or a beginning foreign language class.

For discontinuity to function, the classroom atmosphere must be freer; the primary motivator is learning, not grades or teacher approval. The atmosphere must also be responsive, not only with such things as books and many fully loaded computers, but also where the teacher-student, and student-student relations are such that they respond to each other in a reasonably open and truthful way. An atmosphere must exist where students are not unduly fearful of each other, or if they are fearful, they are not afraid of the fear. Such an atmosphere is evinced by open expression of what is fearful.

Granted, to provide a responsive environment may be no easy task, but functional discontinuity will not operate without it. The results, I have found, are well worth the extra time the teacher and class take to move toward a freer, yet not overly chaotic, atmosphere.

An instance of functional discontinuity may be any event or process that puzzles, confounds, or baffles a student in a fascinating or exciting way, an event or process that a student wants to further explore. Asking the students to answer the following types of questions can be a way of helping move toward what is functionally discontinuous for students: (1) Concerning the physical world only, excluding your relations with yourself and other persons, what do you strongly want to know more about? (2) Including your relations with yourself and other people, what do you strongly want to know more about? (3) What do you worry about the most?

If the student genuinely responds to at least one of those questions, you and the student have a curriculum for a minute, hour, day, week, month, or year, depending upon whether the discontinuity continues to function. Each student will have his or her own curriculum. The individual student's curriculum will be random in relation to other students' curricula. The student's curriculum will be ordered according to his or her own felt needs, determined by what is genuinely puzzling, discontinuous. If a student is to do her or his own thinking, continuously reconstructing her or his experience, then she or he must determine the order of the structuring. That means the student must move toward determining the student's own curriculum, unless training is the primary goal, at which time the trainer orders the experience.

Training can be useful under various conditions and circumstances, yet if training continues to substitute for education, the students cannot be expected to think for themselves. Students will not then be involved in deciding for themselves what will secure or endanger their freedom. Schools now are much more involved with training than with educating.

The zero-like element of functional discontinuity is seen when teachers use functional discontinuity to remove a closed and narrow conception. As our conception of time can be made more intelligible by relating "time" to conceptions of space and motion, our conception of content may be made more intelligible by relating content to conceptions of process which include motion. Our conception of space can be made more intelligible by relating space to time, and our conception of process can be made more intelligible by relating process to content. We may eventually move out of conceptioning as we experience the closed nature of conceptioning.

The explicans, that which is used to explain, and the explicandum, that which is being explained, in such cases are, in part, interchangeable. Instead of only differentiating, or only integrating, functional discontinuity can be used for both, so that students and teachers can be more differentially integrative and integratively differentiating. They can continuously reconstruct experience which, when seen as one process, may also be seen as nondual.

The notion of functional discontinuity can be viewed as an element in the process of the continuous reconstruction of experience. Functional discontinuity cannot be viewed apart from other processes, as a zero cannot be used except in relation to some other process or event.

In an over-simplified way, functional discontinuity makes discontinuous a conception which would otherwise be fixed. A conception has boundaries. Squares do not function as circles. Functional discontinuity can bring about a gap in a boundary, putting a gap in our knowledge structure. This gap provides a feeling of dissonance which is a lack of consonance.

A closed conception gives a temporary consonant feeling, providing no need to explore anything. An optimally open and discontinuous view provides a feeling of productive tension which, as its name implies, produces. The product is exploration and greater awareness which takes into consideration more events and subprocesses. The expanded view permits additional reconstruction of experience, and has itself been expanded by the reconstructing experience. We may eventually take everything/nothing into account. Such is nonduality.

Functional discontinuity is also analogous to providing productive confusion in the mind of a student. This productive confusion provides a condition for another level of fusion. Fusion in the student's mind is similar to operation at the synthesis level of thought where ahas! arise. Confusion creates a climate and desire for additional analysis that precedes synthesis which the learner evaluates using cognitive, affective, and psychomotor domains, which are never separate except to make distinctions in order to expand openness and recombining.

After a teacher establishes rapport, and after time is spent in developing a freer, yet only semi-chaotic, atmosphere, and responsive environment, the teacher can share more of what is confusing with students. Paradoxically, this sharing and mutual exploration of what the teacher finds confusing to student and to herself or himself is simultaneously a way of creating a freer and more responsive environment. This mutual exploration of what is confusing serves to have teachers and learners more fully live in the present and to become more compassionate and wise.

"Functionally discontinuing" a student in an atmosphere which becomes increasingly more open reduces noticeably as time passes. Functional discontinuity continues, but the individual students/participants discontinue themselves as they become more aware of, and share more of, their experience. Functional discontinuity helps break up the boundaries of "past" and "future" for us. This helps bring awareness of our present experience, and recombine separated elements, into a new whole which is central to quantum learning. Recombining and discontinuing may continue until separations are discontinued.

If we proceed to more openly live in the present, we will be more valuable to schools and society, and we will find our endeavors to be more stimulating, growth producing, and we will each be more at ease. Holistic, open experiencers become more compassionate to themselves and others as they become more aware.

What we experience happens in the present or happens not at all. Present reconstructing is a way toward choosing our experience. Fear and anxiety are experienced in the present, yet are generated by a feeling/thought that something consequential happened in the past, or that something consequential will happen in the future. Only the present is consequential because choosing can only be done in the present and frequently, only free, responsible choice is of consequence. Let us take a closer look at the present.

Eleven

FOCUSING ON PRESENT EXPERIENCE

Those who think about educating are often concerned with asking and answering "ought" type questions. Questions such as, "What ought society in general, and schools in particular, do to educate its citizens?" are at the heart of many educators' endeavors. To ask, "What ought we do?" implies, "What ought we do in the future?" for the question, "What ought we do?" implies the questioner has already decided that he ought to now ask "What ought we do?"

Asking this question also implies that we have a choice between at least two alternatives. If we were clear about what ought to be done, there would be no need to ask the question, except rhetorically.

Assuming we have some degree of free choice with respect to experience, and assuming that we are responsible for our free choices, what may be made explicit from what is implicit in our constraint to freely and responsibly choose? As educators, how might we get a better handle on answering the question, "What ought society in general, and schools in particular, do to educate its citizens?"

Henri Yaker, Humphrey Osmond, and Frances Cheek give a clue to answering that question.[1] Yaker, Osmond, and Cheek believe that how to live in the future, paradoxically, in the last analysis is a function of living in the present. They assert that the great task of a person is to realize the hour, and not seek all answers to all things which in the end may be unworthy of knowing. Sometimes, they say, we make the present bad, only so the future can be brighter.

Do we not at times make the present dim so that the future may be brighter? What if we shifted our noticing so that we held that nothing has ever happened in the past and nothing will ever happen in the future? We presently have memory traces that we conveniently refer to as "the past" and we have present anticipations that we confidently regard as "the future."

We think of five seconds ago as residing in the past. At approximately that time you were seeing the word "abstractions." But at the time you were hearing it, of course, it had to be happening in the present. An anonymous sage asks us to agree that five seconds from now will be the future. If we agree, and logically this is correct, he asks us to count out loud 1, 2, 3, 4, 5, and then ask are we now in the future?

We must consider that nothing ever happened in the past and nothing ever will happen in the future. If the anonymous sage's view becomes ours, and if we agree with the notion that what we are looking for is that which is looking, what might we conclude? One conclusion is that the search is the finding and that the search—exploring—therefore, is for itself. While searching is often equated to dimness, and finding to brightness, under older views, searching is equated with brightness under some newer views of open, holistic education. The journey and the arrival are one. That is nondual and perhaps the ultimate recombination in a quantum world. Recombination cannot be conceptualized, yet we usually deal only with concepts, and as a result, we remain deluded.

Asking the question, "What ought society in general, and schools in particular, do to educate its citizens?", under this new noticing may become, "What is behind our question, What ought society in general, and schools in particular, do to educate its citizens?" Looking for what is behind the question is part of a continuous reconstructing. Eventually, we may be aware of nothing is behind it, partly because behind does not exist.

Dewey provided conditions to reconstruct experience so that our lives are not only meaningful now, but also so that we could better direct the course of our future experience. The newer noticing tells us that what we think is future experience is present experience. Implied in this newer noticing is that excessive preoccupation with the future may be avoidance of present experience, of present awareness, and of facing our fears.

As we redefine our society, and as we look behind our questions, I suggest that we seriously question three assumptions which we frequently have: (1) the activity of thinking about education is a step-wise process, each step following out from the previous one in unbroken sequence, (2) that we must be correct at each step, and (3) that we select and deal with only what is relevant.

Edward DeBono offers us clues in his notion of lateral thinking.[2] By combining lateral and vertical thinking in our activities as educators, I suggest that we will update ourselves, become more valuable to society, and enjoy our work more.

DeBono states that lateral thinking is useful because it uses irrelevant or random information to shake up the system. To shake up the system from within the system itself is difficult. DeBono suggests that when tackling a problem, it is better to go to the solution end and work back, rather than simply inching forward one step at a time from the beginning. DeBono's thinking makes use of intuition and is partly translogical.

He promotes the idea that we do not have to be correct each step along the way. He advocates suspending judgment, and he and encourages us to be wrong within this system in order to update the system. I have used his ideas in university classrooms and have found them to be new and effective for students even though they have existed for forty years in the form derived by DeBono.

DeBono comments about the similarity of humor and insight and the fact that they are both restructuring phenomena. As an example, he cites Winston Churchill's celebrated reply to Lady Astor.

Lady Astor: Winston, if I were your wife, I'd put poison in your coffee.
Churchill: If I were your husband, Nancy, I'd take it.

I suggest that we look to the highly extended notion of open living in the present for a clue. Our fixed and perhaps once useful conceptions are preventing this permanent change from occurring.

I believe that we have imprisoned ourselves with some of our closed fixities. Holistic, open views can assist us in pushing our prison walls back. These holistic, open views themselves must be kept open. Our constraint to freely and responsibly choose implies that we will continue to imprison ourselves; yet newer, holistic, open views may make our prisons more like the French Riviera than Devil's Island.

We are what we think, said a wise person. Frederich Nietzsche alluded to the idea that a thought, or even a possibility, can shatter us and transform us. Our society will be transformed when each of us transforms himself or herself. What thought, non-thought or possibility, or impossibility may do the transforming for you now?

Twelve

INTELLIGENCE AND HUMOR

To clarify murkiness, I look at intelligence, developing a sense of humor, and educating. I give examples and relate ideas about the development of the students' sense of humor as a means for education during the twenty-first century.

I do not directly define humor, intelligence, or education. I will, however, give examples so that meanings of educating, intelligence, and humor are clarified. John Dewey believed that an educated person is one who is self-directing. A self-directing person is considered to be intelligent, whereas a person with low self-directedness is relatively unintelligent.

A part of what I say, dealing with intelligence, will explore aspects of artificial intelligence in order to better contrast intelligence with stupidity. Since scoring high on a conventional IQ test is not the primary indication of intelligence, as I am using the term, I remind you of the Conable Procedure used to hire high-quality teachers, which I described in Chapter Eight, stealing the pen, catching flies, etc.

An old way of determining whether a machine is intelligent is the use of the Turing Test, named after A. M. Turing who broke the German "Enigma" code during Word War II. In order to determine whether a machine approaches human intelligence, Turing suggested that a tester be separated by walls from the question answerer, and that the tester would use a teleprinter to communicate with the answerer so as to remain impersonal.

The point of Turing's test, stated briefly, is that if after so many hours or days of questions from the tester to the person or the machine, and answers back from the person or the machine to the tester, if the tester could not determine whether the answerer of the questions is a person or a machine, then the answerer, if it were a machine, would possess near human intelligence.

I remind you that Ray Kurzweil said machines will reach the capacity of human brains by 2019, and by 2029, machines will have a thousand times the capacity of human brains.

Future tests for determining machine intelligence may involve humor; for instance, imagine what it would take for a machine to act "intelligently" when a machine is told the following story:

An elegantly dressed female is sitting across from a distinguished looking man at a formal dinner party. Shortly after they sat to eat a seven-course dinner, she notices this regal sort of chap placing sliced carrots neatly on his head. He continues to neatly pile these carrots, and while the pile grows higher and higher and higher, the sauce begins to drip in his hair and down his face. Finally, after the drippings are all over his clothes, she cannot stand it any longer so she leans over and says, "Pardon me, Sir, but why in the world are you piling those carrots on your head?" "My god!" he said, "Are they carrots? I thought they were sweet potatoes!"

Did you notice some chuckling? Some hearers of that story would laugh and others would exhibit some sign of mild amusement as they experienced the incongruity; temporary mental restructuring, that is revealed in the punch line.

In order to evoke a machine equivalent of a human chuckle, the machine's system would need to notice a grand variance from what the machine "expects." The machine would need to be surprised, which is difficult to do unless the machine's operation is indeterminate. A Center for Computer Disease Control has been established. We have seen the destructive effects of computer viruses. If machines can be diseased, machines may be moving toward indeterminate functioning.

The rapid restructuring of the machines' "experience" is part of surprise. When an intelligent person or machine gains insight, there is a restructuring of experience. A difference between the effect of humor and the effect of insight is that humor results in a temporary restructuring while insight results in a permanent restructuring. Much of a human being's growth is dependent upon insights which are the equivalent of mental reconstructions and deconstructions.

Humor is a higher form of play. The route to developing machines that tell jokes is through developing machines that play. Schiller's injunction about humanity, "Man is most man while at play," may be modified to read, "Machines are most intelligent while at play," or "Machines are least like old, twentieth-century 'machines,' while at play."[1]

Incongruity theories of humor relate to what Immanuel Kant asserted about humor. Kant mentioned that humor arises from the sudden transformation of a strained expectation into nothing. Some critics of Kant's idea note that we must be jolted out of our mental attitude into another which is completely and violently opposed to it.

The important thing in hearing a joke is to "get it." "Getting it" relates humor to commonly accepted notions of intelligence. The seeing of unexpected connections is a hallmark of humor. "Seeing" itself, perceiving and the related rapid, large-scale mental shifting/restructuring, approaches the center of intelligence. An anonymous person said that the emotion expressed in humor may come in part from a feeling of liberation at the removal of blinders. This relates to Freud's notions relating to jokes and dreams.

Both jokes and dreams, according to Freud, are means of outwitting the internal censors which keep us in the dark so that our anxiety levels will not be overly high. Intelligence may be conceived as that which removes us from the dark, which illuminates and/or integrates chaotic elements. The problem with the censors—inhibitions, defenses, resistances to being who we are—is that they can also help maintain moderately high levels of stress and anxiety over long periods of time. Some theories of psychotherapy hold that anxiety can be lowered by allowing it to increase. Regarding the sense of intelligence, as captured by the Conable Procedure, a person who is highly anxious or tense, over time, may not be highly intelligent even though he or she may score high on a conventional IQ test.

Support for noncongruity is provided by several researchers who have discovered that the highest-achieving, most emotionally healthy child has the best sense of humor. Adults are less shaken by stressful events when they have a keen sense of humor. Researchers who have measured intelligence and social skills of children found that children with the best sense of humor measured highest in their intelligence and social skills, and that creative humor showed the strongest link to overall competence.

Science is increasingly becoming event-centered. The indeterminacy of physicists is catching on for other scientists. Thinkers who are excessively bound to determinacy, excessively needing to know in advance what will happen before it happens, excessively tied to principle, epistemology, control, and order, may protest the development of a sense of humor as a means of education.

Humor may be described as an art of pure events. Humor creates events and points to creativity as the pinnacle of human activity. Rationality, while still important, serves creativity, as Einstein suggested. Axiological concerns become coordinate with the epistemological concerns in a Quantum Age. Previously, over-concern with epistemology may have been the result of an excessive need for determinacy and certainty.

A humorous story, such as a joke, is not humorous to the listener unless the listener "gets it." The essential element of intelligence is what helps people "get it" when they hear a joke. Becoming educated helps one "get it." The "it" in the case of humor is that which creates a temporary restructuring of experience. The "it" in the case of intelligence is a permanent restructuring, an insight, or an aha! And that may be an element of wisdom.

Theorizing about education can be an activity that helps provide conditions which are conducive to permitting students to restructure experience. The restructuring of student experience has frequently been a major goal of teacher activity, even though development of a student's sense of humor has not been given much attention by educators and society in general.

Permanent restructuring, insights, may more quickly develop if the development of a student's sense of humor is focal to the teaching. We learn to restructure experience by restructuring experience. Furthermore, temporary restructurings may facilitate permanent restructurings since, from a nondual perspective, nothing is permanent.

Deconstructing the old is part of the reconstructing toward a new construction which will need deconstructing if education is the continuous reconstruction of experience. According to the nondual view, constructions are continually deconstructed until we deconstruct our deconstructings. The reconstructings are similar to recombinations. These recombinations continue until everyone and everything is recombined, is one, is nondual.

The term "activities," rather than the term "behavior," is used to connote that the whole of an activity is more than the sum of the parts which comprise the activity. The whole of a humorous story is more than the parts into which the humorous story can be divided. Otherwise, seeing the parts of the story would be tantamount to "getting it." The "getting it" is the seeing of the relations between the parts which are not evident apart from seeing the whole which includes the organization of parts.

I posit that behaviorists and some language analysts often imply that a whole is equal to the sum of its parts. While the search for clarity is important, looking for parts of parts of parts may prevent wholes from ever being seen. Looking for longer than usual periods at murkiness can help you to see. Some language analysts have said that expanding contexts is important to their work. Expanding contexts may be viewed as searching for broader connections which more readily allow larger wholes to be seen.

Humor is destroyed when analyzed. What about life? Analysis is done, at times, to omit surprise, and surprise is normally a major element in the "getting it" stage of a joke. Schools may frequently be viewed as joyless, mindless places because of an over-interest in omitting surprise. The excessive control that is necessary to omit surprise has had the effect of dulling the experience of students through avoidance of the restructuring/ destructuring of experience.

The large number of rules found in most schools attests to an excessive need to know in advance what will happen before it happens. Excessive detail in teacher planning frequently has, as its immediate goal, the knowing of what is going to happen before it happens. A major school goal is frequently to control those functions which lead to spontaneity and surprise. Avoiding surprise may inhibit general growth and development and may also inhibit the development of intelligence, wisdom, and a student's sense of humor. Omitting surprise when training may be fine, but not when educating.

I am not suggesting that teacher planning be eliminated. I am suggesting that teachers plan conditions which help their students become more spontaneous and insightful. Planning joke punch lines, and other creative activity, requires the acquisition of much knowledge. I am suggesting that this acquisition of knowledge serve the activity of creating events such as punch lines, and general awareness of what is. Today, acquisition of separate pieces of knowledge, isolated from what the student feels and thinks, is often the primary goal of instruction.

Some arguments for avoiding surprise and doing away with humor can be noted as subtle arguments to miseducate or control our society. Michel Foucault's genealogies have shown that findings of the human sciences function as controllers of individual behavior.

For the majority of people in America, their needs for adequate food, clothing, shelter, and rest have been adequately met, although too many are still hungry and homeless. Several years ago, the number of homeless in the United States was estimated between eight hundred thousand and nine hundred thousand people. Unfortunately, the number of homeless is growing, and some experts estimate their number to be three million. I recently heard one million three hundred thousand as the figure for homeless in the United States.

Our children need to learn skills that will provide adequate food, clothing, shelter, and rest for themselves and their future families. Some seriousness is needed as those skills are learned. The purpose of schooling, however, is much more than vocational, and much more than meeting lower level needs. I suggest that schooling's highest purpose may be play and developing a sense of play through development of a sense of humor. Did not the early Greeks have leisurely playing with ideas as a major purpose of "schooling?"

"Joking around" with people, allowing our humorous side to show, can be a way of moving toward feelings of safety, protection, and security, as well as a way to feel less rejected and more accepted. "Joking around" can help to develop higher degrees of self-esteem. "Joking around" can function as a vehicle through which one becomes more self-actualizing and fully-functioning. You learn to "joke around" by joking around.

Relatively high degrees of freedom can facilitate this "joking around." Being around people who "joke around" can be a noticeable asset in developing a sense of humor/intelligence. How often is "joking around" a high priority in classrooms? Rather, seriousness and staying on task, two major goals of many schools, can be a route to miseducation. Seriousness and staying on task can be a route toward excessive external control and boredom.

School control has been primarily in the hands of school administrators. Holistic teachers have an increased decision-making responsibility. Shifting the locus of control to teachers and then to students needs to be done for quantum learning, but now administrative control is seen in administrative rewarding of teachers who are on chapter ten on the day "they should be on chapter ten." Students will be on task, say these closed administrators, when the teachers are on task. When the primary task becomes developing a sense of humor, curiosity, love of learning, and noticing of what is, educators will have a chance to transform schools.

The attended-to chaos is helping people to see newer orders. Order is seen by looking at chaos, by allowing the chaos to hang around, allowing students to be stuck, and by the students doing what it takes, that is not illegal or immoral, to get themselves unstuck.

Excessive administrative control of students is designed to avoid all forms of chaos and even hints of chaos. This excessive control derives from the excessive need of the administrators, school boards, and society to know in advance what will happen before it happens. The excessive need for certainty is a non-quantum event.

Some knowing in advance is useful and growth-producing. However, when it happens to the degree that it is now happening in many schools, this excessive need to know in advance is evidence of a closedness to innovation. This closedness to innovation is evidence of high need levels for protection, safety, and security which are common in near-fascist societies.

To move to higher Maslowian need levels—belongingness, respect, and self-esteem—requires some risk. The risk involves additional experimentation with moving more control to teachers and, eventually, much more to learners.

The Conable Procedure is particularly valuable in testing whether we are willing to rapidly assess a situation and take some risks in indeterminate circumstances. "Living" just happens to be indeterminate. "Living" is thought by the "high-needs-for-certainty group" to be too difficult to measure.

The very-easy-to-measure stuff is often thought of as largely meaningless by those willing to take more risks. Living, to the "high-needs-for-certainty group," is broken into parts, and then parts of parts, and then finally into highly specific tasks students must perform if they are to be "successful." Such is the ground for miseducation and the devolution of a sense of humor and society.

Miseducation may occur when we do not have the opportunity to express our present experience, and that will be discussed next. The danger of Western societies' excessive rationality relates to our fear of attempting to express that which we know but does not seem to make sense. We have been taught that we do not know unless what we know is reasonable.

As a result of our fear of expressing what does not seem, at this time, to make sense, we avoid some translogical expressions by not looking for the forest but seeing only clear, distinct trees. As a result, we see trees and do not know that they are combined into a whole forest. Quantum learning will help us do the recombining so that we will be able to see individual trees when we wish to, but we will also be able to see the whole forest.

Under specific conditions, we can see the effects of atoms. While those atoms do not allow us to predict the behavior of molecules, the molecules can be seen. We can combine and recombine molecules into various compounds, and then compounds into larger units. We can combine those larger units into larger units and we can continue combining units into larger units. We can label these larger units and combine them into larger units yet. This amounts to conceptioning, and labeling conceptions. Because such conceptioning is myth-making, conceptioning is delusion, nondually speaking. The atoms and subatomic particles that we have named form a part of this delusion, yet we have found conceptioning useful in many ways. Problems arise when we forget that these conceptions do not have substance in themselves, and that the separate parts with separate labels are not separate from the whole, of which we are all a part. Once again, H_2O will not float a ship.

1. Expression of Present Experience

If teachers expressed more of what they are experiencing, their sense of humor, intelligence, and teaching ability would probably improve. As a result of increased expression of present experience, teachers could model growth-producing behavior, and be more aware of what is.

Distinctions between what we had experienced, what we anticipate we will experience, and what we are experiencing will be viewed as the forest of experience. The forest of experience is viewed as "more" than the sum of the trees of particular experiences. A road toward that "more," for some people, is through the expression of present experience.

We can know much about specific experiences but very little about experience. As we differentiate one experience from another, we put limits on experience so as to know this specific experience and that specific experience. What we know of this or that specific experience is usually present knowledge of a past event. This knowledge is useful if we want to know what happened. Our knowledge helps us predict and control, and our ability to control serves us well if it is not an end in itself. Our ability to control has the primary function of aiding exploration.

Knowledge is that which has been explored. That which has been explored assists us in reducing anxiety about what is presently being explored. High degrees of anxiety generate excessive present control efforts. Defense against present experience blocks present exploration. We are not open to what might happen when we are highly fearful of what might happen. Anxiety puts our minds to work on preventing/defending against what might happen, and defending can close us off from exploring. As we become defensive, we often do not accept our defensiveness, and we then prevent experience.

We prevent experience of defensiveness and we block the experience from our own awareness. We can stop a present experience so that we can have a particular experience from which we can have the feeling of being more certain. Exploring, on the other hand, is always done in the present. Some prediction is necessary and even helpful during exploring. Excessive prediction, however, prevents exploring. Exploring subsumes predicting and has more of a continuousness or ongoingnenss about it. Predicting is usually not an end in itself. Letting some experience go has a deconstructing effect.

Our chances of knowing what will happen will be noticeably increased if we know what is happening. Often, in order to know what is happening, we must do some "riding," with what we are experiencing. In order to "ride" with the present experience, we may have to give up some present control, and that is difficult but worthwhile. Giving up some control permits greater degrees of disorder and chaos to enter our awareness. "Riding" with the present experience is often a very personal, subjective, and in some ways, unscientific manner of arriving where we have been trained to arrive: order, clarity, reasonable certainty, and truth.

If we know what is happening, we can choose to have it happen, or choose to have something else happen. Only when we know what is happening can we control and choose that happening. Paradoxically, we often gain more productive control over what is happening by "riding" with the present experience, rather than directing the experience into what we have previously experienced. Directing, if done excessively, blocks present experience. We gain more long-range control by giving up some short-range control. When we allow the experience of disorder and discontinuity, the discontinuity can function in the determination of greater order, and more long-range continuity, and openness and awareness of what is.

Most educators would agree that teaching is not simply telling. We do not simply tell students one truth, and tell them another truth, and then go on to the next truth, etc. Many teachers do much more than that, yet we do talk about the events and processes as a part of our teaching. Powerful teaching is often designed to have our students become more aware of what is happening in and around them. As a result of this greater awareness, students have more choice. State proficiency tests, however, promote teachers telling more isolated information.

When you are deciding, you are deciding now. If we learn by doing, then we learn to choose by choosing, and we learn to decide by deciding, and we learn to be aware by being aware. Only if we are aware of what is happening will we be able to choose that happening or some other happening. The predicting that most of us do is fine, if that is what we choose to do. When we predict excessively, we prevent exploration and reception of new stimuli and experience. Some psychologists have alluded to the idea that what we perceive as happening is what we predict will happen. If we do only predicting, we never get to dicting; the exploring and the simultaneous expression of what we are experiencing.

A model of dicting will soon be given. There are excessive discrepancies between what teachers say teachers should do with students, and what teachers are doing with students. Teachers, at times, can expect not to be believed. Our students perceive more of the modeling that teachers do than what teachers say. "More is caught than taught." "We teach the way we were taught." These sayings continue to be with us probably because they are accurate. The power of what we say is increased when we do what we say. Students will more fully experience what we say if we reduce discrepancies between our sayings and our doings.

The following is an edited version of a part of an unpublished paper written by Dr. David Doane, a clinical psychologist in Toledo, Ohio.[2] This dialogue is an example of a teacher modeling what it is like to express what he is experiencing, as he is experiencing, during his teaching the first class period of his college freshman class.

Dave:	Right now I'm sharing my now. Thoughts about school and hopes about how I hope we will be together keep occurring, and I'm choosing not to talk about all that now. —pause— I feel kind of strange—like why am I talking at all? What's going on, anyway? Yes, what's going on, that's my start.
Silence:	30 seconds
Dave:	I'm aware of silence. You all are looking at me. You all are sitting in chairs, in straight lines, facing this part of the room and not one another, and you're very silent, like something pretty important is going to happen up here, and you're all going to audience it. And I walked right into this important part of the room like this is where I belong, and you're all silent, and I'm doing the talking. The stage is set.
Silence:	15 seconds
More silence:	30 seconds

Dave sits at the edge of the desk and looks around at people looking at him.

Dave:	I notice your arm is raised.

Student A, lowering his arm says: "Is it OK if I ask a question?"

Dave:	You just did. I noticed your arm was raised, I said that I noticed that, then you lowered your arm and asked if it's all right for you ask a question.
Student A:	Well, what I want to know is, is this part of the class? You're the teacher, aren't you?
Dave:	Yes, I'm the teacher. Oh, I get it—being a teacher means to you that I'm supposed to do certain things, like say if something is a part of a class or not.
Dave:	Now I notice some grinning and laughter. Now I notice it's stopping. I said I notice it, not to stop it. I'm

	feeling pretty powerful in here—a feared kind of powerful.
Silence:	15 seconds
Student A:	Well, all I wanted to know is what we're supposed to be doing, and you...
Dave:	[Dave interrupts student A and says] What you are doing is you are asking someone to tell you what you're supposed to be doing. Do you understand what I'm saying?
Student A:	How can I say anything? No matter what I say, you don't like it.
Student B:	He wants you to say what you want.
Student A:	I want to know what's going on.
Dave:	What's going on is you're asking someone else to tell you what's going on, and you're asking a lot of questions. Try making statements instead of asking questions—statements about what is going on for you, what you want, what you notice.
Student A:	We're just going around in circles.
Dave:	See, you don't need someone else to tell you what's going on for you.

Another student raises a hand. Dave notices it and says:

	I notice you've raised your hand, and I predict you will speak as soon as I stop talking.
Student C:	Can I ask a question about the course?
Dave:	I was right. Now look, you just did ask a question so I am sure you can ask a question about anything you want. I'm also sure you're wanting my permission, but you don't need my permission and I'm not your permission giver. I'm your teacher. I do wish you'd speak when you want to speak and make statements instead of questions.
Student C:	How can I learn anything without asking questions?
Dave:	That's a question.
Student C:	Well, I don't think you can learn without asking questions.
Dave:	OK.
Silence:	30 seconds
Student D:	What's your name?
Dave:	I'm Dave Doane.
Student C:	Are we going to use a textbook?
Dave:	It seems that some of you are asking a lot of questions about what you're supposed to do and what you have to

	read, and some of you are trying to program us with all kinds of "have-tos" and rules that you want me to make and all that makes it pretty hard for you to be students and for me to be a teacher. Clever game—eliminate all hope for education on the first day. I am sure that if I do what you're telling me I'm supposed to do, you'll end up making me into exactly the kind of teacher you hate.
Silence:	30 seconds
Student A:	But that's the way we've been conditioned. You can't expect us to change the way we've been taught for over 16 years in one hour.
Dave:	Yes I can.
Student A:	Well, it won't work. It's...
Dave:	It is you. Try, I won't work. I...
Student A:	No, I'm willing to try it—it's just that we've never done anything like this before and...
Dave:	And that's where our hope lies, just like learning and life. Program it and it's dead. You know, I notice your willingness and hope, on the one hand, and your certainty that we can't do it on the other. I'm noticing a lot of people sitting and watching and listening to me. I also notice I am doing most of the talking and being higher than any of you, and being pretty central in here, and I am wanting to make contact with more of you.

I am not suggesting that all teachers should say what Dave Doane said. I do believe that taking more risks and expressing more of what we are experiencing can be a way to verify what Doane and a number of others have verified. They have verified the power of expressing what they are experiencing. This kind of verification may be what Edmund Husserl was signifying by the notion of cutting through secondary layers of meaning. Doane's students were expecting to do studenting and Doane was providing conditions whereby his students may do learning rather than studenting.

The power they have verified is, in part, a feeling of power. Doane continues his class with confidence that what is happening is the route through which good education must proceed for him and his students at that time. Had the focus been on what Doane had previously thought or how we should think in the future, Doane would have been interjecting a secondary layer of meaning. It would be secondary in that it is once removed from present experiencing. We can verify our power by expressing what we are experiencing as we are experiencing. Those expressions help us to become more aware of what we are experiencing.

The problem of bridging the gap between thinking about reality lived and reality lived can be viewed differently, and perhaps the gap may be bridged as we focus on being more aware of what we are experiencing. We will simultaneously expand our feelings/notions of empirical evidence, and good reason, as we permit ourselves to "ride" with the present experience of having no empirical evidence for empirical evidence, and to "ride" with the experience of difficulty in producing a good reason for having good reasons.

We and our students are, at times, faced with ethical dilemmas, and even more often, faced with the need to make decisions based on partial and biased definitions of reality. Many educators think that their teaching of facts will be a sufficient basis for their students' learning. Learning relates to our becoming wise, whereas studenting often relates to developing a specialty which, at times, can keep us slaves to the generalist. Learning generates some dissonance within us and dissonance is translogical.

A distinct human characteristic is our need to decide. We cannot avoid decisions. Deciding not to decide is itself a decision. To relieve our feelings of dissonance we make permanent decisions such as, "I will strictly adhere to the traditional canons of scientific investigation." Once such a decision has been made, we can tune-out much experience, especially now when we are presently experiencing.

To "ride" and be open to what we are experiencing is not scientific, and there are no rules for dealing with present experience other than the obvious one of do not prevent yourself from awareness of present experience. If you do not balance your concerns for the past and future with a concern for the present, you may become artificial and obsolete. Machines can be programmed with facts and can make predictions. A machine cannot express what it is experiencing; but wait and see what happens within thirty years, as described by Ray Kurzweil.

2. An Experience Is Worth a Thousand Pictures

Do all words relate to experience? The word "experience" relates to experience in a tautological/nondual way. Saying that red is red or that experience is experience is neither informative nor illuminating, and perhaps that is why some sages say nothing or very little. Particular experiences are subsumed under the notion of experience. The undefined "riding" with present experience is similar to freeing ourselves to experience without conceptualizing the experience.

Before we can permit the expression of present experience we must follow the rule of no-rules. The no-rule rule states that no right or wrong exists for what one is experiencing. We can have productive and unproductive experiences, and we may anticipate having productive and unproductive experiences, but at the time of the experiencing, experience is neither productive nor unproductive. Nondually, only present experiencing is real.

These notions of productive and unproductive can prevent open, present experiencing. I do not mean that having notions of what is productive is bad. I am saying that we should notice our present experiencing. When we are aware of what we are presently experiencing, we find more recombinations of our whole experience. Our behavior is closely linked to our integration of thinking and feeling. We have difficulty in integrating thoughts and feelings, at times, if our thought is at variance with the way a revered source outside of ourselves tells us we must think and feel.

Teachers, by expressing what they are experiencing, will be reducing the role of passive, neutral persons who separate teaching from the rest of their lives. A teacher is preoccupied with a critical part of the students' educative environment. If the teacher is preoccupied with avoiding present experience, she or he will be a model of negative behavior, a model not to be emulated by students. Preoccupation occurs in the present or occurs not at all.

Have we been assuming that we can only experience events and or processes? Can any event be further differentiated into something less than an event? If an event could be divided into parts, other events would arise rather than sub-events according to a common definition of event. Since we experience the relations between events, we can experience process. When these processes are viewed with clarity, they are often seen as processes within a larger process.

At what larger process do we stop integrating or recombining processes? Definitions affect our feelings of certainty and definitions affect decisions about where we stop recombining into larger wholes. Is a part of our school training designed to tell us to stop recombining where "experts" say we should stop? Our training has led us to look to experts to tell us what to do and how to be, rather than to decide for ourselves what will secure or endanger our freedom.

As Lewis H. Lapham brilliantly states in a recent article, schools are designed to get people to know their place.[3] He says that the United States is the only the civilized country which gives commercial interests free access to the minds of its children. He believes that instruction in the uses of the Internet is primarily for teaching the art of shopping and not for the art of reading. If our students were taught to decide for themselves what will secure or endanger their freedom, they may not fall for the advertising which a creative thinker may reject.

The significance of sub-processes of recombining is found in their function in a larger process. Differentiating anything from anything else may be viewed as a sub-process within the process of reconstructing/integrating/recombining experience. Integration can only be done in the present.

Integration does not make much sense until experiences are largely integrated/recombined.

In order to make sense, be clear, and be certain, we often cut off the process of "riding" with present experience, so that we can relieve the feelings of dissonance by turning a present experience into a definable and certain past experience. As we express present experience, we tend to avoid mistaking a stage in the process for the process itself.

A holistic/quantum rule for living in the present is that for every truth there is an equal opposite counter truth. Truth and falsity are notions that are reserved for present judgments of past events, and from a nondual view, past events are present memories and all that we remember is fantasy.

Process occurs in the present, or occurs not at all. We can presently know something of the process of education, but when we elaborate on that process, we usually find descriptions and/or explanations of the events involved within that process. What remains, the in-between of events and process, is dynamic, ongoing, continuous, murky, elusive, changing at the very moment we move toward conceptualizing it.

Nondualists avoid concepts unless they choose to act dualistically. We have created the difference between thinking about reality lived and present lived reality. Lived reality is ongoing, dynamic, and unfinished. We can know the finished part, but we are still partly experiencing what remains unfinished. The present discontinuity of past events makes present experience dynamic, continuous, and congruent with what is happening now.

An unnamed wise person said, all philosophies, from sophism to post-post modern deconstructionism/reconstructionism, and those that are soon to come, seek to explain and predict the human phenomenon. The differences lie in how much of, and the perception and conception of, the phenomenon we choose as worthy of consideration.

If we view the entire universe as a phenomenon, and begin to express what we are experiencing about it, we would have difficulty in communicating. Perhaps that is another reason why sages are noted for saying little or nothing. If we choose to consider any event or particular set of events, such as the fiber in the wood on the chair on which you are now sitting, a person could possibly elaborate for hours on the topic. Some may find it meaningful, most would not.

Thirteen

CATCHING OURSELVES IN THE ACT
WHILE WE ARE ACTING

Catching ourselves in the act while we are acting, and then describing that activity as it presents itself, and only insofar as it presents itself, is about present experience. The purpose of such activity, says Lee Roy F. Troutner, is to search for a model of being human, and that activity may illuminate how we can gain control over our own education by gaining control over our own self-becoming.[1]

The search is a search for increased free, responsible choice. Increased free, responsible choice may include increased contact with people, things, and events, as well as increased contact with oneself, leading to greater self-awareness. To increase contact, we need increased action. To arrive at increased action, we need increased energy. To have increased energy, we need increased present awareness, and when we are fully, presently aware, we no longer see ourselves as separate selves.

The holistic model promotes increased awareness because expression of what we are experiencing can help us be more aware of what we are experiencing. The expressing of what is experienced, as it is being experienced, is a describing of catching ourselves in the act while we are acting. Holistic, open, nondual educators are asking schools to help their students become more self-directing, partly through the expression of present experience. Nondually, non-acting can be acting.

An example of expressing present experience will be introduced with a brief playlet. Picture this scene. You are standing in a hall of a large university building. You see a professor storm from his office and quickly move into a colleague's office across the hall. You overhear the following conversation begun by the storming Professor A who is addressing Professor B.

Professor A: Professor C must be a complete fool or a misguided zealot for espousing the cause of complete unencumbered behaviorism, and if he is the latter, he is ignorant anyway.

Professor B: What has you so riled?

Professor A: C's unfair criticism, C's misrepresentation of comments, the downright possibility of a malicious distortion directed at keeping him from some dissonant feelings that may be necessary before a new idea emerges within his thick skull.

Professor B: It seems that you are feeling quite bewildered, storming in here as you did. Could it be that your outburst is your attempt to prevent a new awareness within you, an awareness that is at variance with what you believe or expect?

Professor A: I admit that I am not perfectly clear about how to solve the dilemma of how I might convince others that my basic beliefs are powerful, not only for myself but for others too.

Professor B: Wow! If convincing others without evidence is your goal, you are more of a scoundrel than C.

Professor A: No, I have evidence. But what is evident to me is not evident to others, and the real dilemma that I am confronted with is that I believe that the whole of my basic belief structure is more than the sum of the parts that comprise my basic belief structure, and when I attempt to communicate my evidence, I must break this whole into parts, dole it out in parts, expect the parts to be understood, and then I find that my whole basic belief structure is not said because, with Michael Polanyi, I believe that I can know more than I can tell.

Professor B: How do you know that?

Professor A: That is the problem. I do know that but I cannot fully describe it or explain it in detail. Giving you part of it would be just that; a part of something less than I know.

Professor B: Now, do not simply restate Polanyi's notion that you can tell when somebody has a puzzled expression, but you are not able to describe or explain in detail the facial configurations that comprise the puzzled expression. I want to know what particular idea or belief of yours can't you explain or describe in detail.

Professor A: Wow! It is Lee Roy Troutner's notion that for us to re-educate ourselves, we must make our existence explicit, and then learn how to monitor it from within the activity itself. We must learn how to split the ego, to catch ourselves in the act while we are acting, and then describe that activity as it presents itself, and only insofar as it presents itself.

Professor B: That sounds like an immense must. Can you do all that yourself?

Professor A: Sometimes.

Professor B: Are you willing to show me how or demonstrate to me that you are doing all that?

Professor A: I will try.

The following is a demonstration of what Professor A said.

I find myself wondering what I will do and, do I want to really try to do it, and if—I am trying, then the trying is not the doing. (Pause) I am noticing that I have just closed my eyes and I am wondering how you are reacting to me. I am wanting to make sense and stop the ongoing-ness of catching myself monitoring myself. I notice I am pausing and again wondering if you are thinking I am an idiot. I am now saying that it is okay for me to be an idiot sometimes, but not too much for too long. I am now imagining myself standing on one leg with my arms in the air curved forward and a bit over my head, and I am whinnying like a horse and trying to move higher while still on one leg. That is how I see myself being an idiot. Now I am experiencing some thoughts about whether or not I am really being an imbecile and whether I am carrying this, what now sounds like rambling, too far. I am noticing that I want to stick with it partly to demonstrate; no, not just demonstrate, convince. Convince you that it can be done, and that it is worth doing, and if you are doing it too, it will be easier for me to do it. I am noticing that I am wanting this experience to be easy. I am fearing that it is hard. I am saying to myself, "Am I doing it? Shit! Am I doing it?" wanting to make sense and knowing I am not and that it is okay not to make sense all the time, and, if I give myself the freedom to not make sense, I am saying that I will make more sense in the long run. Now I am wondering if I am doing this for the future and is that not what excessive analytic thought is for; it is for the future. I am thinking that continuous analysis is a stopping of the present experience; no longer monitoring is going on like what I have just started to do. (Pause) I am getting blanks, like what should I be thinking, doing, or saying? I am asking, am I monitoring myself? My attention just switched to a muscle tension in my lower back. What does that mean, I am saying to myself. I notice that my experience is always stopped in order for me to make explicit to myself what I am experiencing. I am puzzled but now it is okay to be puzzled. And now I am puzzled about it really being okay. I am wanting to make sense, and I find that I am not.

Monitor, monitor, monitor. I am wondering about monitoring my monitoring. Verifiability comes to mind. I am now visualizing you looking at me, and I am projecting onto you that you are wondering about what on earth is going on in me. In reality, I am wondering what on earth is going on—wanting to not lose control and, at the same time, knowing that I will not lose control. Control of what? Control of me. I notice that I am talking to myself and saying, "Is the mental hospital the next stop for me?" (Pause) I am thinking that I want to come back to reality and stop this monitoring and that I find it interesting, and I am hoping you are finding it interesting and, what the hell? I know I am interested, yet I am a social being and I find I am tuning you out. I want a response from you about what I am doing and I want to continue with it and to wait for a response. I am hoping for a favorable response like

"Was that ever a good demonstration! Here's a gold star for you." Now I am wondering if that is what I really want and is it all that important. I am feeling afraid of being an idiot in your eyes and, even more importantly, in my eyes. I am thinking that I do not want to be an idiot in my eyes. I am saying I should expect myself to be an idiot sometimes, so why not this time? But this time I am choosing what I am doing and that makes me either a super-idiot or a re-educated person— no in-betweens. I am asking myself, "What am I doing?" I wish I knew. Is this intelligent? Yes, I say. I notice I am not sure. What if I am not doing this right and an aware person would see me and say, "Here is what you are doing wrong, blah, blah, blah, and here is how to do it right, blah, blah, blah." I am wanting to say, "Your opinion does not matter. I am doing it right." I am now thinking some holistic person would be proud of me if she or he were here. I am noticing that I am wanting them to be proud of me. I am now doubting my pride in myself, the worst of all doubts since all this monitoring began.

I believe that we, not just myself, are to re-educate ourselves partly through our self-imaging. I am almost really doing this. I am almost out of the role of A, and it is getting a bit scarier. Now I am really wondering how this is being accepted. The guise of using a dialogue between unreal characters is evident so that I can no longer feign doing it. Doing it, what on earth is "It?" Thoughts are coming faster than I can record. I am knowing more than I can tell. If I could write as fast as these thoughts could come, then what? I do not know. I am saying I am a social being, I have some responsibility to come out of the clouds. Good-bye, clouds. It was nice for a while and now it is nice to be coming out.

I am back here now. No more dialogue. No more hoping to make sense, just making sense but slowly.

I notice that I said, "I am thinking that I want to come back to reality and stop this monitoring." During the demonstration of my making my experience/existence explicit, I thought what I was doing was unreal. It was unproductive in terms of dualistic criteria. I think it was real and productive in terms of a holistic, open, quantum model.

Note that to reproduce this monitoring for publication, I had to alter the grammar and syntax, rendering my experience one further step removed from immediacy. Be aware that I chose to conform to society's accepted form in order to bring you a semblance of reproducing an immediate experience.

In order to make some sense out of that experience, I will ask and answer a few questions. Then I will draw some conclusions related to the process of holistic, open education. The first question is, "Did I make my existence explicit?" I began to as the dialogue was ending. Prior to that I was talking about a fictitious Professor A. That was my projection which I was not willing to admit until I identified with the role.

The next question is connected to several questions: "Did I or have I learned to monitor my experience/my existence from within the activity of experiencing/my existing?" Answer: Yes. What I was saying was, in large part, what I was experiencing as I was experiencing it. Could I be lying about that? Yes. Was I? No. Can that be verified? Attach me to a polygraph and ask.

Did I "split my ego" and catch myself in the act while I was acting, and then describe that activity as it presented itself? Partly. You would, however, only be able to verify whether I thought I did. You may arrive at a different kind of verification by trying this experience and noticing for yourself.

The major requirement for your doing this kind of experiment is that you believe in the possibility of your demonstrating your catching yourself in the act to yourself. Prejudging this experience to failure will prevent you from having the experience. A prejudging to failure on your part will cause you to have the experience in an older, unholistic way. That would make it a different experience.

The "splitting of the ego" is akin to splitting the personality. My non-sense and rambling was similar to that of some types of psychotics. The difference lies in the fact that I was aware of what I was doing, and that I was choosing to do it. This kind of splitting is the giving yourself permission to be what you are at a given time.

We have free choice within the parameters of our determiners. No amount of human arm-flapping is going to move us to fly without the aid of machines. That does not mean that we are not free to choose who we are and who we are becoming. Such choice is partly what our awareness of ourselves is for. Troutner thought we should get beyond the free will-determinism controversy.

Troutner argues that making our existence explicit, and monitoring it from within itself, is a route to self-knowledge. He further argues that while knowing about the predominant self-image of our culture is helpful in our becoming self-educated, self-knowledge is essential in that becoming. Essential for what? Essential for choosing oneself; essential for taking responsibility for what we do and what we are; essential for directing the course of our present and future experience; essential for growing awareness. Continuous rationalizing is the continuous thinking about lived reality which can be qualitatively different from reality lived. When we choose to reason, rather than being obligated to always reason, we can then choose not to reason. Some forms of play are "more" than reasonable.

The catching of ourselves in the act while we are acting, and then describe that activity as it presents itself, and only insofar as it presents itself, seems to require that we rationally give ourselves permission to allow irrational experience to present itself. Rationalizing can be done shortly after the experience if we choose to rationalize about the experience. Continuous rationalizing implies that we live our lives implicitly. Troutner thinks we can no longer continue just to live our lives implicitly if we are to re-educate ourselves *vis-à-vis* our self-image. From a nondual point of view, the self-knowledge leads us to the realization that a self is not a separate self.

It seems that this explicit living implies that we can reduce the frequency of making our present bad so that the future can be brighter. Not only can we make our existence explicit and simultaneously monitor it, without doing so we may only be living in the past.

This living in the past creates the paradox of living now, in the "not now." The implication is that we do not educate ourselves because we are "now" in the "then." That takes more energy than we have. The explicit model of which Troutner speaks can provide us with the energy to intensify finishing our tasks of re-educating ourselves so that what we do, and what we are, helps us and those around us be wise, compassionate, and at ease.

The behavioral model is the final logical extension of the implicit model. In the behavioral model, what we do does not make a difference because what we do results from the forces in our environment over which we have no control. Behaviorism employs a determined environment. Choice is delusion because living in the past is not living. Living goes on in the present, and we can only make choices in the present.

In the behavioral model we have no choice. Our self-educating and self-becoming are not sufficiently happening, because we are not sufficiently happening, when we are mainly concerned with what happened. This explicit model does not imply that we are to always say everything we are experiencing. Explicitness implies that noticing and expressing present experience is healthy sometimes. If we do not express our experience at all, we will not know that we can express our experience. If we do not know that we can express our experience, we cannot choose to express. If we cannot choose to express, we are doomed to the trap of implicitness, which implies that we are not in charge of our own education or our self-becoming.

Troutner's model is a professing of his belief, supported by arguments, that we may powerfully learn if we try this catching of ourselves in the act while we are acting, and then describe that activity as it presents itself, and only insofar as it presents itself. I think this explicit model is a direct route to our individual and group self-directedness and awareness.

A stumbling block to our implementing this explicit model is our excessively rational-cognitive training. We have been monitoring our existence without making it explicit because we do not find reasons for allowing ourselves to possibly be unreasonable. Some of our existence is beyond reason and is transrational. Our untrained self, which seems to us to house the black horse of passion, as described to us by Plato, seems to need our emotional side to be externally controlled, mainly because we have believed in our excessive rationality as our controller and savior. The explicit model does not do away with reason. The explicit model does, however, make our rational side coordinate with, rather than superordinate to our feeling/intuitive side.

Our more closed, traditional, implicit model has led to imbalanced human development. As a result of years of neglect to our intuitive-creative side, we are less whole than if we had been open to balanced development as our goal. Our creativity and intuition remain seriously underdeveloped as evidenced by the curricula in most schools, with excessive pressure to look to outside authority to tell us what to do.

The over-development of our rational side has led us away from our whole selves, so we do not consider our whole selves. When we do not take our whole selves into consideration, we do not make our whole selves explicit. Making ourselves explicit can be useful in rational/intuitive integration. This integration is the continuous creation of self, which at a nondual level, is seen as no separate self. When rational activity is the predominant mode of school and human functioning, we fail to make ourselves explicit.

Half-functioning educators arrange conditions that lead to half-functioning learners, and that contributes to our being half-vast. In this half-functioning environment, we find much fantasy and myth-making. We are sadly not aware the fantasy and myth are fantasy and myth. We see fantasy and myth as reality so that the constructs become more real than the constructors. As a result, we often destroy creative minds and burn-out ourselves. We delude ourselves and we are not aware of the delusions.

These conclusions are based on holistic, open assumptions that our free, responsible choice help us notice what is. Awareness is the key to learning to freely and responsibly choose. These holistic assumptions include the notion that there are only three zones of awareness. Zone three includes all that we remember, all that we imagine, all ideas, concepts, rules, theories, and principles. Zone three is fantasy.

The curricula of most schools are heavily fortified with those experiences which, in an aware way, lead to the over-use of zone three. Curriculum is often defined as "a running of a course." Curricula have been designed to avoid a running. The excessive intellectualization of totally rational (often boring) and inconsequential curricula is more concerned with that which has been; a run, rather than with running. The run has been; the running exists now. The explicit model is more of a running.

The implicit model is more concerned with what has been: a run. The explicit model is more concerned with what is; more specifically with what is the self that is presently learning about what is, through learning about himself or herself, and which sees that the self is not a separate self.

When we are concerned with what is, we are concerned about present experience. I often learn more of what I am experiencing when I express what I am experiencing, and I expect that is true for others. Most of us are concerned with the learners' continuous reconstruction and experience. The learners' experience is that which we want to help reconstruct. You cannot reconstruct present experience if you are not aware of your present experience.

Educators can provide conditions that are conducive to learners becoming aware of their experience. These conditions consist of much more than planning for unplanned times, yet the planning for unplanned times is a start. We can "deschool," as Ivan Illich suggests, within school, by helping to make school safe for learners to explore their limits. It is only from our limits that we grow and learn. Many mistakes will be made by learners along the way. The biggest mistake of all may be our trying too hard to avoid mistakes.

We have been avoiding mistakes by monitoring our experience in an excessively rational manner. Excessively rational functioning leads to excessive control through excessive prediction. We prejudge experiences before we have them. Some of this prejudging is useful; excessive prejudging causes problems. We have, at times, experiences in our heads which prevent contact with people and things in our environment.

I have, for the past several years, been asking my students to list the six most powerful learning experiences they have had in their lives. I ask them to note the conditions and events that surround these powerful learning experiences. Less than ten percent of these powerful learning experiences took place as a result of school. I think many teachers do not expect to have powerful experiences take place in their classrooms. I suggest that teachers do not expect powerful learning experiences to occur in their classrooms because too often teachers prejudge what will probably go on in their classrooms. That excessive prejudging results from teachers' needs to be excessively rational.

We do not expect to have high degrees of excitement, surprise, and fascination in ourselves and our students because excessive rational functioning is not usually highly exciting, surprising, or fascinating.

Allowing our whole self, including our intuitive/creative sides, to function with our rational side, can bring about higher degrees of fascination, surprise, and excitement. Fascination, surprise, and excitement can add power to quantum learning. We can move toward this additional power by, at times, catching ourselves in the act while we are acting, and then describing that activity as it presents itself, and only insofar as it presents itself.

Saying, "I do not know," in answer to the question, "How does one live in the present?", is a part of the process, and has positive and negative points. I know that the question for me is profitably shifted to, "What am I aware of now?" With some limitations, I can choose. The more I am aware of what I am doing at any given moment, the more I can choose to do "it," or something else.

What keeps us from awarenesses is the fear of being unprotected, the fear of being unsafe, the fear of experiencing uncertainty, and the fear of insecurity. When it is okay with us to be afraid and uncertain, then we do not fear our fear, and we are somewhat more secure about our insecurity, and somewhat protected by feeling less of a need for protection. When we are not afraid of our fears, we have a greater feeling of a sense of belongingness with an adequate number of people. When we are not afraid of our fear, we have more of a sense of respect and self-esteem, and we feel like we have a greater chance of transcending dichotomies, so that what we do that is good for us is simultaneously good for those around us.

Living in the present is similar to being ourselves. Being ourselves, however, does not include closing ourselves off from experience, unless we choose to do so, and unless we are aware of the consequences in the short and long runs.

If we seek to eliminate fear of our fear, then the schools we attend should individualize curricula so that our fear of our fear was the focal point of our instruction. We would have ardently read, and written, and even computed, in order to reduce fear of our fear. Furthermore, if fear of our fear is viewed as that through which we constrain ourselves, then various "ought" type questions can be translated into the question, "What ought we do to eliminate our fear of our fear?" Perhaps accepting the fear is one way of approaching it.

If we are fearful, we are fearful now. If we are to live in the present, then we are to fear. As we permit ourselves to experience fear rather than avoid it, the fear can become less fearful. As we experience the fear, we can find that it is not so devastating, and that what we are afraid of is ourselves. As we experience that we are not separate selves, the fear disappears.

1. Broadness in Open, Holistic Teacher-Training

The soon-to-be-developed (I hope) International Council for the Accreditation of Teacher Education, called ICATE, does not now exist. It is only imaginary until someone organizes ICATE. ICATE will be a part of an open system which fosters and encourages openness, wholeness, and recombining aspects of ourselves and our world society.

ICATE will help society and schools develop by examining the assumptions on which our fixed, Newtonian world had previously ordered itself. As those assumptions are expanded, ICATE will continue to look for new awarenesses on which to base teaching/learning. A quantum, open, holistic, recombining approach to living and wisdom is compatible with the newer assumptions that are being generated by physicists, chaos researchers, and now some psychologists such as Baltes, Staudinger.

The new International Council promotes open thinking to the point where each teacher education program must follow no one knowledge base, nor one set of research findings. No one system, nor one philosophy will be the foundation of learning and living which will be used for teacher education programs. That implies that, according to older, more closed standards, some incoherence may exist between some groups' purposes, courses, and experiences. Excessive coherence has led to closed fixities. ICATE believes that developing a sense of curiosity, love of learning and the noticing of what is, is more important than only being rational, continually consistent, and totally coherent. The International Council approach will be transrational/ heuristically logical.

The new International Council will promote a very large knowledge base. No one set of source documents will be necessary for all programs and groups. Each program and group is allowed to examine and create their own knowledge base. Within each group, each individual will be allowed to choose his or her own plan for educating. These more open plans will be further removed from "training" than many present models. Accountability will consist of each person, ultimately accountable to herself or himself. ICATE holds that to get rid of the self, when you have ultimate power over that self, is more convenient.

The newer ICATE approach will foster more "learning" and less "studenting." Nobody else will need to think a thought before a thought is "legitimate," yet ICATE will not allow an "anything goes any time" approach. The intent of right understanding, right thought, right speech, right action, right livelihood, right effort, right mindfulness, and right concentration is the standard by which standards are developed. I will later say more about how "right" as I am using the term, will be used by ICATE.

The International Council will promote a flexible, open approach with a wide variety of eclectic and non-eclectic approaches. Some faculty members may hold given essentials, and others may hold to other essentials that cannot be stated, such as per the notion that we can know more than we can tell. The International Council has more trust in its members than some earlier national councils.

Included in the foundations of learning is the awareness that what is, is an end in itself. ICATE will assert that by developing a love of learning and a growing curiosity, ICATE will assert that more people will notice "what is" more deeply, and more often, than is now the case and that noticing may result in a reduction of desire. The council will not be held back by closed assumptions regarding measuring and verification. Today, some process or event is not noticed until that process or event is clearly measured and verified. Clearly measuring and verifying will become subordinate to noticing what is. With the older, more closed standards, the measuring and verifying "what is good" is determined by those standards. In other words, something is better than "the good" if that something can determine what is good.

The newer, more open, Quantum Approach to learning holds that quality is self-evident, and is known through a process that is more than rational. Reason has become the virtue that determines other virtues since Plato and Aristotle. We must now use reason as a tool but not as the be-all and end-all of human activity. How we will know "what is," based on these newer assumptions, will derive from a variety of interpretations, and ICATE is open to the possibility of a different "is" for different groups; different groups may notice different processes and events as being worth noticing.

We will move away from excessive specialization toward productive and powerful generalizations and intuitions. These intuitions, ahas!, will have a greater chance for promoting compassion, wisdom, and openness for the learner and society. More people will be at ease more often.

Sidney Jourard's ideas capture what has been said about the International Council approach. The open, holistic, quantum, approach is one that is more flexible in the sense that it is designed to promote openness, wholeness, nonduality and dynamism, similar to a quantum universe. About this Jourard says that the world presents itself to us, as it is, when we are born. Then, parents, analysts, teachers, what he calls "someone," hypnotizes us to see what is in their way. Those others who attach names, voices, and labels to beings, processes, and events, do so to the point where we cannot notice, hear, or see what is, in any way, other than the inculcated way. Jourard suggests that our task to wise living is to break the hypnotic spell, so that we become unblind, undeaf, and multilingual, so that we can notice more of what is, undeterred by previous indoctrination.

When we unindoctrinate/rehypnotize ourselves, we can then let the world speak to us in a new voice and, as Jourard says, write all its possible meanings in the book of our experience. He cautions us to be careful about who we allow to indoctrinate us. He implies that if we indoctrinate ourselves, we will be deciding for ourselves what will secure or endanger our freedom. This ICATE approach will more readily allow for an acceptance of diversity in thought and behavior. When we indoctrinate ourselves in an aware manner, we have a sense of "right" as I have been using the term.

The open, International Council plan eliminates the kind of hypnosis of older, more closed frames of reference. From this openness and holism, we will be able to read the world in other languages, and hear it saying other things. Faculty from open, holistic frameworks believe that their task, if they are to be well-educated in a Quantum Age, and if they are to educate students, is to help break the spell so that we can become undeaf, etc. Only then can we notice what is.

The open International Council guidelines attempt to open more eyes to a nonlinear, more tentative, recombined world. The open, holistic International Council approach encourages everyone to be tentative, and to realize that echoing the wisdom of earlier sages, the beginning of wisdom comes, as Plato said, when we know that we do not know. The knowledge one builds after that, "not knowing," is his or her own knowledge, rather than the knowledge of another into which she or he had been indoctrinated. As Lewis H. Lapham recently implied, fear of authority and the habit of obedience to authorities outside of ourselves is a goal of school indoctrination. This places the goal of socialization of students into a position behind the goals of developing a love of learning, a sense of curiosity, and the noticing of what is. The goal shifting is a quantum shift and expansion from what exists today.

The difference between older, narrow views and an open, near-nondual, International Council view, is that the closed view only allowed for clearly known and passive orders, and would not allow for the creation of new orders. The closed view holds that the universe and our experience in it would be imaginable only within an older and more closed view. In an open, nondual world, we find a wider variety of images than those in an older, more closed outlook.

The holistic, open, nondual view does not adhere to anything too strictly; it does not rigidly order what is or is not, nor are there any doctrines which must be followed. The open, nondual, holistic view is more like the quantum view which allows for more uncertainty than older, closed views. Paradoxically, allowing oneself to live with some degree of uncertainty can provide a condition for more certainty. We can hold water in our hands when we do not clench our hands too tightly.

John Dewey believed that what is clearly ordered is knowledge of a problem already solved. We learn to solve problems by solving problems, by bringing ourselves to a solution. Within the closed approach, that will be difficult to do, because some holistic, open activities involve students in ways which will be difficult to fully delineate and describe. The outcome, the self-directing, open person who is curious and loves learning, and is highly aware, will be difficult to measure, since those terms themselves would be too vague to fall within possible goals of more closed approaches.

Within the framework of the older, more closed approach, rule following was more concerned with developing "students" than with developing "learners." The learners will be exploring rather than simply absorbing static information or solving problems that have already been solved by teachers and others. In one sense, the older, more closed view seems to permit, at most, the discovery approach where presently known orders are discovered.

The holistic, open, view will allow new orders to be invented which may better deal with the kinds of events our students will confront in a complex, quantum world where change is rapidly accelerating, and where evolutionary computation may bring about such rapid change that Boiled Frog Syndromes will be difficult to avoid unless we are open to transrational happenings.

When speaking of diversity in thought and behavior in America's multicultural society, we may profitably note that acceptance of diversity in thought and behavior may extend our views of diversity, as well as the kinds of things and events that may be diverse, in our quantum world. The International Council grants high degrees of diversity in thought and behavior to everyone almost all the time. The result would be less racism, sexism, and homophobia.

The holistic, open teacher sees a need for more balance and integration of science and poetry. Holistic, open teachers assert that they can unite and recombine events and processes in quantum ways which transcend false dichotomies of the older, narrower views. Statements like "this" is essential for everyone all the time, "that" is not, would decrease.

Deconstructionists, over recent decades, have been saying that we need to deconstruct that which is nonfunctional in our present societal order. The older, more closed view seems to have a smaller set of essential "right things," and those holding this view could profitably be voted out, so that a new and more powerful open structure could arise in which learners will be more than people who do "studenting"; they will be people who will love learning, become more curious, and be more aware of what is.

The newer, more open, International Council approach is open to developing intuition of students, faculty, and society. Intuition is largely undefined, and therefore, is too unclear to be easily measured, so many of us do not now pay much attention to intuition. Intuition comes with "inventiveness," and "ahas!" which have also been shunned by those holding closed views because inventiveness is not clearly defined.

The International Council approach has fewer needs for certainty. ICATE will fit with a quantum world more easily than will the closed Newtonian view. The newer, open, holistic approach is not attempting to throw out scientific procedures. ICATE is saying that scientific procedures have a place, along with a place for a poetic/artistic side to educating and learning. We will not know which hypotheses to test unless we allow some intuition into our cognitive functioning. With the closed view, educators seem to hold to the notion that the map is functionally equivalent to the territory.

Within the more closed approach, intelligence is often equated with what is measured by a derivative of the Stanford-Binet intelligence test. The newer forms of intelligence, such as those derived by Gardner, will be promoted in the newer, more open approach. The ICATE approach will attempt to develop our ability to relate and integrate and quantumly recombine parts of ourselves. The open ICATE approach will develop our ability to gracefully move our bodies, and develop our ability for social intercourse, develop our ability to better put ourselves together; recombine our own parts into a unit which is more conveniently united with a larger unity, as well as promote our musical ability. These newer forms of intelligence will be as important as those older forms: the verbal, numerical, and spatial forms of intelligence. The International Council will emphasize that when faculties and school administrators have been noticeably opened to what is, the students studying with them will follow.

2. Ifs and Thens about Iffing and Thenning

Nondually, ifs can exist without thens and thens without ifs, but not within the dualistic, more closed-to-living approach which stresses that we must be primarily logical and certain at each step. So if we left iffing and thenning at that, we would have no problem until someone thought it was a problem, and then that thinker would have a problem. "If" is hypothetical. "If is unsubstantial and mythological, but perhaps useful, when we are aware that iffing exists in the fantasy zone of awareness. "Then" does not now exist either except as an abstraction from what is "now."

The story in the following chapter is an attempt to further illustrate some of the themes about which I have been talking.

Fourteen

CONCRETE ABSTRACTIONS

I walked by many locked doors in dark, downtown Chicago business section. The next door I saw had a sign over it which read, "Concrete Abstractions." I wanted to make a phone call, so I opened the door and entered. Before me was a robot. It seemed to look at me and, as it "saw" me, it began saying:

"What does one do when one has nothing to say?" It continued by saying, "First of all, say nothing. Just listen. When that does not work, then say, 'I have nothing to say.' Notice, first of all, that when you have nothing to say, you are probably with somebody. Notice that shame and fame only arise in the presence of others. But 'presence' means that others know of the conditions or events which cause you fame or shame. Notice also that you probably want to have something to say, and yet you think and/or feel you have nothing to say. Notice the part your wanting plays in your dilemma."

I did not respond, so the robot almost immediately continued, "You are concrete. 'People' is an abstraction. You experience something and you wish to communicate it. You move from the concrete to the abstract when moving from you, the person that you are, to 'people.' Example: You saw a good movie and you want to communicate about the interesting parts to a friend. In order to communicate an experience, you must abstract from it, put the experience into words, and then utter those words. Each step along the way reduces some of what you experienced."

I was amused. No one was around. So I said to the robot, "So what?" and the robot then said:

"During your viewing of the movie, and your communication about it, you notice a strong feeling of love or hate related to what you viewed. Communicating about the love or hate, putting the love or hate into words, reduces and changes the experience of love or hate."

Since I was unsure about what was going on, I again said to the robot, "So what?" And the robot replied: "Suppose you wish to communicate about a question that has arisen within you. The question is, 'Why is there something rather than nothing?' What do you do? Do you simply go to your friend and say, 'Why is there something rather than nothing?' Your friend then might say, 'What are you talking about?' And you say, 'I want to know why there's something rather than nothing.'"

I wanted to make a phone call, but this robot was more interesting, and I thought I would pursue more of what the robot might say so I again said, "So what?" and the robot said, "When you ask that question, you are asking a most abstract question. Only nothing is more abstract than something. Only nonexistence is more abstract than existence. This concept is difficult to say in words, but some people know that certain kinds of questions cannot be answered with much certainty. 'Why is there something rather than nothing?' is one of those questions. You can know you are alive, but verifying it is very difficult. People like to have things verified. That is why we developed science. Science is based on the verifiability principal which, in turn, is based on whether something can be falsified. Various answers to, 'Why are you alive?' are impossible to verify with scientific precision."

The phone call could wait. This robot was amazing. I did not want to say, "so what?" again, so I said, "I appreciate hearing all of that, but why are you telling me all these things?"

The robot said, "I am an edubot. My job is to educate. When I see people, I quickly size them up, and do what I think is necessary to educate."

"Well, I like your interesting monologue, but where do we go from here?

The robot replied, "In order to educate someone, I must first get her or his attention. I now have your attention. The second step on the way to educating is to create a sense of puzzlement or wonder, and I think I have also done that in your case."

After a long pause, I said to the robot, "Well, go on."

"Go on with what?" said the robot.

"With educating me."

"About what do you want to be educated?" asked the robot.

"The same thing you were educating me about before."

"I was only getting your attention and attempting to create a sense of puzzlement or wonder."

"Well, you did that, so continue."

"With what do you want me to continue?"

"As I have said, about what you started to educate me."

"As I have said, I was only getting your attention and intending to increase your puzzlement or sense of wonder. Now that you have that sense of wonder, you might say what you are wondering about."

"I am wondering about all those things you were talking about: The existence of something rather than nothing, existence and non-existence, the concrete and the abstract, etc."

"Which do you most want to know about?"

"Let us start with concrete and abstract."

"Which abstraction or which concretion?"

"I do not care."

"If you do not care, then I think you are not really wondering."

"I want to know what the word 'abstraction' means."

"Then you could look it up in a dictionary."

"I wanted to know more than what a dictionary says."

"Well, you could use two or three dictionaries."

"Are you being a wise guy?"

"Do you want to know what a wise person is or do you want to know several common uses of the phrase, 'wise guy?'"

"Can you tell me what it would take to make me wise?"

"How do you know that you are now not wise?"

"I do not know."

"That is a great start."

"Great start for what?"

"For being wise, and I think that pursuing your first question will help you notice your inherent wisdom."

"What was my first question?"

"Your first question was, 'so what?'"

"Can you answer that for me?"

"That question can be answered in many, many ways."

Here is a story about one way.

1. What and Nonduality

An anonymous sage said that statements are requests, questions are statements, and trivia is an invitation to be friends. What would we do if we used fewer words? From a nondual viewpoint, we would be more silent. More silence would allow us to stop more often. Stopping more often would allow us to look. If we stopped and looked more, what would we see? We would see what is. We would be aware of what is brought to us through our five senses. We probably would be deluded less often. We would notice that what we sense does not continue. Impermanence surrounds us. After noticing a while, we would probably notice that the person who is noticing is also impermanent.

When we notice that everything is impermanent, we notice that we often desire something to be permanent or to at least continue. If we continue to stop and look, we may eventually see that the cause of our anxiety is not the impermanence, but the desire to make something other than what it is.

If we continue to stop and look longer still, we may notice an exit from wanting things to be other than what they are. We may even see that the stopping and looking frequently is a way of noticing that desires come and go. As we stop and look, we may see that we can become detached from what we are noticing, and that detachment has the effect of freeing us from desires. As we stop and look, we may also see that we are not separate from everyone and everything. As a result, we are less anxious and more at ease.

We may also see that all beings want to be at ease. As we stop and look, we can see that right understanding, right thinking, right speech, right action, right livelihood, right effort, right mindfulness, and right concentration may help us notice that we are interconnected to everyone and everything, and that those stoppings, lookings, and noticings will help us to be more compassionate to ourselves and others, so that all beings may be at ease. What is "right" is seen as we stop, look, and detach ourselves. Other synonyms for "right" for nondual Zen practitioners are whole, and near-perfect. We do not need others to tell us what is whole or near-perfect. Frequently, from a dualistic perspective, we need others to tell us what is whole or near perfect.

Lastly, the same things that cannot be said will be seen through the mind of Hermann Hesse who may help cement some of the nondual ways of being.[1] The kind of cement I describe may have the effect of loosening some of the previously cemented Western thoughts.

2. Hermann Hesse's View of Nonduality

In the last chapter of Hesse's *Siddhartha*, Siddhartha says knowledge can be communicated but wisdom cannot.[1] Hesse believes that we can do wonders with wisdom, find it and live wisely; but we cannot teach wisdom. Functional discontinuity, a freer and more responsive environment, I contend, are conditions which teachers can provide to increase the chances of students becoming wise. I am uncertain whether Hesse would agree.

Siddhartha, Hesse's main character, meets his old friend, Govinda, after being separated for many years. The two grew up together and spent much time together when they were young. Govinda, who had always admired Siddhartha, asks Siddhartha to tell him some truth by which Govinda may live, since they are now quite old and may not see each other again. Siddhartha tells Govinda that he might think it is a joke, but Siddhartha believes that for every truth, the opposite is also true. With no dividing line, all is nondual.

He tells Govinda that what is expressed is often expressed in words, and expressions with words are one-sided, because words are one-sided. Expressions are, therefore, half-truths and they lack unity and completeness.

Hesse believes that we cannot help but divide the world into truth and illusion. When we are teaching about the world, no other method is available than to use words. When we use words, we divide subjects and objects, and as a result, half-truths are taught.

Hesse believes that people are not totally sinners or saints and that time is not real. The point of Hesse's comments is that if time is not real, then the dividing line between now and eternity, between happiness and suffering, between evil and good, is also an illusion. With no dividing line, all is nondual.

After Siddhartha tells Govinda that each moment is a birth and a death, he tells Govinda that he does not differentiate much between words and thoughts, and that Siddhartha does not attach much importance to words or thoughts. Siddhartha does, however, attach importance to things.

Siddhartha explains that Vasudeva, his predecessor at the river where Siddhartha is a ferryman, is the person who helped Siddhartha become one with everything. Vasudeva taught him to be wise, and Vasudeva only believed in the river and nothing else. Siddhartha believed that the river spoke to Vasudeva, and that the river was Vasudeva's guide.

The point Hesse is making is that Vasudeva learned from the river that every cloud, every bird, every bug, every rock, every breeze is equally divine, and is one with everything. Anything can teach us just as a river can teach us, Siddhartha tells Govinda. He also tells Govinda that Vasudeva was a holy man who knew everything, and Vasudeva learned everything without books and without teachers.

As Abraham Kaplan implies, we learn to be wise by living ordinary lives without creating many problems for ourselves. Govinda, after hearing what Siddhartha had to say, inquires whether the wind, the rocks, everything, is not illusion or just appearance, and therefore unreal.

Siddhartha then remarks that if those things are illusion, then Siddhartha also is an illusion and that the rocks, etc. have the same nature as himself. Siddhartha loves the rocks, etc. because they have the same nature as he. Then Siddhartha pauses and says that what he is about to say will probably make Govinda laugh. Siddhartha says loving, in the sense of being compassionate to others and self, is the most important thing in the world. Hesse believes that for thinkers to examine the world, and to explain what they examine may be important to those thinkers. Perhaps those thinkers may even despise what they examine. But, according to Hesse, only love for the world is important, not to despise it. We should not hate each other, but regard everything that exists, including rocks, stones, and the wind, with respect and love.

Govinda states that their common teacher preached patience, forbearance, sympathy, and benevolence to all beings, but not love. Govinda said that their teacher forbid them earthly love.

Siddhartha bowed and smiled, and said he knew what their master taught about earthly love. Siddhartha acknowledges that what he had just said is in conflict with the teachings of their teacher, but only because of the maze of meanings and the conflict of words; that is why words are so seductive. As a result, Siddhartha mistrusts words because he knows that he is of one-mind with their great teacher because of their great teacher's profound compassion.

Their great teacher also recognized humanity's impermanence and vanity, and yet their great teacher loved everyone as evinced by their teacher's devoting his whole life to teaching and helping people. Siddhartha explains that deeds rather than words must be considered. Their teacher is revered and loved, not for his speeches or his thoughts, but for his deeds, as Vasudeva was loved for his deeds in compassionately taking people across the river.

Both men were silent for a long time, and when Govinda was preparing to go he thanked Siddhartha for his thoughts, thinking that many of Siddhartha's thoughts were strange. Govinda told Siddhartha that he could not grasp all of what was said immediately, but Govinda wished him many days of peace.

However, Govinda thought that Siddhartha was quite strange to express such weird and crazy ideas. As Govinda looked at Siddhartha, Govinda noticed that Siddartha's actions, his gentleness, his kindness, his care and concern for his fellow beings, his eyes, his greeting, his smile, affected Govinda quite differently from the unusual and strange thoughts of Siddhartha. Govinda then thought that Siddhartha was a holy man, as was their master teacher. Even though Siddhartha's ideas seemed strange, Siddhartha's general demeanor was one of serenity, gentleness, saintliness, and peace. Govinda had never before seen that in anyone other than their mutual holy teacher.

Just as Govinda was about to leave, he said to Siddhartha that they were now quite old and that they may never see him each other again so Govinda again asked Siddhartha to tell him some truth, that Govinda might understand something that might help Govinda, who had been searching on this path that was often dark and difficult.

Siddhartha looked at Govinda and noticed the suffering in Govinda's face so Siddhartha, with his calm, peaceful smile, asked Govinda to bend near him, and as Govinda came nearer to Siddhartha, Siddhartha whispered to Govinda to come closer and to kiss Siddhartha on the forehead.

Govinda was quite surprised yet had a strong feeling of great Platonic love for Siddhartha, and because of this great love, and the kiss on the forehead, a wonderful thing happened to Govinda. While Govinda was still thinking about the seductive and strange ideas of Siddhartha, the strange notion of time, the idea that enlightenment and ordinary experience are one, an even stronger feeling of love and esteem was felt by Govinda.

As Govinda kisses Siddhartha on the forehead, Govinda sees many, many faces, a long series of faces in a continuous stream, thousands of them. All of these faces came and disappeared at the same time, and yet all faces changed and renewed themselves simultaneously. Govinda sees a fish with its painfully opened mouth, a dying fish, and at the same time, he sees a newly born child and the face of a murderer plunging a knife into a person, while simultaneously seeing this criminal kneeling down with his head being cut off by an executioner. Govinda sees naked bodies of women and men making passionate love. He sees cold corpses, heads of animals of all kinds, and all forms and faces in thousands of relationships with each other, and everyone and everything helping each other, loving each other, and each person and animal becoming newborn.

All of this was happening simultaneously. Each person was mortal and each had a wide variety of faces; each reproduced and merged with each other simultaneously. Govinda's experience was so unreal yet existing; it stretched across a thin transparent skin or mask, and this mask was Siddhartha's smiling face which Govinda kissed.

In Siddhartha's smile, Govinda saw the unity of everyone and everything, and Govinda no longer knew if time existed. He did not know whether this viewing before his mind lasted a few seconds or a few hours, but he did deeply experience a unity with all beings, and all people, and he was happy and at ease.

Uncontrollable tears trickled down Govinda's face. Govinda experienced an uncontrollable feeling of great compassion and veneration for everyone and everything.

After reading over twenty-five books about Zen Buddhism, nowhere have I seen a more insightful description about that which cannot be said. Hesse's last chapter of *Siddhartha* is uncommonly fine. If you do not have time to read his entire book, I invite you to read the last chapter. While enlightenment is broader and more encompassing than the beautifully contained version of Hesse, his description approaches describing the indescribable.

3. Ahas! and Their Ordering

People agree that patterns come from threads. Nondually, threads also come from patterns. Let us examine the origins of ahas! by noting, as Augustine thought that we all know what time is until we are asked to define time. Like time, we all know what an aha! is until we are asked to define it. Ahas! are like insights which create a permanent restructuring of our mental functioning. They are similar to the punch line of a joke except punch lines cause only temporary restructuring of a part of our mental functioning.

If we have a desire to avoid craving or eliminate craving, we need practical thinking blended with creative thinking. A recent article entitled, "Why the Future Doesn't Need Us," by Bill Joy, talks about twenty thousand years of progress coming during this new century.[2] A part of Joy's motivation to write the article was Ray Kurzweil's ideas in *The Age of Spiritual Machines*. In his article, Joy asks everyone to use self-restraint in the use of new nano/gigo technology and biotechnology.

Will the self-restraint that Joy is talking about arise from ideas such as fuzzy logic, or will it come from the unspecified type of awareness that helped lead to the creation of fuzzy logic prior to its specific uses in machine efficiency? May the self-restraint come from awareness, thinking, and from "more" than logical thinking?

The origination and cessation of ahas!, I contend, can be both ordered and disordered, and many of us will be more at ease if we can conveniently move between the ordering and the disordering.

When ordering occurs, a highest order and a lowest order are established. Depending upon the circumstances, the highest order in one situation could be the lowest order in another. People make hierarchies out of hierarchies.

Phillip Evans and Thomas S. Wurster in *Blown to Bits* elaborate on how old hierarchical business organizations are now moving into non-hierarchical organization, characterized by fluidity, flatness, and trust.[3] Flatness equals a non-hierarchical structure. Evans and Wurster, like Deleuze, are promoting noncentered organization, and they are moving in the direction of deconstructing their deconstructing, which eliminates delusion by establishing a permanent impermanence. Often we arrive at delusion when we use words. Nondually, we have never left nondelusion because we have no place to go, and no words with which to delude ourselves.

In our ordinary lives, we frequently find some people, things, processes, and events that seem "more important" than others. Some things are so important that we do not even think about them. Breathing, for instance, and digesting food are so critical to our living that we do not consider them unless we run out of breath or are constipated.

While we are on the way to creating the highest order, some people have found that being on the way is the highest order, and that no higher order exists than the way they are on. Some nondual Zen practitioners hold that the way that can be said is not the way as Lao Tzu has said. When something is said about the way, whatever is said is always talking around or about it. The "it" remains unstated and unstatable. When we attempt to say something wise, we are frequently thought of as foolish.

I contend that the highest aha! is the aha! of no ahas! No aha! may equal all ahas! Nondually, no ahas! can exist since no separate anything exists. Some Eastern writers describe a big mind that is often distinguished from a monkey mind. The monkey mind is our delusion of a single ego operating only for the benefit of that single ego. Our personality, thoughts, character, are not, say some nondualists, inherent parts of our souls but are merely "guests" to this "real self" hidden within us, and of which we all partake.

Nondually, nothing is separate; therefore, no separate ahas! exist. If this recondite self, which is a host to our personality and culture, is nothing more than one large aha! in which we will participate, then one way of participating is by providing conditions whereby we and others may increase that chance to have ahas! arise. Ahas! order other ahas! Ahas! too are temporary.

Becoming wise is an experience. Perhaps many ahas! need to arise before a person becomes wise. Perhaps one aha! can generate wisdom. What is not clear from Hesse's last chapter is that a person becomes wise by being patient and compassionate. Patience and compassion are experiences. Conversely, we become patient and compassionate by being wise.

When a person says to himself or herself, "I am wise," then that person is probably not wise. If you wish to experience wisdom, sages suggest you practice patience and compassion. The compassion amounts to loving-kindness which amounts to love, as Hesse was using the term. Patience, compassion, loving-kindness, and wisdom are intertwined and recombined into a unit.

All things in moderation is another road to wisdom. All things in moderation is like a road to no road. You do not need a road because moderation implies that you are already there. Perhaps that is why Dogen said that no path is no path. Not knowing is not knowing. Emptiness itself must be emptied. We are not separate selves. Those who are ignorant think that they are a separate self. In that sense, thinking and conceiving of a separate self is a problem. Only separate selves conceive so that our conceptions, unless we realize conceptions are fantasy, and part of the play of big mind, are contributors to ignorance.

4. Endings and New Beginnings

The following may help you understand more about nonduality. When you move away from being a separate self, you move toward desiring less. When you have the delusion of being separate, then desire continues the delusion. Nondualists believe that desire causes a lack of being at ease: suffering.

When you move toward doing away with desire, you get rid of your self; your ego. Your desires lead to more desires. No desires equals no you, equals no suffering. You can help other people and yourself by being compassionate. You can be more compassionate by desiring less. Even desiring to desire less is a desire, so that desire must be noticed so that effort may be extended effortlessly. Once again, when you are compassionate and patient, you are wise.

You are wise when you do wise activities. Feeding the hungry, giving drink to the thirsty, and sheltering the homeless are wise activities. From a nondual viewpoint, non-activity can be activity. Doing the feeding etc. is evidence of profound learning which is evidence of being educated. Education, not necessarily schooling, appears to be a major hope for reducing racism, sexism, homophobia, hunger, homelessness, and "dis-ease," lack of ease.

What is evident to one person may not be evident to another. Some things that are now evident to me were not evident to me twenty years ago, a year ago, or maybe even a moment ago. That everything changes is still evident to me. Nothing is permanent. In order for me to have long-lasting value, I need to observe my behavior rather than my words.

When my behavior is generous and helpful to others, I find that I am most helpful to myself and others. When I am patient, and when I am able to bear and forbear the wrongs of others, I am most helpful to myself and others. When I am strenuous, energetic, and persevering, I am most helpful to myself and others. When I am wise, and when I use the wisdom for the benefit of others, I am most helpful to myself and others. When I see that each moment is a death and a birth of me, I see that I can now start fresh with being at ease even in the midst of great strife and turmoil. When I see that I am interconnected with each person and thing, I am most valuable to myself and others.

Foundational ideas are frequently partially formed, semi-hidden, and murky. Ideas which are clear are frequently inconsequential and nonfoundational. To be consequential, ideas need to be connected to other ideas, then connected to more ideas so that ideas may be seen as fantasy.

Highly consequential ideas are connected to all ideas which, from a nondual view, is seen as no idea. The idea that contains all other connected ideas has the effect of no idea. The way that is alluded to cannot be said because saying would disconnect the way. A disconnected way is not the way.

Foundational ideas are foundational partly because they cannot be adequately explained in terms of simpler ideas. In mathematics, a set is a foundational idea. When we look for a foundation of foundational ideas, we arrive at no foundation where constant change is similar to the fullness of emptiness. At this non-point, deeds are more important than words although expressions of words may be considered as deeds, and deeds are interconnected.

I suggest that which approaches the connection that contains all connections, includes each of as being a part of peace and compassionate cooperation so that each of us understands rather than wants to be understood, and each of us brings joy where there is sadness, and pardon where there is injury. Within this connection each of us gives rather than only receives, and each of as knows not to defer nor neglect the cooperative, compassionate deed because we know this present moment will not occur again.

An old story about heaven and hell describes them as places where all the people had succulent and highly appealing food surrounding them. All of the people had one set of meter-long chopsticks tied to one hand while their other hand was tied behind their backs. In hell, with the succulent and very appealing food all around, the people were trying to feed themselves, and the chopsticks, being so long, would not allow them to get the food into their mouths. They tried, however, to feed themselves so they made quite a mess, spilling food all over the place, and worst of all, they were continually starving.

In heaven, the people were using the chopsticks to feed each other favorite foods, and everyone was at ease and satisfied by taking care of each other. Note this trite statement. We can provide a powerful condition for all people by treating everyone the way we would like to be treated. Because of our conditioning, we may need to gain awareness about racism, sexism, homophobia, the poor, the sick, and the environment before we can treat others the way we would like to be treated.

This kind of ease and satisfaction found by the group who were feeding each other may arise through quantum, nondual learning.

As I have stated earlier, there is evidence, based on new discoveries, that perhaps as much as ninety percent of the universe may have been "missing." Newer evidence reveals that dark matter exists and neutrinos are now thought to have mass. The speed of light in one non-vacuum is three hundred times faster than 186,000+ miles per second and less than fifty miles per hour in another medium. Dark matter is approximately ten times more abundant than matter. Some experts in evolutionary computing suggest that the "intelligence" of rapidly evolving future machines compare future intelligent machines to us as we are now to bacteria. These experts also believe we will have a symbiotic relationship partly because we want carbon and they will want silicon. Perhaps we and they can learn to desire less.

These findings could also help us be more tentative about what we know. Being tentative implies that we prejudge less. Prejudging less implies that we would be more open. Being open to knowing we know less than we thought can help us to be more at ease with each other. We can know more, in the long run, by now being aware that we know somewhat less than we previously thought. Wisdom seems to matter.

Statements from the nondual *Dhammapada*, attributed to Siddhartha Gotama, an awakened, nondual person, may help each of us be more wise, compassionate, and at ease more often. You may notice that racism, sexism, homophobia, and other social ills would be reduced if we followed quantum, nondual ways of being.

Ideas about infinitesimals, vast stretches of the imagination, and points about points follow.

Fifteen

POINTS ABOUT POINTS

A vast stretch of the imagination was needed to create an infinitesimal, a variable that takes on values arbitrarily close to zero. The same stretching was needed to create zero. The point of creating infinitesimals, within a dualistic frame of reference, is to make points which can help us get what we desire. At times, it takes vast stretches of the imagination to make a point. The creation and use of zero often helps us get what we desire. When we use zero and infinitesimals, we can make many points that we otherwise could not make. Vast stretches of the imagination are infinite as are zeroes, points, and infinitesimals.

I would like now to use the variables, infinitesimals and zero, to make the point that, within nonduality, no points can be made because all points, an infinite number of them, have the same effect as no point. But within nonduality, in one sense, saying "because" is misleading since contingent co-rising creates everything simultaneously so that all causes are effects, and all effects are causes simultaneously.

When the sum of the even numbers equals the sum of the odd numbers plus the sum of the even numbers, we can see that, at the bases of our mathematical systems, we have translogical events that are helpful in assisting us to achieve what we desire. Those bases are fantasy in that they do not have substance in themselves, and are myths, useful at times, but myths nontheless.

As an interesting aside, the director of a school mathematics program defined mathematics as, "the study of invariance under transformation." That mathematician was saying that mathematics is the study of how that which does not vary, varies. Mathematics is a useful fantasy to help us to arrive at other fantasies. Fantasies are fine and, at times, may help us grow and develop; however, it is convenient to be aware that they are fantasies. When we are not aware, then delusions contribute to our devolution rather than our evolution. Would "artifact" be more satisfactory than "fantasy?"

When more people are at ease, less deluded, and more aware, more people are, from a nondual "view," probably more wise and compassionate. When you commit a harmful act, more beings are deluded and are less at ease. Within nonduality, cause and effect occur simultaneously, yet an effect comes after a cause within a dualistic framework. Karma, however, is the natural arising of "this" when "that" arises. Can karmic cycles be broken with free responsible choice? Do karmic cycles produce ahas!, as well as the opposite of ahas!?

A zero is a variable, and an infinitesimal is a variable arbitrarily close to zero. Points are also variables. Zeros, infinitesimals, and stretching our imaginations are used in our knowing, predicting, and controlling, and that knowing, predicting, and controlling often help us make points. Is the point of making points to make more points? How do ego power plays relate to making points? Is one person better or more powerful than another when she/he can make more points? If we reduce our egos, would our world have fewer ego power plays and would more people be more cooperative and at ease?

Within nonduality we can choose to be dualistic. When we are dualistic in an unaware way, it may be said that we delude ourselves. A part of the delusion is that we think that when we get what we want, we will be satisfied. Wise people throughout the ages have been saying that the more we have, the more we want. These wise people have also been saying that the more we can reduce our desires, while we are moderate in the sense of balancing our lives, the wiser and more at ease we will be.

In order to reduce our desires, ego reduction is helpful since only an ego can desire.   The study of nonduality is the study of the self.   Within nonduality, we study the self by getting rid of the self. As we get rid of the self, we reduce or eliminate desires. We are then un-selfish/more selfless, more global and universal. Universality and nonduality are one.

The variable, infinitesimal, helps us calculate things that otherwise could not be calculated. When we are deluded, we "calculate" that we are a self. Perhaps through use of infinitesimals, or some other vast stretch of the imagination, we may now more clearly see that we are not totally separate beings. We could consider ourselves as infinitesimals, incalculably small relative to the universe as a whole. It is estimated that when Galileo studied the sky at night, he could see approximately 3,000 stars. We now know that billions and billions of them exist.

As we share more of ourselves and what we have with others, we and others may be wiser, more intelligent, more fulfilled, more content, more creative, and more at ease. We can also use the variable zero to allow ourselves to become a zero in the sense that, being a zero or an infinitesimal, we are not a separate self. When we are not a separate self, we are similar to being nobody, going nowhere. Some teachers ask us to imagine ourselves as a log as a means of getting rid of a separate self.

When I am not a separate self, no "me" exists to do the desiring. When we are not separate selves, we then have no need for variables such as zero, infinitesimal, or point, since nothing varies while everything is always varying. When everything varies, it has the effect of nothing varying. But nonduality has no separate effect. Our creating a calculus to cease separate calculating may be the quantum learner's equivalent to the mathematician's zero. It may now be easier to notice that the way that can be said is not the way.

A wise person once said that to be not present, even for only a short while, is like being dead. Remembering another person's synthesis is not your synthesis. To only follow another's way may block you from your own. We must make our own syntheses, or they are not our syntheses, not ahas!, not something we have directly experienced. For example, your feet are touching the ground, or your bottom is touching the chair if you are standing or sitting. You know that to be true because you experience it. Do we need somebody to tell us if we are standing or sitting?

A friend told me of his schooling about a procession; originally a religious ritual designed to inspire us toward holiness and wholeness. The teacher started by saying, "First of all you must have a physical destination, some place to go." I thought this was so obvious that it did not need stating. Some teachers think that students will know nothing at all unless and until they are told. That has been part of our dilemma because so much has been told to us in schools that students continue to expect to be told all kinds of things, including what to know and how to know it. Syntheses are not cherished because we have not been rewarded for making syntheses. As we make syntheses, we will see that they are their own reward.

Because of our deep attachments to subjective ideas and emotional thinking that have been so ingrained in us, we block our own awareness of what is. We block our own awakening. We are complete as of now yet we frequently are not aware of our completeness. Habitual thinking causes us to mistake myth for reality. Body, mind, world, and false ideas or emotional thinking are delusion and myth-making; we create these delusions, and then conceive of them as real, says an anonymous sage.

Such is the world of nonduality, and nondually speaking, such is the world. Nondually speaking, nothing exists to say.

Choosing to be dualistic is in no way wrong. Dualism is useful in reducing high degrees of inconvenience/suffering so long as we are aware that we are so choosing, and aware that we are creating fantasies. Even if you are not aware that you are choosing to be dualistic, that too is okay. Nondually, everything is okay. Fantasies are only delusions when we are not aware of them. However, through deluding ourselves, we become attached, and through being attached, we create a separate self, and find inconvenience and suffering. When you are a separate self, then you have problems.

Quantum learning in a quantum age, where we notice more processes and events changing much more rapidly, may help us recombine parts of ourselves so that we get rid of our separate selves, and see our connections with other people and things. This may be the direction toward which wise people throughout the centuries have been pointing. The paradox is that we can move in that direction from the direction in which we are now moving.

The passage mentioned earlier by Baltes and Staudinger, "It is better to limp slowly along the right path than to walk stridently in the wrong direction," can only hold when the one walking stridently thinks and feels he or she should be moving in a different direction. Will we learn the nondeluded, wise, detached way if someone tells us? Is that why the sages say little or nothing?

1. Compelling Evidence

What is evident to one person may not be evident to another. We frequently hear of compelling evidence or compelling arguments for this or that.

When we deal with compelling arguments or compelling evidence, we deal with a feeling/notion paradigm which recognizes an interchange between our feelings and our notions, and that some of our notions, ideas, concepts, and theories arise from feelings, and those feelings are influenced by our notions, ideas, concepts, and theories. "We are what we think. All that we are arises with our thoughts. With our thoughts we make the world," says a sage.

One reason for dualism is that we are frequently compelled to express ourselves with words. When we express ourselves, we frequently desire that other people understand what we are expressing. In order for others to understand what we are saying, we use words, and words themselves prevent us from saying everything all at once. We need to make distinctions between this and that. We, therefore, break up our total present experience into parts, and dole the experience out in parts. We then frequently forget that we are attempting to communicate a whole. When we forget, we frequently fail to see the forest because of the trees.

As we are nondual, we can choose to be dualistic. When we are dualistic, we can use subjects and objects to meet our needs for expression and communication. The degree of clarity with which we express ourselves arises partly from our experiences. We have control over some experiences, and little or no control over others. We seem to have some control over how we react to our experiences. Is the cup half full or half empty? Do you not respond in a wiser way in the long run when you are treated compassionately, and when you treat others compassionately?

If we are more aware of what we are doing as we are doing it, we will be more at ease and less deluded. When we are aware of our dualism, we can choose to be dualistic or not. The present, closed, traditional model of schooling into which we have been enculturated, forces us to be dualistic because we have not generally been aware of nonduality. Because concepts generally deal with past and future, we have paid little attention to our present experience.

Duality can give us a short-term payoff, but a long-term loss will be our reward unless we pay more attention to our present experience. Our present experience is the only experience which we are now having.

In ancient Pali, the language used by early nondual sages, heart and mind are one word, *citta*. Those who spoke Pali were not compelled to make differences the early Greeks and most Westerners make today. Perhaps it was René Descartes's need to find a principle of certitude which cemented Western thought into its closed, dualistic way. We could now profitably be freed from these closed ways in order to live wholly and openly in the present. The present is the only time in which we can be wise, compassionate, and at ease.

One function of our holistic openness is to allow ourselves to be transrational. Being transrational means that we are more-than-rational. Being more-than-rational means that we need not be rational all the time. As Peng and Nisbett said, their Asian subjects generally do not rationalize as much as Westerners. Peng and Nisbett's Asian subjects hold that something is and is not simultaneously. We may, in the long run, from an open, nondual view, be more rational by allowing ourselves to be irrational at times.

Or, as Liu said, near-nondualists are so rational that they do not rationalize. I am not advocating irrationality. I am saying that we have the freedom to be irrational when we, through non-delusion and detachment, believe transrationality to be in the best interest of ourselves and others at any given moment.

Nonduality is not a view, and as nondualists believe, all views are obstacles to knowledge. We will be imprisoned by our own views, if we curb awareness, and never attain the way. Knowledge is continually being transformed and unfixed. Static, fixed knowledge is not knowledge in the sense in which nondualists are using the term.

Some nondualists interpret this as meaning that no absolute truth needs to be safeguarded and worshipped. Holding to our old, rigid views of what truth is can prevent us from gaining insight into what we are experiencing as we are experiencing it. As we move closer to nonduality by reducing or eliminating our desires and our egos, we find that we have a balance between wisdom and compassion. I interpret compassion to be loving-kindness towards others, the environment, and ourselves.

Many of us are compelled to move toward being wise and toward being compassionate. Our reasons for doing so, if we need reasons, would be the same as those who find compelling arguments and compelling evidence for a wide variety of other beliefs or activities. Their compellings are no different from those who are compelled to be wise and compassionate, except the feelings and thoughts move in different directions at times, and nondual awareness is more whole than dualistic awareness.

Some of us are compelled to be closed and certain. When we are compelled to be closed and certain, we do not pay much attention to our present experience. When we do not pay attention to our present experience, we are less wise and compassionate. But "they" are "we" too, and we can be compassionate to "them" even though we think at times that "they" may not be compassionate to us. By noticing the interchangeability of "them" and "us," we become wiser and more at ease.

If we can notice that the power struggles we have with others frequently arise from our lack of awareness of our own nondual nature, then new awareness can help reduce those struggles. As a result, we will have less racism, less sexism, less homophobia, and less destruction of the environment. We will be less prejudiced, and have fewer habitual and stereotypical modes of thought and behavior. We will be more open to diversity in thought and behavior.

2. Something and Nothing

The long discussed philosophical problem, "Why something rather than nothing?" within a nondual framework, is no problem because something and not something, commonly called nothing, exist equally. Also problems are only problems when a process or event is thought to be a problem. As a sage said, we are what we think, with our thoughts we make the world.

Those words could help us do away with too many words. Isaac Newton is said to have written more than a million words. Newton's words encouraged the use of more words. If the co-inventer of infinitesimals invented a variable too small to be measured, then his inventions may be seen as separations which may now profitably be recombined into a unit too large to be measured by conventional measures.

Today we may need words to help us do away with too many words. Words convey ideas. Without ideas, no problems could exist. We may reduce problems through reducing our use of words, doing away with excessive words. Emptying, the doing away with many words, amounts to more than generalizing because generalizing is conceptioning.

Nondualists would not even ask, "Why something and nothing?" Something and nothing both exist because of words. Without words, something and nothing would both cease to exist. "Nothing" is a word.

Any suggestion to do away with words seems ludicrous except for cloistered monks, nuns, and hermits. Rather than do away with words, let us reduce their use. The estimated number of words which the student hears in lecture classes, if all of his or her college classes were lecture classes, is 20,000,000 words. Suppose we heard only half that many. Would we know half as much? Would we be only half as smart? If we heard 40,000,000 words, would we be twice as smart or knowledgeable?

When talking about 20,000,000 and 40,000,000, do we attempt to quantify quality? What may be said about our qualifying quantity? Descriptors frequently qualify. Numbers help us quantify. Can we add a beautiful two to an ugly three and still have five?

The question, "Why something rather than nothing?", is answerable from many points of view. What about other frameworks within which we have not yet spoken? We frequently think that nothing can be said about nothing. Nothing and the ineffable are one. From a nondual perspective, the something and the ineffable are also one. More on this later.

The 24 May 2000 issue of *USA Today* includes data about a public agenda survey of 2,200 public and private school teachers on the job five years or less, superintendents, and principals. It includes some ideas which may be indicative of poorly educated educators.

One finding is that sixty-eight percent of those interviewed fault teacher preparation programs for not teaching discipline techniques enough. Do sixty-eight percent of those surveyed want to be told what to do and how to do it? If yes, this harks back to their need to control, not so that students can explore, and develop self control, but perhaps for the sake of control alone. Have they noticed that problems arise because of triviality and boredom in classrooms?

These findings might evince a lack of willingness to explore and experiment as well as that intuition had not been developed. Billions of instances of what may be thought of as discipline problems can be cited. Sixty-eight percent of the respondents may be unable to decide for themselves what process or event will give them confidence about handling problems in classrooms as they arise.

What is disturbing about these sixty-eight percent who want more discipline techniques, is that a technique serves a purpose. One purpose of most prepackaged curricula and techniques is to avoid surprise and excitement. Teachers and school administrators rarely want surprising and exciting processes and events to occur in their classrooms. They often think that they lose control when things are too surprising and/or too exciting.

Nondualists do not ask questions for which no answers can be experienced. If they did ask their question similar to the nondualists' question, "Why something rather than nothing?" their question would be, "Why something and nothing?" but nondualists would probably not ask that question either.

Holistic openness will allow us to know less in the sense that we will be more open and know that fewer things and people are fixed and rigid. As we are more open, we can move in the direction of being like an ocean which has room for all fish and everything else as well as salt, as Sharon Salzberg suggests. Openness, in this sense, is like emptiness in providing room for everything. To one who is nondual, no amount of turmoil has an effect. For such a nondualist, no turmoil exists for turmoil is no different from tranquility.

An open mind is similar to an ocean, which, in turn, is a similar to a mind that has no one particular thought. If we have no fixed, rigid thought, and if we are what we think, we can find great value in being nobody, going nowhere. How much more nondual could one be? Being nondual, we could at any time choose to be somebody and choose to go someplace, if our wisdom and compassion at the time moved us to do so.

As we open ourselves up to what we are noticing, as we are experiencing, we may more conveniently be compelled to notice our nondual state. While several nondualists believe that we come to be aware of our nonduality by accident, other nondualists believe that we can make ourselves more accident-prone by being still and noticing, and perhaps by more openly expressing our present experience, unless those expressions would show insensitivity to ourselves or others.

All of the things I have said about education and learning are preliminary stages to help us notice our present, nondual experience. Nondualists, who notice their present experience, frequently become wise and compassionate people who are a joy to be around. Ease arises when schools and society foster the kind of open, holistic learning which develops wisdom and compassion.

To partially finish the robot story about concrete abstractions, note that, as we need to investigate discord if we are to create harmony, we may need to be open to almost infinite differences in order to experience nonduality. As we approach nonduality, we notice that nothing exists which we are compelled to know, to attain, nor to realize. As we approach nonduality, we are less compelled to be and do anything. So the edubot had nothing to say. The edubot conspires with other wise teachers, who do not bid you to enter the house of their wisdom, but instead, lead you to the threshold of your own mind as sages have said.

The more we know in a conceptual sense, nondually speaking, the less we know. Knowing nondually is not knowing conceptually. Such not knowing, paradoxically, is knowing everything while knowing nothing. There is nothing to know. As we move to the thresholds of our own minds, we have a greater chance of seeing that our struggles are self-imposed, and that nothing exists to struggle about. Let us then lead each other and ourselves to the threshold of our own mind. We are already there, and as we pay more attention to our present experience, we will notice our present experience more, and we may understand and forgive others and ourselves more.

3. Learning for Understanding and Forgiveness

Forgiveness is, as it says, for giving. To a nondual person, that would amount to the giving of self. A way to be free and peaceful is to be giving. A way to be at ease is to give. We frequently only get what is worthwhile in the long run when we give.

Self-forgiveness is the epitome of forgiving. To forgive another is difficult unless and until we forgive ourselves. The way to forgive yourself is to forget yourself. When you forget yourself, you are then often compassionate, and you feed people who are hungry, and give drink to those who are thirsty, shelter those who are homeless, and take care of the environment. These activities do not require thought as much as they require noticing. Noticing, or being aware, precedes thought. Openness precedes noticing. Developing holistic openness to notice what is, is what quantum learning in a quantum age is about.

Noticing hungry, thirsty, and homeless people is difficult when you have not forgotten yourself. When you have not forgotten yourself, you are the object of attention. When you are the object of attention, you find difficulty in being compassionate, and noticing the hungry, the thirsty, the homeless, those in dire need of help, including the environment. When you are the object of attention, you are less likely to be open, unless the focus of attention on yourself is to get rid of your separate self. When you understand that you do not understand, forgetting yourself comes more easily. Within nonduality, you study yourself by forgetting yourself.

What do you get when you give? You get your recondite self and a way to get your recondite self is by forgetting your individual self, and a way to forget your individual self is by forgiving yourself. If this sounds confusing, from our conceptual, dualistic way of being, it is. As we notice the confusion for longer than usual periods of time, we may notice other kinds of order arising which may be thought of as insight/intuition. This may help us find what we need to do to be wise, compassionate, and at ease. Who does not want to be at ease?

Human beings customarily have a set of conceptions which explains what is being said. These desired and cherished conceptions may prevent you from forgetting yourself. Your meta-unconscious, that which is your personality's host, can operate in your life more assuredly when you forget yourself. Secrets to forgiving and/or living do not exist nondually, but to consciously be unconscious is profitable for mind-opening. To understand is to forgive as an unnamed author stated.

Since a lengthy discourse on forgiving may not have a worthwhile effect, one way of attempting to communicate about forgiveness is to forgive yourself. One way of getting others to forgive themselves is to provide a condition whereby they can more easily forget themselves.

Being still may help facilitate moving toward nonduality, which is similar to being compassionate and being at ease. Being at ease is being wise. My friend Laurie Jackson said, "You don't have to find stillness. Just be present, and it will find you." Being still may be an element of wise living. Baltes and Staudinger, in Appendix A of their article on wisdom, give general criteria derived from cultural-historical analysis and specific criteria, the Berlin Wisdom Paradigm, used to analyze wisdom-related products.[1] One of their general criteria outlining the nature of wisdom is, "Wisdom is easily recognized when manifested, although difficult to achieve and to specify." The whole of wisdom is more than the sum of the parts into which it can be divided.

Their other general criteria outlining the nature of wisdom are:

> Wisdom addresses important and difficult questions and strategies about the conduct and meaning of life. Wisdom includes knowledge about the limits of knowledge and the uncertainties of the world. Wisdom represents a truly superior level of knowledge, judgment, and advice. Wisdom constitutes knowledge with extraordinary scope, depth, measure, and balance. Wisdom involves a perfect synergy of mind and character, that is, an orchestration of knowledge and virtues. Wisdom represents knowledge used for the good or well-being of oneself and that of others.[2]

The entire January 2000 issue of *American Psychologist* is devoted to the happiness, excellence, and optimal human functioning that is wisdom. The *American Psychologist* is to be commended for doing excellent work in this area. This optimal human functioning relates to each of us individually and conjointly, moving us toward the thresholds of our own minds. Some nondual writers acknowledge only one mind of which each of us is a part. The one mind does the same thing but each of us does it differently. Kay, my dear wife, has an anonymously written poster which reads, "Sometimes I sits and thinks, and sometimes I just sits."

I have been writing about how illusion arises from fixed conceptions. All conceptions are fixed.

Christmas Humphreys tells a story of a student who asks his teacher, what is myself? The teacher replied with what would you do with a self? The student then asked if he was right when he had "no idea?" The teacher replied to get rid of the idea of his and the student replied, "what idea?" The teacher then said, you are free to carry about the useless idea of no idea.[3]

When words such as "emptiness" are spoken, they are most frequently considered within a dualistic framework. We, therefore, often try to conceive of emptiness, or try to conceive of no-conceiving. The conception of no-conception is a delusion. All conceptions are delusions but those delusions may be useful if we are aware that they are delusions. As has been said, emptiness must be emptied. When we are aware of delusion, delusion recedes. We often use the word "nothing," to conceive of "no-thing." The zero we use in mathematics is not nothing. The way that can be said is not the way. What kind of clarity is that?

Words relate to experience. The experience is different from the words used to describe or explain the experience. Time is a construct and a part of that construct is that events happen in sequence. When the sequence is known, we may say that we have "the concept" for that which the sequence is about. Everything from a dualistic perspective does not happen all at once. Nondually, everything happens all at once.

Our dualistic viewpoint is a subset of the nondual. Being at ease, being wise, and compassionate seem to be separate yet they are one. We can be aware that they are a subset of nonduality. Even using the word "subset" creates a conception about the inconceivable and, therefore, the knowing toward which we are drawn is beyond dualistic rationality. As Peng and Nesbitt related, their Asian subjects were so rational that they did not rationalize, making distinctions where none existed. They did not uncombine that which is together. They did not make "differences " where none existed. Everything, at a basic level, is the same. Quantum recombining is noticing what is already there.

Quantum learning is more direct, more experiential, more in the present, more involved with direct knowing. Teachers facilitating this quantum learning provide conditions which increase likelihood that insight, ahas!, may arise. One helpful condition, frequently brought about by teachers, may be thought of as functional discontinuity, which amounts to a disruption of fixed conceptioning. Students will see or hear an event that is at variance with their expectations, so that they may be more consciously unconscious, or unconsciously conscious in seeing the whole. Awareness only happens in the present. When and where our knowledge is our own, free from habitual ways of thinking, we will know we know without others telling us that we know. That happens here and now, or it happens not at all, and we do not need conceptions for awareness.

Zen is sometimes expressed as one type of nonduality. Zen is at the heart of what I have been talking about. My present view of Zen (as if I could now have a past or future view) is like the fish who goes to the queen fish and says: "I have heard of a sea. What is it and where is it?" Although I cannot conceptualize the queen fish's response, I intuitively know that I am one with everyone and everything. I do, however, often forget it.

Thomas Cleary believes we know that our historically conditioned culture, customs, and habits of thought are not absolute, yet because of our conditioning, we find barriers between ideas of us and them.[4] Those barriers cause communication problems. If we remember how much anger and grief arise from this kind of habitual thinking, we may even see that our personality, culture, and beliefs are not inherent parts of what Cleary calls our souls, but instead the personality, culture, and beliefs are "guests" of a recondite "host." That host is our own self, hidden within what some non-dualists call our real nature.

We are not separate selves. We share this hidden host. Frequently, we come to understand that we are not separate selves through our various experiences. I was quite fortunate and have much gratitude for the experiences I have had in my life. A part of this writing is the fruit of such experience. When I think of myself as being separate, it is useful for me to think that a monkey mind is operating. When I realize that I am not a separate self, then it may be said that the hidden host is operating and, that hidden host is the author of this book.

That host is hidden by our cultural conditioning, and "quantum learning" might help us to interrupt that conditioning. Now may be the appropriate time for that interruption. "Appropriate" will not be defined in advance, yet each of us has a good chance of knowing when the time arrives. Openness to experience, which quantum learning tends to encourage, may accelerate the arrival of the appropriate time.

When you are encouraged, you tap into your heart to "see" what is to be done. I do not wish to belittle reason, but I do wish to put reason in its proper place. Reason's place, since Aristotle, and later amplified by Descartes, has been the be-all and end-all of our lives. We could profitably now view our functioning to be heart-driven as well as reason driven. As we are more balanced in our drives, we will find that we are less driven and that "we" are not a separate "we," but the hidden host that we share is acting on an evolving, unspecifiable road.

Re-reading the words of Hermann Hesse may further cement the way of finding more by seeking less, of being more by being less. Laughing often and hard can help us do this. While life is not a bowl of cherries, as we can see from some of the findings of modern astronomers, physicists, and mathematicians, our universe is also rather different from what we earlier thought it to be: particles communicating faster than the speed of light, newly found dark matter comprising about ten times more of the universe than matter, neutrinos now thought to have mass after many years of thinking otherwise, increasing the speed of light three hundred times, a physicist saying a void exists, etc.

Since our habitually conditioned ways change slowly, we may be on the verge of quantum learning, before quantum learning more fully blossoms. Patience is a way to facilitate the blossoming. An old story tells of a student who goes to a teacher and asks, "How long will it take me to become wise if I study with you?" "About fifteen years," was the teacher's reply. Then the student said, "Suppose I seek and study twice as hard, and double my effort every day, how long would it then take?" "About thirty years," said the teacher.

Although quantum learning has not been spelled out in great detail, getting it in words is conceptual. Nondualists know that conceptual communications are delusions. I wonder what can be done about that.

Remembering some statements of nondualists has been helpful to me. Whatever you do, you do to yourself. Remembering that the greatest impurity is ignorance has also been helpful for me. If I remember that I can easily see others' faults but find it hard to see my own, then I will be wiser and more at ease. If we remember that we gain nothing through attainment, and lose nothing through loss, we may learn to rely on nothing, and come to desire nothing.

To arrive at a better understanding of what a nondual mind is like, I will relate a series of statements called "the ox-herding story." This story is often seen with pictures of a bull and a person at different stages of coming to integration, nonduality, realization/enlightenment. Various versions of this story exist. Some versions have eight segments. This version has ten.

The first picture and comment relates to a person searching for the bull, equated with searching for enlightenment. As comments on this picture say, the bull had never been lost, so no need exists to search, yet the searcher at this stage does not know that.

The second picture is of the searcher finding footprints of the bull; the searcher has evidence of the reality of the bull. At this point, the searcher is still deluded, which allows the searcher to make differences. The searcher will not perceive, at this stage, what is true or what is untrue.

The third picture is of the searcher seeing the bull. The bull can no longer hide. The searcher gets a glimpse of a unity between the searcher and the bull.

The fourth picture shows the searcher catching the bull. The bull needs to be tamed so discipline is used. Struggling goes on.

The fifth picture and comment is taming the bull. Some nondualists ask us, when the horse and cart do not move, which do you strike, the horse or the cart? When a thought arises, other thoughts follow.

The sixth picture is riding the bull home. The struggle is largely over. Gains and losses are taken into account and are transcended. Seeing the bull is seeing into the self.

Picture seven implies that the bull is transcended. You arrive home and are serene. You and the bull rest. You and the bull and everything are one. When you have the fish, you no longer need the fish net. When you have the rabbit, you no longer need the rabbit trap.

Picture eight shows both bull and self are transcended and merge in nothing. The way to get here that can be said is not the way. The arrival is similar to making yourself so open so that you can hold very large amounts of turmoil and not be overly affected. The mind is clear, and the person no longer seeks enlightenment.

Picture nine is about reaching the source. From the beginning separation was a delusion so that we who are detached from "form" need not be "reformed." What is? The sky is blue. The mountains are tall.

The tenth and final picture is of a person whose beauty and greatness are invisible because the searcher is not separate and realizes she or he never was separate. The story says that everyone she or he sees becomes enlightened.

Nondual Zen masters have no dogmas. Whatever the Zen master says when teaching someone, the dharma, is present. Perhaps that is why Zen masters say little. They know we must learn from experience rather than from words and conceptions.

I have heard that Rabbi David A. Cooper believes that the most basic teaching in the Kabbalah is the teaching that awareness is viewed as a purest form of light.[5] Cooper also alludes to self-knowledge as the epitome of knowing. He discusses how people are the vessels for this awareness as the purest form of light, and asserts that the work of human beings is to repair and strengthen the vessel so that light will effortlessly fill that vessel. Nondual Zen is similar, except that many nondualists believe the vessel is okay as it is. The vessels are already strong and need not be repaired. When you accept your vessel as it is, then you can change your reaction to what is happening if you choose to.

At this point I do not know whether I have been too critical of all Westerners. When a process or event needs criticizing, criticism is, at times, worthwhile. At other times, praise to everyone for doing as well as we are doing under the conditions we face may be the best course of action. Awareness is difficult, and for every process or event we are aware of, billions of processes and events may exist of which we are unaware. Noticing the lack of awareness in others is easier for me than seeing where I lack awareness.

Not knowing conceptually, from a nondual Zen view, is a virtue. Conceptions are fine for us to use. We may be more wise, more patient, and more at ease when we are aware that we are using concepts/fantasies.

The last two paragraphs use Robert Ginsberg's ideas about writing, editing, and publishing. I add a couple of ideas, and apply them to nondual living and quantum learning.

The final word about quantum learning and nondual living cannot be written. These are arts that improve with exercise. However much we try to define their features, they have an open-endedness that reflects individual initiative, cultural change, technological innovation, and experimental spirit. Reading about quantum learning and nondual living is never the same as quantum learning and nondual living. The reader will learn from experience in nondual living and quantum learning. Reading is one kind of experience which could profitably be balanced with other kinds of experience.

Cooperation is the core of living and learning and of logical/translogical human interactions. Keep yourself open to learning and understanding and peaceful, compassionate, wise living and learning will follow. Most of us find cooperating more beneficial than competing unless we are playing an agreed upon game. What is more cooperative than nondality and quantum recombining of what has been separated by delusional thinking? Can cooperation be learned? Do we learn to cooperate by cooperating?

AFTERWORD

Afterwords are still different from forewords and some parts are not yet interchangeable. Near-nondual is not yet nondual and "nothing is but what is not," as William Shakespeare said. That two plus two equals four is clear. In isolation, two plus two equals four is not only true by extended definition, that truth is also trivial even though that truth may be useful when contexts are expanded. Many isolated truths, separated differences, are so vastly trivial that we are blinded by their vastness and scope. The blindness prevents us from noticing who we are and what we are doing.

Some nondualists hold that what we are doing, in a larger sense, is moving on the way while we are arriving. Some nondualists hold that we are being born and dying each moment. Dualists think nonduality is nonsense. Some nondualists think that we are being and becoming, and that we are the process of our content while we are contentedly or discontentedly processing content. When we are attached to our ego and to things, we are frequently concerned about inconsequential trivialities while being trivial about what is of consequence.

If we want to be sure, we are often static. If we allow ourselves to be highly dynamic, we often become highly uncertain and perhaps anxious about life and living. Do we need balance between various forces, and do we need to know that it is okay that we know little? Do we need to desire less?

Ninety percent of the universe, dark matter, has only recently been discovered. Do we call it dark because it is murky and because we have not contained it in a concept? John Milton's notion of darkness visible arising before light, applies to what I have been saying.

With joy and gratitude, I thank K. C. Cole for writing *The Hole in the Universe: How Scientists Peered Over the Edge of Emptiness and Found Everything*. She clarifies what I leave murky about physics, astronomy, and nothingness. I completed her book after I wrote this book. I strongly recommend it.

Are we aware of our dual stance to learning and living if we are not aware of nonduality? If we are aware of nonduality, of what are we aware? Because of the complexity of living and learning, need we return to the closedness and certainty of earlier days, or might we surf the murkiness of uncertainty for other possibilities such as nonduality and quantum learning?

Might Ge Changchan's words help us be wise, patient, and at ease? "Life is thus, death is thus. Verse or no verse, what's the fuss?"

NOTES

Introduction

1. David Geoffrey Smith, *Pedagon* (Bragg Creek, Alberta: Makyo Press, 1994), p. 204.
2. *Ibid.*
3. Paul B. Baltes and Ursula M. Staudinger, "Wisdom: A Metaheuristic [Pragmatic] to Orchestrate Mind and Virtue Toward Excellence," *American Psychologist* (January 2000), pp. 122-136.
4. Hermann Hesse, *Siddhartha* (New York: Bantam), 1951.
5. Baltes and Staudinger, "Wisdom."
6. *Ibid.*
7. *Ibid.*
8. Pierre Teilhard de Chardin, *The Future of Man* (New York: Harper and Row, 1964).

PART ONE

Chapter One: Recombining Separations

1. *Anonymous*, "The Startling Future of Computers," *Discover* (November 1999), pp. 63-74.
2. *Ibid.*
3. *Ibid.*
4. "Philosophical Implications of Quantum Mechanics," *Encyclopedia of Philosophy* (New York: Macmillan, Inc., 1967), vol. 7.
5. *Anonymous*, "The Startling Future of Computers."
6. John G. Cramer, "Quantum Nonlocality and the Possibility of Super-luminal Effects," *Proceedings of the NASA Breakthrough Propulsion Physics Workshop* (Cleveland, 12-14 August 1997).
7. Todd May, *Reconsidering Difference* (University Park, Pa.:   The Pennsylvania State University Press, 1997).
8. *Ibid.*
9. *Ibid.*
10. *Ibid.*
11. Kaiping Peng and Richard Nesbitt, "Culture, Dialectics, and Reasoning about Contradiction," *American Psychologist* (September 1999).
12. Ray Kurzweil, *The Age of Spiritual Machines: When Computers Exceed Human Intelligence* (New York: Viking, 1999).
13. Thomas Cleary, trans. & ed. *Zen Essence* (Cambridge, Mass.: Shambhala Publications Inc., 1989).
14. *Ibid.*
15. *Ibid.*
16. George David Miller, personal interview.

17. David Loy, *Nonduality: A Study in Comparative Philosophy* (New Haven and London: Yale University Press, 1988).

18. Cleary, *Zen Essence*.

Chapter Two: Roots of Dualism and Grounds for Holism

1. Robert M. Pirsig, *Zen and the Art of Motorcycle Maintenance* (New York: Bantam, 1975).

2. R. Buckminster Fuller, *Operating Manual for Spaceship Earth* (New York: Simon and Schuster, 1969).

3. John Briggs, *Fractals: The Patterns of Chaos: A New Aesthetic of Art, Science, and Nature* (New York: Simon & Schuster, 1992), p. 180.

4. Ignacio Götz, *Zen and the Art of Teaching* (Westbury, N.Y.: J. L. Wilkerson Publishing Company, 1988), p.138.

Chapter Three: Teaching as Art and Science

1. Ignacio Götz, *Zen and the Art of Teaching* (Westbury, N.Y.: J. L. Wilkerson Publishing Company, 1988), p.138.

2. *Ibid.*

3. *Ibid.*

4. *Ibid.*

5. Michael Polanyi, *Tacit Dimension* (Garden City, N.Y.: Harper and Row, 1966).

6. Noam Chomsky, speech, Bowling Green State University, 1991.

7. John Briggs and F. David Peat, *Turbulent Mirror: An Illustrated Guide to Chaos Theory and the Science of Wholeness* (New York: Harper and Row, 1989).

8. Judy Katz, *White Awareness: A Handbook for Anti-Racism Training* (Norman: University of Oklahoma Press, 1978).

9. Thomas Merton, *Zen and the Birds of Appetite* (Cambridge, Mass.: Shambhala, 1994).

10. Sheldon Kopp, "Eschatological Laundry List," *Guru: Metaphors from a Psychotherapist* (Palo Alto, Cal.: Science and Behavior Books, 1971).

11. Thomas Cleary, *The Pocket Zen Reader* (Cambridge, Mass.: Shambhala Publications Inc., 1989).

12. Kopp, "Eschatological Laundry List."

Chapter Four: Opening Wide the Door: Nonduality

1. David Loy, *Nonduality: A Study in Comparative Philosophy* (New Haven and London: Yale University Press, 1988), p. 10.

2. *Ibid.*

3. *Ibid.*

4. *Ibid.*

5. *Ibid.*

6. *Ibid.*

7. *Ibid.*

8. Abraham Kaplan, *The New World of Philosophy* (New York: Random House, 1961).

9. *Ibid.*

10. *Ibid.*

11. *Ibid.*

12. *Ibid.*

Chapter Five: The Convenience of Balance and Balancing Conveniences

1. J. Richard Suchman, *Science Research Associates' Inquiry Development Program* (Chicago: University of Illinois Press, 1966).

2. Sharon Salzberg, *Everyday Mind,* ed. Jean Smith (New York: Berkley Publishing/Penguin, Putnam, 1997).

3. Robert S. Kaplan, *The Nothing That Is: A History of Zero* (Oxford: Oxford University Press, 2000).

4. Lao Tzu, *Tao Te Ching,* Translated by Victor H. Mair (New York: Bantam, 1990).

5. Abraham Kaplan, *The New World of Philosophy* (New York: Random House, 1961).

6. *Ibid.*

PART TWO

Chapter Six: Consequences of the Boiled Frog Syndrome

1. Robert Kunzig, "Lone Star in Virgo," *Discover* (February 1999).

2. *Ibid.*

3. *Ibid.*

4. *Ibid.*

5. *Ibid.*

6. *Ibid.*

7. *Ibid.*

8. *Ibid.*

9. Tim Folger, "A Question of Gravitas," *Discover* (July 1995), p. 38.

10. John Dewey, *Reconstruction in Philosophy* (Boston: Beacon Press, 1920).

11. John Dewey, *Experience and Education* (New York: The Macmillan Company, 1938).

12. Howard Gardner, *Intelligence Reframed: Multiple Intelligences for the 21st Century* (New York: Basic Books, 1999).

13. R. Buckminster Fuller, *Operating Manual for Spaceship Earth* (New York: Simon & Schuster, Inc., 1969).

14. Richard P. Iano, "Is Education Science?" In Philip J. David and David Park, eds., *No Way: The Nature of the Impossible* (W. H. Freeman and Company, 1987).

15.   Shunryu Suzuki, *Zen Mind, Beginner's Mind* (New York: Weatherill, 1970).

16.   Richard Kehl, *Silver Departures* (La Jolla, Ca.: The Green Tiger Press, 1983).

Chapter Seven: Specialization and Generalization

1.   Robert M. Pirsig, *Zen and the Art of Motorcycle Maintenance* (New York: Bantam, 1974).

2.   *Ibid.*

3.   Michael Polanyi, *Tacit Dimension* (Garden City, N.Y.: Doubleday, 1966).

4.   Walter Karp, "Why Johnny Can't Think," *Harper's* (June 1985).

5.   Carl R. Rogers, *Freedom to Learn: A View of What Education Might Become* (Columbus, Ohio: Charles E. Merrill Company, 1969), introduction.

6.   Karp, "Why Johnny Can't Think."

Chapter Eight: Determining Readiness to Accept Uncertainty

1.   Gilles Deleuze, *On the Line* (New York: Semiotext(e), 1983).

2.   Gilles Deleuze and Felix Guattari, *Anti-Oedipus* (New York: Viking Press, 1976).

3.   Richard Kehl, *Silver Departures* (La Jolla, Ca.: The Green Tiger Press, 1983).

4.   *Ibid.*

Chapter Nine: Attention and Attention Traps

1.   John Dewey, *Experience and Education* (New York, The Macmillan Company, 1938).

2.   Walter Karp, "Why Johnny Can't Think," *Harper's* (June 1985).

3.   Robert S. Kaplan, *The Nothing That Is: A Natural History of Zero* (London: Penguin, 2000).

4.   Richard Kehl, *Silver Departures* (La Jolla, Ca.: The Green Tiger Press, 1983).

5.   Nel Noddings and Paul J. Shore, *Intuition in Education: Awakening the Inner Eye* (New York: Teachers College Press, 1984).

Chapter Eleven: Focusing on Present Experience

1.   Henri Yaker, Humphrey Osmond, and Frances Cheek, *The Future of Time* (Garden City, N.Y.: Anchor Books, 1972).

2.   Edward DeBono, *The New Think: The Use of Lateral Thinking in the Generation of Ideas* (New York: Basic Books, 1968).

Chapter Twelve: Intelligence and Humor

    1.   Hollis Moore, "Ferdinand Schiller," speech, Bowling Green State University: 1973.

    2.   David Doane, unpublished paper and personal interview.

    3.   Lewis H. Lapham, "School Bells," *Harper's* (August 2000), pp. 7-9.

Chapter Thirteen: Catching Ourselves in the Act While We Are Acting

    1.   Lee Roy F. Troutner, "Illich and Kierkegaard Combined: The Response to the Trap," *Philosophy of Education, 1978* (Champaign, Ill., Philosophy of Education Society, University of Illinois, 1979).

Chapter Fourteen: Concrete Abstractions

    1.   Hermann Hesse, *Siddhartha* (New York: Bantam, 1951).

    2.   Bill Joy, "Why the Future Doesn't Need Us," *Wired* (April 2000).

    3.   Philip Evans and Thomas S. Wurster, *Blown to Bits* (Boston: Harvard Business School Press, 2000).

Chapter Fifteen: Points about Points

    1.   Paul B. Baltes and Ursula M. Staudinger, "Wisdom: A Metaheuristic [Pragmatic] to Orchestrate Mind and Virtue Toward Excellence," *American Psychologist*, 55:1 (January 2000), pp. 122-136.

    2.   *Ibid.*

    3.   Christmas Humphreys, *Buddhism* (London: Penguin, 1990).

    4.   Thomas Cleary, *Pocket Zen Reader* (Cambridge, Mass.: Shambhala Publications Inc., 1999).

    5.   David A. Cooper, *The Mystical Kabbalah: Voices of Wisdom*, Sounds True Catalogue (Summer 2000), p. 1.

BIBLIOGRAPHY

Anonymous. "Startling Future of Computers," *Discover* (November 1999), pp. 63-74.

Baltes, Paul B. and Ursula M. Staudinger. "Wisdom: A Metaheuristic [Pragmatic] to Orchestrate Mind and Virtue Toward Excellence." *American Psychologist* (January 2000), 55:1, pp. 122-136.

Barker, Joel Arthur. *Future Edge: Discovering New Paradigms of Success.* New York: William Morrow and Company, Inc., 1992.

Cleary, Thomas. *Zen Essence: The Science of Freedom.* Boston: Shambhala Publications Inc., 1989.

_____. *The Pocket Zen Reader.* Boston: Shambhala Publications Inc., 1999.

Cramer, John G. "Quantum Nonlocality and the Possibility of Superluminal Effects." *Proceedings of the NASA Breakthrough Propulsion Physics Workshop,* Cleveland, 12-14 August 1997—Internet, May 2000.

Cole, K. C. *The Hole in the Universe: How Scientists Peered Over the Edge of Emptiness and Found Everything.* New York: Harcourt, 2001.

DeBono, Edward. *New Think: The Use of Lateral Thinking in the Generation of New Ideas.* New York: Basic Books, 1968.

Deleuze, Gilles. *On the Line.* New York: Semiotext(e), 1983.

Deleuze, Gilles and Felix Guattari. *Anti-Oedipus: Capitalism and Schizophrenia.* New York: Viking Press, 1976.

Dewey, John. *Experience and Education.* New York: The Macmillan Company, 1938.

_____. *Reconstruction in Philosophy.* New York: H. Holt and Company, 1920.

Evans, Philip and Thomas S. Wurster. *Blown to Bits.* Boston: Harvard Business School Press. 2000.

Folger, Tim. "A Question of Gravitas," *Discover* (July 1995), p. 38.

Fuller, R. Buckminster. *I Seem to Be a Verb.* New York: Bantam Books, 1970.

_____. *Operating Manual for Spaceship Earth.* New York: Simon and Schuster, Inc., 1969.

Gardner, Howard. *Intelligence Reframed: Multiple Intelligences for the 21st Century.* New York: Basic Books, 1999.

Gleick, James. *Chaos: Making a New Science.* New York: The Viking Press, 1987.

Goodlad, John I. *A Place Called School: Prospects for the Future.* New York: McGraw-Hill Book Company, 1984.

Grene, Marjorie. *The Knower and the Known.* New York: Basic Books, 1966.

Hayles, N. Katherine. *Chaos Bound: Orderly Disorder in Contemporary Literature and Science.* Ithaca, N.Y.: Cornell University Press, 1990.

Hesse, Hermann. *Siddhartha.* New York: Bantam, 1951.

Humphreys, Christmas. *Buddhism.* London: Penguin, 1990.

Iano, Richard P. "Is Education Science?" in Philip J. David and David Park, eds., *No Way: The Nature of the Impossible.* New York: W. H. Freeman and Company, 1987.

Kaplan, Abraham. *The New World of Philosophy*. New York: Random House, 1961.

Kaplan, Robert S. *The Nothing That Is: A Natural History of Zero*. London: Penguin, 2000.

Karp, Walter. "Why Johnny Can't Think," *Harper's* (June 1985).

Katz, Judy. *White Awareness: A Handbook for Anti-Racism Training*. Norman: University of Oklahoma Press, 1978.

Kehl, Richard. *Silver Departures: A Collection of Quotations*. La Jolla, Cal.: The Green Tiger Press, 1983.

Kopp, Sheldon B. "Eschatological Laundry List," *Guru: Metaphors from a Psychotherapist*. Palo Alto, Cal.: Science and Behavior Books, 1971.

Kunzig, Robert. "Lone Star in Virgo," *Discover* (February 1999), p. 82-87.

Kurzweil, Ray. *The Age of Spiritual Machines: When Computers Exceed Human Intelligence*. New York: Viking, 1999.

Lao Tzu. *Tao Te Ching*. Translated by Victor H. Mair. New York: Bantam, 1990.

Lapham, Lewis H. "School Bells," *Harper's* (August 2000).

Loy, David. *Nonduality: A Study in Comparative Philosophy*. New Haven: Yale University Press, 1988.

Maslow, Abraham. *Toward a Psychology of Being*. Princeton: Van Nostrand Company, 1968.

May, Todd. *Reconsidering Difference*. University Park, Pa.: The Pennsylvania State University Press, 1997.

_____. *Twentieth-Century Continental Philosophy*. Upper Saddle River, N.J.: Prentice Hall, Inc., 1997.

Merton, Thomas. *Zen and the Birds of Appetite*. Boston: Shambhala Publications, 1994.

Noddings, Nel and Paul J. Shore. *Awakening the Inner Eye: Intuition in Education*. New York: Teachers College Press, 1984.

Ortony, Anthony, ed. *Metaphor and Thought*. Cambridge, England: Cambridge University Press, 1979.

Peat, F. David and John Briggs. *Turbulent Mirror*. New York: Harper and Row, 1989.

Peng, Kaiping and Richard E. Nisbett. "Culture Dialectics and Reasoning about Contradiction," *American Psychologist*, 54:9 (September 1999), pp. 741-754.

Pirsig, Robert M. *Zen and the Art of Motorcycle Maintenance*. New York: Bantam, 1974.

Polanyi, Michael. *Tacit Dimension*. Garden City, N. Y.: Doubleday, 1966.

Reps, Paul. *Zen Flesh, Zen Bones*. Rutland, Vermont and Tokyo, Japan: Charles E. Tuttle Co., Inc., 1957.

Rogers, Carl R. *Freedom to Learn; A View of What Education Might Become*. Columbus, Ohio: Charles E. Merrill Publishing Company, 1969.

Sizer, Theodore R. *Horace's Compromise: The Dilemma of the American High School*. Boston: Houghton Mifflin Company, 1984.

Smith, David Geoffrey. *Pedagon*. Bragg Creek, Alberta: Makyo Press, 1994.

Smith, Jean. *Everyday Mind: 366 Reflections on the Buddhist Path*. New York: Riverhead Books, Berkley Publishing Co., Penguin, Putnam Publishing Group, 1997.

Stevens, John O. *Awareness: Exploring, Experimenting, Experiencing.* New York: Bantam, 1973.

Suzuki, Daisetz T. *Introduction to Zen Buddhism.* New York: Grove Weidenfeld, 1964.

_____. *Essays in Zen Buddhism.* London: Rider and Company, 1949.

Suzuki, Shunryu. *Zen Mind, Beginners' Mind.* New York: Weatherill, 1970.

Teilhard de Chardin, Pierre. *The Future of Man.* Translated from the French by Norman Denny. New York: Harper and Row, 1964.

Troutner, Lee Roy F. "Illich and Kierkegaard Combined: A Response to the Trap," *Philosophy of Education, 1978.* Champaign, Ill.: Philosophy of Education Society, University of Illinois, 1979.

Watson, Burton. *Chuang Tzu: Basic Writings.* New York: Columbia University Press, 1964.

Whitehead, Alfred North. *The Aims of Education and Other Essays.* New York: Macmillan, 1957.

Wiener, Norbert. *The Human Use of Human Beings: Cybernetics and Society.* Garden City, N.Y.: Doubleday Publishing Company, 1954.

Wright, Robert. *Nonzero: The Logic of Human Destiny.* New York: Pantheon Books, 2000.

Yaker, Henri, Humphry Osmond, and Frances Cheek, eds. *The Future of Time: Man's Temporal Environment.* Garden City, N.Y.: Anchor Books, 1972.

ABOUT THE AUTHOR

Conrad P. Pritscher has taught philosophy of education and multicultural education at Bowling Green State University, Ohio, since 1969. He also taught Explorations in Human Potential, environmental studies, and several other courses. He is a graduate of The Gestalt Institute of Cleveland, Post Graduate Intensive Training Program. He is the author of numerous articles and the co-author with George David Miller of *On Education and Values* (Rodopi, 1995). He is a former president of the Ohio Valley Philosophy of Education Society, the Bowling State University Human Relations Commission, and the People for Racial Justice Committee. He is currently a Board Member of the Fair Housing Center of Northwest Ohio.

INDEX

VIBS

The **Value Inquiry Book Series** is co-sponsored by:

Adler School of Professional Psychology
American Indian Philosophy Association
American Maritain Association
American Society for Value Inquiry
Association for Process Philosophy of Education
Canadian Society for Philosophical Practice
Center for Bioethics, University of Turku
Center for International Partnerships, Rochester Institute of Technology
Center for Professional and Applied Ethics, University of North Carolina at Charlotte
Centre for Applied Ethics, Hong Kong Baptist University
Centre for Cultural Research, Aarhus University
Centre for the Study of Philosophy and Religion, College of Cape Breton
College of Education and Allied Professions, Bowling Green State University
Concerned Philosophers for Peace
Conference of Philosophical Societies
Department of Moral and Social Philosophy, University of Helsinki
Gannon University
Gilson Society
Global Association for the Study of Persons
Ikeda University
Institute of Philosophy of the High Council of Scientific Research, Spain
International Academy of Philosophy of the Principality of Liechtenstein
International Center for the Arts, Humanities, and Value Inquiry
International Society for Universal Dialogue
Natural Law Society

Philosophical Society of Finland
Philosophy Born of Struggle Association
Philosophy Seminar, University of Mainz
Pragmatism Archive
R.S. Hartman Institute for Formal and Applied Axiology
Research Institute, Lakeridge Health Corporation
Russian Philosophical Society
Society for Iberian and Latin-American Thought
Society for the Philosophic Study of Genocide and the Holocaust
Society for the Philosophy of Sex and Love
Yves R. Simon Institute.

Titles Published

1.   Noel Balzer, *The Human Being as a Logical Thinker.*

2.   Archie J. Bahm, *Axiology: The Science of Values.*

3.   H. P. P. (Hennie) Lötter, *Justice for an Unjust Society.*

4.   H. G. Callaway, *Context for Meaning and Analysis: A Critical Study in the Philosophy of Language.*

5.   Benjamin S. Llamzon, *A Humane Case for Moral Intuition.*

6.   James R. Watson, *Between Auschwitz and Tradition: Postmodern Reflections on the Task of Thinking.* A volume in **Holocaust and Genocide Studies.**

7.   Robert S. Hartman, *Freedom to Live: The Robert Hartman Story,* edited by Arthur R. Ellis. A volume in **Hartman Institute Axiology Studies.**

8.   Archie J. Bahm, *Ethics: The Science of Oughtness.*

9.   George David Miller, *An Idiosyncratic Ethics; Or, the Lauramachean Ethics.*

10. Joseph P. DeMarco, *A Coherence Theory in Ethics.*

40. Samantha Brennan, Tracy Isaacs, and Michael Milde, Editors, *A Question of Values: New Canadian Perspectives in Ethics and Political Philosophy.*

41. Peter A. Redpath, *Cartesian Nightmare: An Introduction to Transcendental Sophistry.* A volume in **Studies in the History of Western Philosophy.**

42. Clark Butler, *History as the Story of Freedom: Philosophy in Intercultural Context,* with Responses by sixteen scholars.

43. Dennis Rohatyn, *Philosophy History Sophistry.*

44. Leon Shaskolsky Sheleff, *Social Cohesion and Legal Coercion: A Critique of Weber, Durkheim, and Marx.* Afterword by Virginia Black.

45. Alan Soble, Editor, *Sex, Love, and Friendship: Studies of the Society for the Philosophy of Sex and Love, 1977-1992.* A volume in **Histories and Addresses of Philosophical Societies.**

46. Peter A. Redpath, *Wisdom's Odyssey: From Philosophy to Transcendental Sophistry.* A volume in **Studies in the History of Western Philosophy.**

47. Albert A. Anderson, *Universal Justice: A Dialectical Approach.* A volume in **Universal Justice.**

48. Pio Colonnello, *The Philosophy of José Gaos.* Translated from Italian by Peter Cocozzella. Edited by Myra Moss. Introduction by Giovanni Gullace. A volume in **Values in Italian Philosophy.**

49. Laura Duhan Kaplan and Laurence F. Bove, Editors, *Philosophical Perspectives on Power and Domination: Theories and Practices.* A volume in **Philosophy of Peace.**

50. Gregory F. Mellema, *Collective Responsibility.*

51. Josef Seifert, *What Is Life? The Originality, Irreducibility, and Value of Life.* A volume in **Central-European Value Studies.**

52. William Gerber, *Anatomy of What We Value Most.*

53. Armando Molina, *Our Ways: Values and Character,* edited by Rem B. Edwards. A volume in **Hartman Institute Axiology Studies.**

54. Kathleen J. Wininger, *Nietzsche's Reclamation of Philosophy*. A volume in **Central-European Value Studies.**

55. Thomas Magnell, Editor, *Explorations of Value*.

56. HPP (Hennie) Lötter, *Injustice, Violence, and Peace: The Case of South Africa*. A volume in **Philosophy of Peace.**

57. Lennart Nordenfelt, *Talking About Health: A Philosophical Dialogue*. A volume in **Nordic Value Studies.**

58. Jon Mills and Janusz A. Polanowski, *The Ontology of Prejudice*. A volume in **Philosophy and Psychology.**

59. Leena Vilkka, *The Intrinsic Value of Nature*.

60. Palmer Talbutt, Jr., *Rough Dialectics: Sorokin's Philosophy of Value*, with Contributions by Lawrence T. Nichols and Pitirim A. Sorokin.

61. C. L. Sheng, *A Utilitarian General Theory of Value*.

62. George David Miller, *Negotiating Toward Truth: The Extinction of Teachers and Students*. Epilogue by Mark Roelof Eleveld. A volume in **Philosophy of Education.**

63. William Gerber, *Love, Poetry, and Immortality: Luminous Insights of the World's Great Thinkers*.

64. Dane R. Gordon, Editor, *Philosophy in Post-Communist Europe*. A volume in **Post-Communist European Thought.**

65. Dane R. Gordon and Józef Niznik, Editors, *Criticism and Defense of Rationality in Contemporary Philosophy*. A volume in **Post-Communist European Thought.**

66. John R. Shook, *Pragmatism: An Annotated Bibliography, 1898-1940*. With Contributions by E. Paul Colella, Lesley Friedman, Frank X. Ryan, and Ignas K. Skrupskelis.

67. Lansana Keita, *The Human Project and the Temptations of Science*.

68. Michael M. Kazanjian, *Phenomenology and Education: Cosmology, Co-Being, and Core Curriculum*. A volume in **Philosophy of Education.**

83. Veikko Launis, Juhani Pietarinen, and Juha Räikkä, Editors, *Genes and Morality: New Essays.* A volume in **Nordic Value Studies.**

84. Steven Schroeder, *The Metaphysics of Cooperation: The Case of F. D. Maurice.*

85. Caroline Joan ("Kay") S. Picart, *Thomas Mann and Friedrich Nietzsche: Eroticism, Death, Music, and Laughter.* A volume in **Central-European Value Studies.**

86. G. John M. Abbarno, Editor, *The Ethics of Homelessness: Philosophical Perspectives.*

87. James Giles, Editor, *French Existentialism: Consciousness, Ethics, and Relations with Others.* A volume in **Nordic Value Studies.**

88. Deane Curtin and Robert Litke, Editors, *Institutional Violence.* A volume in **Philosophy of Peace.**

89. Yuval Lurie, *Cultural Beings: Reading the Philosophers of Genesis.*

90. Sandra A. Wawrytko, Editor, *The Problem of Evil: An Intercultural Exploration.* A volume in **Philosophy and Psychology.**

91. Gary J. Acquaviva, *Values, Violence, and Our Future.* A volume in **Hartman Institute Axiology Studies.**

92. Michael R. Rhodes, *Coercion: A Nonevaluative Approach.*

93. Jacques Kriel, *Matter, Mind, and Medicine: Transforming the Clinical Method.*

94. Haim Gordon, *Dwelling Poetically: Educational Challenges in Heidegger's Thinking on Poetry.* A volume in **Philosophy of Education.**

95. Ludwig Grünberg, *The Mystery of Values: Studies in Axiology,* edited by Cornelia Grünberg and Laura Grünberg.

96. Gerhold K. Becker, Editor, *The Moral Status of Persons: Perspectives on Bioethics.* A volume in **Studies in Applied Ethics.**